American Exceptionalism

The American Ways Series

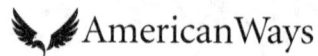

General Editor: John David Smith,
Charles H. Stone Distinguished Professor of American History
University of North Carolina at Charlotte

From the long arcs of America's history, to the short timeframes that convey larger stories, American Ways provides concise, accessible topical histories informed by the latest scholarship and written by scholars who are both leading experts in their fields and polished writers.

Books in the series provide general readers and students with compelling introductions to America's social, cultural, political, and economic history, underscoring questions of class, gender, racial, and sectional diversity and inclusivity. The titles suggest the multiple ways that the past informs the present and shapes the future in often unforeseen ways.

Current Titles in the Series
How America Eats: A Social History of U.S. Food and Culture, by Jennifer Jensen Wallach
Popular Justice: A History of Lynching in America, by Manfred Berg
Bounds of Their Habitation: Race and Religion in American History, by Paul Harvey
National Pastime: U.S. History through Baseball, by Martin C. Babicz and Thomas W. Zeiler
Wartime America: The World War II Home Front, Second Edition, by John W. Jeffries
Enemies of the State: The Radical Right in America from FDR to Trump, by D. J. Mulloy
Hard Times: Economic Depressions in America, by Richard Striner
We the People: The 500-Year Battle Over Who Is American, by Ben Railton
Litigation Nation: How Lawsuits Represent Changing Ideas of Self, Business Practices, and Right and Wrong in American History, by Peter Charles Hoffer
Of Thee I Sing: The Contested History of American Patriotism, by Ben Railton
American Agriculture: From Farm Families to Agribusiness, by Mark V. Wetherington
Years of Rage: White Supremacy in the United States from the 1920s to Today, by D. J. Mulloy
Germans in America: A Concise History, by Walter D. Kamphoefner
American Exceptionalism, by Volker Depkat

AMERICAN EXCEPTIONALISM

Volker Depkat

ROWMAN & LITTLEFIELD
Lanham • Boulder • New York • London

Published by Rowman & Littlefield
An imprint of The Rowman & Littlefield Publishing Group, Inc.
4501 Forbes Boulevard, Suite 200, Lanham, Maryland 20706
www.rowman.com

86-90 Paul Street, London EC2A 4NE, United Kingdom

Copyright © 2021 by The Rowman & Littlefield Publishing Group, Inc.
Paperback Edition 2024

All rights reserved. No part of this book may be reproduced in any form or by any electronic or mechanical means, including information storage and retrieval systems, without written permission from the publisher, except by a reviewer who may quote passages in a review.

British Library Cataloguing in Publication Information Available

Library of Congress Cataloging-in-Publication Data

Names: Depkat, Volker, 1965– author.
Title: American exceptionalism / Volker Depkat.
Description: Lanham : Rowman & Littlefield, [2021] | Includes bibliographical references and index. | Summary: "In engaging and lucid prose, Volker Depkat offers general readers and students of American history an invaluable lens through which they can evaluate for themselves the merits of the many ways in which Americans have understood their country as exceptional"— Provided by publisher.
Identifiers: LCCN 2021041234 (print) | LCCN 2021041235 (ebook)
Subjects: LCSH: Exceptionalism—United States. | National characteristics, American. | United States—Civilization.
Classification: LCC E169.1 .D464 2021 (print) | LCC E169.1 (ebook) | DDC 973—dc23
LC record available at https://lccn.loc.gov/2021041234
LC ebook record available at https://lccn.loc.gov/2021041235

ISBN 978-1-5381-0118-6 (cloth : alk. paper)
ISBN 978-1-5381-9995-4 (paper : alk. paper)
ISBN 978-1-5381-0119-3 (electronic)

For my wife, Irmgard Depkat

Contents

Acknowledgments   ix

Introduction   xiii

1   The American Land: Landscapes of Abundance, Wilderness, and Beauty   1

2   The West and the South: Exceptional Regions and Regions of Exceptionalism   25

3   Cities upon Hills: The Colonial Foundations of American Exceptionalism   51

4   Sacred Fire of Liberty: The American Revolution and the Transformation of American Exceptionalism   71

5   The American Way of Empire: Exceptionalism and U.S. Foreign Policy   93

6   Promissory Notes: Exceptionalism and African American Self-Empowerment   135

7   Perfectible Union: American Exceptionalism and Reform   157

8   People of Plenty: American Exceptionalism and Affluence   185

9   Crisis of Disorientation: Contested Exceptionalisms in Contemporary America   213

Bibliographical Essay   237

Index   265

About the Author   281

Acknowledgments

BACK IN 1972, when my grandmother (who was born and raised in northern Germany without ever leaving her small hometown in the vicinity of Lübeck) learned that we would be moving to the U.S. to live in El Paso, Texas, for a while, she warned me of the Apaches and other American Indians. When we had finally set up shop in Sun City in 1973, one of the first Americans I met there asked me whether we had orange juice in Germany already. At the age of seven, both episodes defined my first encounter with American Exceptionalism—although I would not have been able to call it such in those days.

My three years of childhood in El Paso were neither my first nor my last extended stay in the U.S. I was born in El Paso in 1965, and, with both of my parents being German, I moved to and from the U.S. repeatedly, to the effect that I have spent much of my private and professional life explaining America to Germans, and Germany to Americans. This record of cultural brokerage, which is carried by my teaching U.S. history at German universities for almost twenty-five years now, puts me, I think, in a unique position to write about American Exceptionalism as a key concept of U.S. cultural history: I have an intimate, biographically substantiated firsthand knowledge of the U.S. as well as a lot of book learning about it, and yet look at the U.S. primarily from the outside.

I am, therefore, not so much interested in whether or not the U.S. indeed was, has been, or is exceptional. In one way or another, all nations think of themselves as unique, special, and distinct. Nationalisms do not work without a sense of exceptionality among those who imagine themselves as a nation. Therefore, the debate about whether or not the U.S. indeed is exceptional is primarily a matter of identity politics and social battles in the U.S. itself; with this book, I neither can nor do want to relate to that.

What this book can do and aims to do is provide answers to the questions of how the U.S. was, has been, and is imagined as exceptional—by whom, when, where, why, for which reasons, and to what effects. These questions are what I, as a Germany-based historian of the U.S., am most interested in, and I have been pursuing them for quite a while now.

In my dissertation on images of America in the political discourses of German magazines from 1789 to 1830, I investigated the highly controversial debates between German liberals and conservatives about whether American-style freedom, democracy, and capitalism were wanted in Germany. In these debates, notions of American Exceptionalism surfaced in multiple ways: Some liberals looked at the U.S. as an exceptional country of freedom and self-government that had already realized what they themselves were aspiring to in Germany. Others, liberals and conservatives alike, saw the U.S. as a land of exceptional depravity, where an excessive materialism kept people wallowing in an endless mud of shallowness, where a pervasive egalitarianism had put the *rabble* in political power, and where free individuals were actually imprisoned by the liberty they championed. Finally, there were Germans in both political camps who argued that the U.S. was so unique that it could not serve as model for anyone else at all.

The book you are holding is not about how America was imagined as exceptional from abroad. Rather, it is about how the concept of exceptionalism figured and functioned as a cultural force shaping U.S. history from its colonial beginnings to the present. It will identify the major elements of American Exceptionalism as a highly malleable set of ideas, images, and narratives defining concepts of American identity that were always contested among Americans themselves. In the multiple contexts of U.S. history, American Exceptionalism was put to multiple uses to justify the most different, partly outright contradictory, versions of what it means to be American.

I started thinking about this book six years ago, on July 3, 2015, to be precise, when the general editor of the American Ways series, John David Smith, and I were in Heidelberg for the conference "The Challenges of Doing Biography," organized by Manfred Berg for the Heidelberg Center of American Studies. Although John David and I had been invited to talk about biography, we ended up discussing American Exceptionalism over dinner and breakfast. Shortly afterward, he invited me to contribute this book to his series, and I am more than grateful that he did. His unerring support and vast knowledge of American history in combination with his dedicated editorship has made writing this book a truly wonderful and rewarding intellectual experience, and I want to thank him for that.

ACKNOWLEDGMENTS

Furthermore, I would like to thank Jon Sisk, vice president and senior executive acquisitions editor for political science, American government and public policy, religion, and American history at Rowman & Littlefield, who in many respects turned out to be John David Smith's congenial Other in terms of dedication to and professionalism in book making. Thank you, Jon, for this transatlantic cooperation of like minds. There are others at Rowman & Littlefield who I am grateful to: Barbara Stark for her conscientious and dedicated job of copyediting my manuscript, and Hannah Fisher for her professionalism in seeing me through the production process of my book.

Over the past six years, I have presented parts of this book to colleagues and students at Karl-Franzens University (Graz, Austria), and Masaryk University (Brno, Czech Republic). In this context, I would like to thank Nassim Balestrini, Klaus Rieser, Silvia Schultermandl, Katharina Fackler and their advanced and not so advanced students at Graz for their relentless interest in and contributions to the progress of this book. Many thanks also to Tomáš Pospíšil, professor of American studies at Masaryk University, for giving me the chance to discuss chapters of this book with him, his colleagues, and students in Moravia. In addition, I have also learned a lot from the ongoing discussions with Susanne Lachenicht, professor of early modern history at Bayreuth University here in Bavaria.

A thanks also goes to my own University of Regensburg in Bavaria, Germany, where I have been teaching U.S. history in national, continental, and transatlantic perspectives for fifteen years. Here, especially, the Regensburg European-American Forum (REAF), with my colleagues Birgit Bauridl, Stephan Bierling, and Udo Hebel, has offered me a vibrant and stimulating platform of intellectual exchange. I am particularly grateful for the REAF Book Project Presentation event of June 12, 2018, which gave me the welcome chance to discuss my emerging manuscript with Stephan Bierling, Udo Hebel, and Ben Chappel, professor of American Studies at Kansas University, in a marathon event of more than two hours. It was as exhausting as it was exciting. My largest thanks, however, go to my students at Regensburg University, with whom I have discussed the book's themes and arguments in a series of lectures—American Exceptionalism, parts 1 through 4. Their questions, remarks, comments, and exam answers over the course of four semesters have contributed tremendously to the book as it now stands, and I am deeply indebted to them.

Speaking of Regensburg students, my two able student assistants, Anja Kurasov and Annika Pauly, have done a great job conscientiously checking quotes and bibliographical references. Thank you for your work.

My final and most heartfelt thanks are reserved for my wife, Irmgard, and my son, Simon, for providing me with a private environment of love, solidarity, and partnership that carries me along in my scholarly work. While I tried to be a good husband and father, I am fully aware that both of them suffered through yet another book that I was writing on weekends and at times when other people would make merry with their loved ones in whichever pastime pursuits. While I cannot promise that I will not write another book again, I do want to dedicate this book to my wife, Irmgard, who has been at my side for the longest parts of my exciting transatlantic life.

Introduction

EVENTS IN THE U.S. since the spring of 2020 have shed a sharp light on the many facets and multiple paradoxes of American Exceptionalism. The COVID-19 pandemic hit the U.S. as it did every other country. Exceptionalist claims and pretensions did not make Americans immune to the virus, and the U.S. responded to the global disease in pretty much the same way as all other countries falling prey to it: Businesses, schools, theatres, and other institutions went into lockdown, public life died down, and people retreated to the isolated safety of their private homes, while wearing face masks and experimenting with forms of social distancing elsewhere. Many Americans revived old hobbies, or discovered new ones, perfected their home-cooking skills, watched Netflix until they dropped, and hoarded toilet paper in unprecedented amounts. There was nothing exceptional about this in any way. Rather than following trajectories only to be had under North American skies, American responses to the coronavirus were but a variation of international themes.

At the same time, if there was something that was exceptional about the pandemic in the U.S., it was the rapidity with which the disease could spread, the scale it could reach, and the deaths it could cause. The U.S. as the strongest, richest, and technologically most advanced country in the world had far and away the largest number of infections and the highest number of deaths caused by COVID-19. Compared to other developed countries, the U.S. was exceptionally ill prepared to confront the coronavirus. It revealed that the U.S. was anything but an invincible country, and it seriously undermined the myth that the U.S. was the best country on earth.

A couple of weeks into the rapidly spreading pandemic, another event exposed another dynamic of American Exceptionalism: On May 25, 2020, George Floyd, a forty-six-year-old black man, died during his arrest by four Minneapolis police officers after one of them, Derek Chauvin, put his knee on Floyd's neck and pressed his handcuffed body to the ground for nine and a half minutes. This act of police brutality set off a series of nationwide protests against the continuing racism in the U.S., highlighting the fact that liberty in the U.S. is, was, and has always been inseparably tied to slavery, racial discrimination, and other forms of unfreedom. This tension has shaped and structured the conceptual history of American Exceptionalism from its colonial and revolutionary beginnings to today in complex and contradictory ways.

And then came the presidential election of 2020, the climax of Donald Trump's disruptive presidency that had posed a dangerous right-wing populist and authoritarian challenge to all notions of a liberal American Exceptionalism revolving around concepts like "a city upon a hill," a "beacon of light," or "the last best hope of mankind." The 2020 elections witnessed a sitting U.S. president blustering about election fraud even before the first ballots had been cast; Americans saw a president refusing to accept regular election results and trying to manipulate certification procedures in the states; and they experienced a populist mob of violent Trump supporters, let loose by *their* president, sacking the U.S. Capitol on January 6, 2021, to halt the congressional confirmation of the election results. This last attempt to disrupt a legitimate electoral process was not only the final and most glaring in a long series of presidential acts undermining the integrity of a constitutional order that Donald Trump, like forty-four presidents before him, had sworn to protect in his oath of office. It also deepened the already deep crisis of disorientation in the U.S., which, to a very large extent, is anchored in a widely shared uncertainty about whether American Exceptionalism is still a valid concept and an acceptable identity narrative in the U.S. today.

Without knowing what was yet to come, Viet Thanh Nguyen, in an opinion piece published in the *New York Times* on April 10, 2020, suggested that American Exceptionalism was among the ideas that would not survive the pandemic. COVID-19, he argued, had awakened Americans "to the pre-existing conditions" of their body politic. "We were not as healthy as we thought we were," he wrote. "The biological virus afflicting individuals is also a social virus. Its symptoms—inequality, callousness, selfishness and a profit motive that undervalues human life and overvalues commodities—were for too long masked by the hearty good cheer of American exceptionalism, the ruddiness of someone a few steps away from a heart attack."

Nobody can seriously make any predictions as to whether the coronavirus, or any of the other events of 2020 and 2021, for that matter, have killed the concept of American Exceptionalism, but Nguyen's arguments did not come out of the blue. Belief in the exceptionality of their country has been declining rapidly among U.S. citizens since 2000. According to the "American-Western European Values Gap" survey conducted by the Global Attitudes Project at the Pew Research Center in 2011, only 49 percent of Americans still held their culture to be superior. This was a decline of 11 percent compared to 2002, when the survey was first conducted.

Viewed against this backdrop, President Donald Trump's inaugural address of January 20, 2017, was remarkable for its refusal to sing the song of American Exceptionalism. In his first speech as forty-fifth president, Trump did not celebrate the U.S. as a singular nation with a unique history and a manifest destiny to protect, support, and spread liberty, democracy, and affluence at home and abroad. Nor did he mention the Constitution even once.

With the whole world watching, Trump painted a bleak and gloomy portrait of today's America as a desolate wasteland of decline, destruction, and despair. He highlighted "[m]others and children trapped in poverty in our inner cities," pointed to "rusted-out factories scattered like tombstones across the landscape of our nation," saw the educational system depriving America's students of knowledge, and spoke about "the crime and the gangs and the drugs that have stolen too many lives and robbed our country of so much unrealized potential." Instead of American Exceptionalism, Trump spoke of an "American carnage" that needed to be stopped.

The America that Trump promised to put first had overstretched its political power by its global military presence and had overstretched its economic might through a policy of free trade, open borders, and global economic entanglements that made other countries rich while impoverishing the U.S. In light of this diagnosis, Trump advocated an "America First" nationalism, built not on the strength of American institutions, values, and ideals, but on the "red blood of patriots," a nationalism that did "not seek to impose our way of life on anyone, but rather to let it shine as an example [. . .] for everyone to follow" because it accepted the right of any nation to put its own interests first.

Roughly 230 years before President Trump's dark inaugural address, John Hector St. John de Crèvecœur had rendered a radically different description of the American condition. In the third of his *Letters from an American Farmer*, titled "What Is an American?," written in 1782, the

French-born agriculturist from colonial New York represented America as a land of exceptional freedom, affluence, and progress. Its landscape offered a scenic view of "fair cities, substantial villages, extensive fields, an immense country filled with decent houses, good roads, orchards, meadows, and bridges, where a hundred years ago all was wild, woody, and uncultivated!"

Crèvecœur saw North America as a "new continent" peopled by a "modern society" that was radically different from Europe's. American society, he wrote, was "not composed, as in Europe, of great lords who possess everything, and of a herd of people who have nothing." In America, there were "no aristocratical families, no courts, no kings, no bishops, no ecclesiastical dominion, no invisible power giving to a few a very visible one, no great manufacturers employing thousands, no great refinements of luxury." Colonial North America thus appeared as a negation of Europe. It lacked everything that was constitutive of Europe's monarchies and aristocracies. In America, individuals were free to determine themselves, accumulate property, and pursue their notions of a good life. This, for Crèvecœur, was the reason the colonies were experiencing the most dynamic growth the world had never seen before. For eighteenth-century observers on both sides of the Atlantic, America was exceptional because it was *not* Europe. As such, it was a miracle.

Crèvecœur's reflections on the Americanness of America were an early manifestation of the concept of American Exceptionalism, which Byron Shafer, in his 1991 collected volume *Is America Different?*, defined as "the notion that the United States was created differently, developed differently, and thus has to be understood differently—essentially on its own terms and within its own context." This view was seconded by Seymour Martin Lipset in his chapter "American Exceptionalism Reaffirmed" in Shafer's collected volume; he summarized: American Exceptionalism "basically means that America is unique, is different in crucial ways from most other countries," and especially "distinct from other Western countries."

Notions of exceptionality have been crucial for the intellectual construction of America from its colonial beginnings; the current uncertainty about America's national identity, the meaning of America, and its place in the world has a lot to do with the idea of American Exceptionalism having become increasingly problematic. It is, however, not only the declining belief in America's exceptionality that feeds into the present crisis of disorientation. The uncertainty about the meaning of America is anchored to a very large extent in the concept of American Exceptionalism itself, its inner contradictions and paradoxes.

All of this calls for a new look into the conceptual history of American Exceptionalism as a phenomenon and factor of U.S. history from a *longue durée* perspective. Based on the definitions cited above, such an investigation could go in two directions. It could, first, take America's exceptionality as a given, look for indicators to measure it, compare them to other countries in the world, identify the factors that explain the distinctive and unusual trajectories of U.S. history, and from there assess the situation in the U.S. today. That is *not* what this book will do.

Rather, it takes the second investigative path opened up by the above-cited definition of American Exceptionalism. Instead of pursuing the question of *in which respects* the U.S. indeed *was, has been,* or *is* different from other world regions, this book is interested in the questions of *how, when, why, by whom, for which reasons*, and *to what effect* America was *imagined* as exceptional in the course of U.S. history. This means approaching American Exceptionalism not as an objective fact but as a socially constructed system of meaning that makes sense out of the world people live in, that gives them a place in this world, that defines who they are and who they want to be. American Exceptionalism is thus treated here as a cognitive map. As such a map, American Exceptionalism is, as Deborah L. Madsen wrote in her book *American Exceptionalism*, "one of the most important concepts underlying modern theories of American cultural identity" that has contributed substantially "to the evolution of the United States of America as an ideological and geographical entity."

Still, American Exceptionalism is not, and has never been, a monolithic, coherent, and stable intellectual concept. Rather, it is a highly malleable system of meaning that took on different shapes and forms in the changing contexts of U.S. history, serving different purposes and functions in each of them. In his 2009 book *The New American Exceptionalism*, Donald Pease identified American Exceptionalism as a "metaconcept" that puts a frame around a complex, multifaceted, and ever-changing assemblage of myths, symbols, themes, and narratives suggesting America's uniqueness, and as such a metaconcept, this book will treat the phenomenon it seeks to investigate.

Defining American Exceptionalism as a notion, a metaconcept, or a system of meaning, however, does not mean that this book is dealing with bloodless matters of the mind, relevant only as a phenomenon of America's intellectual history. That is way off the mark because, as a cognitive map, American Exceptionalism organized American perspectives on the world and shaped the way in which Americans acted in it. Notions of America's exceptionality and uniqueness have been a "cultural reality" and, as such, a "potent force" throughout U.S. history, as Michael Kammen argued in his *American Quarterly* article "American Exceptionalism: A Reconsideration" in 1993.

American Exceptionalism meant different things to different people at different times; there was hardly ever a shared understanding as to what it was, what defined it, and how to interpret it. The history of the concept actually is a history of competing versions of exceptionalism that became the subject of social struggles over the meaning of America. This book, therefore, will be concerned with identifying the many competing and sometimes outright contradictory versions of American Exceptionalism. Integrating a broad range of very different source materials, the chapters combine in-depth readings of key documents, literary texts, and visual materials with thick descriptive reconstructions of the historical contexts in which exceptionalist notions were constructed, negotiated, transformed, and put to multiple uses for different—sometimes mutually exclusive—political, social, economic, and cultural agendas.

In doing so, the book offers a problem-conscious synthesis of a vast and multidisciplinary scholarly literature that, basically, since the beginning of the American Studies project in the 1920s, has investigated single themes, aspects, dimensions, and major problems of American Exceptionalism for the various periods and epochs of U.S. history. Two of the most important subjects discussed by scholars in the field are the religious foundations of American Exceptionalism in Puritan New England and the political transformation of the whole conceptual field in the course of the American Revolution. Other scholars have analyzed the American land as a formative factor of exceptionalist mindsets, while still others have explored the role of exceptionalism for different periods and themes of U.S. foreign policy. Furthermore, the problems of exceptionalism and race, exceptionalism and abundance, and exceptionalism and labor history have been scrutinized for single periods of U.S. history. Yet still missing is a comprehensive, systematic, and still accessible conceptual history of American Exceptionalism from the colonial beginnings to today for the general reader.

The book's nine chapters are thematically organized around key ideas, thematic threads, and dimensions of American Exceptionalism, with each of the chapters being structured by chronological arches of different temporal length. Readers will thus get repeated marches through U.S. history, although not every march will take them from the colonial times to the present.

Chapter 1 explains how America's landscapes and natural environments have triggered, shaped, and structured the exceptionalist imagination of explorers, travelers, writers, artists, photographers, and, most importantly, immigrants since the start of European-American encounters in the late fifteenth century. Notions of America's exceptionality were to a very large extend tied to the features of the American land and the opportunities it offered—but in very different and even contradictory ways.

Chapter 2 takes another spatial approach to the problem by reflecting the frontier West and the South as two regions in U.S. history with their own distinct exceptionalisms. It will show how the frontier, as a place, process, and myth of U.S. history, was identified, constructed, and discussed as the allegedly single cause America's Americanness. Next, the chapter takes readers to the American South, whose exceptionalism was forged by slavery, plantation culture, the Civil War, and Jim Crow. While the significance of frontier exceptionalism for the creation of a national identity in the U.S. can hardly be overestimated, the dynamics of Southern exceptionalism had the potential of undermining, questioning, and even destroying all pretensions to national unity in the U.S.

The following two chapters trace the colonial origins of American Exceptionalism and the transformation of the conceptual field in revolutionary America. Chapter 3 reconstructs how notions of exceptionalism were planted in colonial soils in the seventeenth century. They came to North America with the Great Puritan Migration of the 1630s and 1640s, led by John Winthrop, whose famous sermon "A Model of Christian Charity" of 1630 not only stands at the beginning of the Puritan project to create a God-fearing ideal society in the woods of New England but also marked the powerful beginning of the conceptual history of American

Exceptionalism. Yet John Winthrop and his Congregationalists were not the only ones striving to realize model societies in colonial British North America. Many other early modern Europeans migrated to North America to realize social utopias there, that is, societies that could only be anticipated for some distant future in Europe, if they could be realized there at all. These utopian quests were anchored in a sense of chosenness and mission, but at the same time, they were inseparably tied to the possibility of failure, which created a distinct set of anxieties specific to the history of American Exceptionalism moving between utopian visions and the specter of failure.

Chapter 4 analyzes the history of the concept in revolutionary America. It will show how exceptionalist notions circulating in colonial British North America were secularized and tied to the American experiment in liberty, self-government, and political participation. The chapter identifies the American Revolution as the point from which the combination of natural-rights liberalism, the institutions of America's democracy, and a future-oriented rhetoric of progress became central elements of an exceptionalist thinking that traced the uniqueness of the U.S. to its revolutionary founding act.

The role American Exceptionalism played in the formulation, justification, and conduct of U.S. foreign policy is the subject of chapter 5. Treating U.S. foreign policy as a matter of identity politics, it will trace the presence and significance of the concept in U.S. foreign policy agendas in a broad historical sweep from the Early Republic to the War on Terror. This *longue durée* history of U.S. foreign policy will show that exceptionalist persuasions were used to justify the most contradictory policy agendas.

American Exceptionalism not only served to structure and legitimate U.S. foreign policy, but it also was a powerful cultural resource for domestic reform, as the following two chapters will show. Chapter 6 looks at the African American struggle for civil rights through the prism of American Exceptionalism and demonstrates how a marginalized group empowered itself by using the founding documents' universal concepts to claim its own right to self-determination and political participation. American Exceptionalism thus had a counter-hegemonic potential, emerging from the well-known paradox that the radical egalitarianism of America's founding ideology, which declared all men to

INTRODUCTION

have been created equal, was never applied to *all* persons living in the U.S. for most of the country's history. This always only partial realization of the American Revolution's emancipatory promise was one of the major forces driving and shaping the civil rights agendas of marginalized groups, and the African American freedom struggle is a very powerful case in point. Yet there were clear limits to the counter-hegemonic power of American Exceptionalism insofar as it allowed for only integrationist visions of racial justice, forcing the hitherto marginalized to assimilate to America's liberal founding credo of individual liberty and equal opportunity.

Chapter 7 expands the argument by critically reflecting on the presence, function, and effect of American Exceptionalism in three reform movements: the women's suffrage movement, welfare reforms of the New Deal, and the labor movement. The chapter shows how both the struggle for women's right to vote and the New Deal reforms were borne by an exceptionalist self-awareness among the reformers, who saw the U.S. as a perfectible union whose exceptionalism still lay ahead and would materialize only if their reform initiative was successful. A look into the history of the labor movement in the U.S., however, reveals an altogether different facet of American Exceptionalism and reform, that is, the one defined by the question of why there is no socialism in the U.S.

Chapter 8 analyzes prosperity and abundance as central elements and themes of American Exceptionalism from the colonial period to today. It traces the history of the American Dream and shows how it put American Exceptionalism on a very fragile basis that could carry exceptionalist notions only as long as Americans could actually accumulate wealth, or at least anticipate it in the future.

Chapter 9 will look into the multiple and contested meanings of American Exceptionalism in contemporary America. It will identify radically different and mutually exclusive versions of the concept that not only mirror the deep frictions and social cleavages between the conservative and liberal America of today but also contribute to deepening the existing divisions. Looking at the political polarization in the U.S. through the lens of American Exceptionalism, and relating it to the fundamental social, economic, and cultural transformations of the U.S. since roughly the mid-1970s, the chapter argues that instead of being a potent cultural force unifying the country, the diverging conservative and liberal variants of American Exceptionalism are currently dividing the country even further.

Overall, this book offers a comprehensive cultural history of the U.S. through the prism of American Exceptionalism, which paves many paths to the central features, key themes, major problems, and contradictions of the American way of life, which has either fascinated or shocked both Americans and non-Americans throughout the ages but which has hardly ever left anybody indifferent. The history of why, how, when, by whom, and to what effects America was imagined as exceptional, therefore, provides much more nutritious food for stimulating thought about U.S. history than the rather sterile question of whether the U.S. indeed is, was, or has been exceptional.

I

The American Land

Landscapes of Abundance, Wilderness, and Beauty

THE NORTH AMERICAN land has triggered the exceptionalist imagination throughout U.S. history. The land's vastness and topographical diversity, landscapes and scenery, fertility of its soils, and rich wealth of its natural resources, and let's not forget its geological marvels—the Grand Canyon, Niagara Falls, or Monument Valley—have formed the material basis for concepts of American Exceptionalism from the early modern period to today.

It was the eminent scholar Perry Miller who famously identified Americans as "nature's nation," whose sense of identity as a nation was deeply rooted in North America's natural environments. While Europeans had history, tradition, and hoary legends to base notions of identity on, Miller argued, Americans, living in a young country lacking historical depth, drew on North America's geography and its nature to imagine, negotiate, and contest notions of Americanness. With the North American continent being as geographically diverse as it is, however, it was not at all clear which land Americans referred to when they talked about America as exceptional.

Still, North America's geography and nature were a major factor in the conceptual history of American Exceptionalism, and in the wide web of nature-related narratives, three different landscapes feature most prominently: First, landscapes of abundance, second landscapes of wilderness, and third landscapes of beauty. In all of these landscapes, nature was imagined as either benevolent or hostile to humanity, but whichever way it was framed, nature always appeared as exceptional; it was either uniquely rich in its fertility and natural resources, extraordinarily hostile, or beautiful and sublime to an unprecedented degree.

CHAPTER 1

LANDSCAPES OF ABUNDANCE

Landscapes of abundance celebrated the unique ability of the American land to provide sustenance and wealth to those who worked hard to tap its resources. Fertile soils, extensive forests full of game animals, rivers full of fish, and a rich wealth of mineral resources in a seemingly empty land—all of these were recurring elements of imagined landscapes of abundance, feeding hopes of opportunity, limitless wealth, and social rising in this world.

In the sixteenth century, however, when Europe began to expand to what, only for Europeans, was the New World, it was highly unlikely that North America's natural abundance would figure prominently in the conceptual history of American Exceptionalism—and that it would do so for so long. The first European explorers, such as John Cabot, Jacques Cartier, Hernando de Soto, or Francisco Vásquez de Coronado, hoped to find in North America what Spanish conquistadores had found in Central and South America before them: gold, silver, and a large indigenous population they could rule over as feudal lords. They did not find any of this in North America, and what they did find, they were not interested in: dense forests teeming with wildlife, gigantic shoals of fish off the Atlantic coast and in the inland waters, fertile soils, and abundant natural resources. These promised neither glory nor quick riches, so Spain and Portugal, the leading European colonial powers, quickly lost interest in North America.

When England entered the race for the Western Hemisphere as a new player at the end of the sixteenth century, it did so with a new form of colonization, the settlement colony. In contrast to the Iberian model of conquest and aristocratic rule, the English colonies in North America were to be systematically peopled by large numbers of European immigrants who would exploit the natural resources of the continent through their own work. Instead of seeking instant wealth in the form of silver and gold, the settlers would engage in agricultural pursuits to patiently extract commodities from North America's lush nature for commercial profit. This gave new meaning to the continent's natural abundance, which was now seen as an economic asset.

In one of the very first descriptions of America, Christopher Columbus had already established this economic gaze on the natural riches of the Western Hemisphere. Writing to Luis de Santángel, his supporter at the Spanish court of King Ferdinand II of Aragon and Queen Isabella I of Castile, on February 15, 1493, Columbus described the Caribbean island of Hispaniola as a "marvel" featuring "large tracts of cultivatable lands," which were "very fertile to a limitless degree." The island was "filled with trees of a thousand kinds," so tall that they seemed to "touch the sky." He counted "six or eight kinds of palm," and recorded a "beautiful variety" of "other trees and fruits and plants." This letter became the basis for the first printed descriptions of America circulating widely in the whole of Europe, and the image of the New World as a land of milk and honey shaped the European imagination for several centuries.

While Columbus was speaking of the West Indies, English explorers like Thomas Harriot or John Smith used his conceptual frame to depict the natural environments of Virginia in a very similar way. In his *A Briefe and True Report of the New Found Land of Virginia*, Thomas Harriot (a mathematician, astronomer, and ethnographer, who in 1585–1586 was involved with the lost colony of Roanoke) admitted that Virginia was not rich in gold. It was, however, endowed with the greatest wealth in natural resources. Painstakingly charting the abundance of commercially viable plants and animals, Harriot described dense pine forests teeming with game animals, wrote about rivers and lakes full of fish, and praised the fertility of the soil in the most celebratory of words. North America thus appeared as a land of potential wealth for those willing to work hard as farmers, fishermen, hunters, and artisans.

Roughly thirty years later, Captain John Smith, the key figure in the founding of Jamestown, Virginia, published his *A Description of New England* in 1616. Describing the experiences of his expedition to what today are Maine and Massachusetts in 1614, Smith informed his readers about the rich fishing grounds off the Atlantic coast and the abundance of beavers, otters, black foxes, and other animals valued for their furs in the thickets of New England's forests. There were "all sorts of excellent good woods for building houses, boats, barks, or ships." The land in New England was "so fertile that questionless it is capable of producing any grain, fruits, or seeds you will sow or plant." In addition, cattle could easily be bred and fed for nothing, and there was also an abundance of fruits and berries worth a fortune in England. These natural resources, Smith suggested, were there for everybody to exploit for a profit, and every person unable to make a comfortable living in New England was deserving of starvation.

Descriptions like these served promotional purposes. They were written to attract European investors and immigrants to North America. This was necessary because England relied heavily on private initiative and enterprise to undertake the colonization effort. The Crown issued charters to private persons, granting them a certain territory in America, authorizing them to govern over it, and privileging them with exclusive trading rights. These charters established the English Crown as supreme authority over the new colonies in America—but the royal government would not get heavily involved itself, leaving it to merchants and other investors to bear the financial risks and organizational burdens of colonization. England's colonies in North America all began as investment objects of European businessmen, who had to see that their colonies were peopled and made a profit. Featuring the abundance of North America's natural resources, and representing the economic chances and possibilities connected to them in bright colors, was a means to attract European settlers and persuade them to take the enormous risks to life, health, and happiness connected to the adventure of settling in America.

After critical and highly chaotic beginnings that brought many a colonial project to the brink of disaster, the colonies of British North America began to consolidate toward the end of the seventeenth century, and in the eighteenth century, they experienced a period of massive and sustained growth that appeared to be unprecedented to many contemporaries. In his "Observations Concerning the Increase of Mankind," written in 1751 and widely read in America and Europe, Benjamin Franklin calculated that the population in the American colonies was doubling every twenty years, while population growth in Europe was stagnating. Franklin saw two reasons for this development: one was European immigration, and the other was the high rate of natural reproduction, which he understood to be the result of the economic opportunities colonial North America offered. In Europe, Franklin argued, people could not afford to marry because all trades, occupations, and offices were full, all land was taken, and wages were low due to the oversupply of labor. In America, however, land was plentiful, "and so cheap as that a labouring Man, that understands Husbandry, can in a short Time save Money enough to purchase a Piece of new Land sufficient for a Plantation, whereon he may subsist a Family." Marriages in America, therefore, were "more general," and they occurred at an earlier stage in life, which is why Americans tended to have more children than Europeans. Franklin argued that the territory of America was so vast and supposedly empty that it would require many ages "to settle it fully."

Depictions of the American colonies like Franklin's attracted a lot of attention in Europe, and in 1750 Gottlieb Mittelberger was one of the many Germans who came to Pennsylvania in search of a land of milk and honey. He did not find it, however, returned to Germany, and published his report *Reise nach Pennsylvanien im Jahr 1750 und Rückreise nach Deutschland im Jahr 1754* (Journey to Pennsylvania in the Year 1750 and Return to Germany in the Year 1754) in 1756 to counter the many idealized images of America circulating in Europe at that time. Still, Mittelberger used many words in praising Pennsylvania's lush nature, the fertility of its soils, and the abundance of its natural resources, claiming that Pennsylvania was "der Bauren ihr Himmel" (the heaven of the farmers), and "der Handwerksleute ihr Paradies" (the paradise of the mechanics).

In revolutionary America, the continent's natural abundance helped structure the debates about independence. In his pamphlet *Common Sense*, published in January 1776, Thomas Paine called for an immediate break with England, and he argued that America's natural abundance would provide the basis for America's military strength in the inevitable war with the mother country. "No country on the globe is so happily situated, or so internally capable of raising a fleet as America," Paine suggested, and he went on: "Tar, timber, iron, and cordage are her natural produce. We need go abroad for nothing." As long as America's strength and natural riches played into each other's hands, "we need fear no external enemy. In almost every article of defence we abound."

When the Revolutionary War was over, the founders of the American republic continued to reflect on North America's topography and its natural resources as both economic and political assets. In the second of the *Federalist Papers*, published on October 31, 1787, John Jay wrote that Providence had blessed the "fertile, wide spreading country [. . .] with a variety of soils and productions, and watered it with innumerable streams, for the delight and accommodation of its inhabitants. A succession of navigable waters forms a kind of chain round its borders." America's rivers were "the most noble [. . .] in the world"; they would serve as arteries of communication and trade, as "highways for the easy communication of friendly aids, and the mutual transportation and exchange of their various commodities."

The geography, flora, and fauna of the North American continent thus became the material base for the experiment in liberty and democracy that was started with the American Revolution. The American republic and the American land were seemingly made for each other, and only because of the American land would the daring experiment in self-government succeed. In the Early Republic, concepts of American Exceptionalism were closely linked to an agrarian myth that envisioned the U.S. as a rural republic inhabited by self-reliant, freedom-loving, sturdy and virtuous farmers working their own land. These exceptionalist narratives celebrated the American land not only as the source of economic riches but also as the source of a republican virtue that distinguished the U.S. from Europe.

It was Thomas Jefferson who, in "Query XIX" of his *Notes on the State of Virginia*, theorized agrarianism to be a source of republican virtue that was needed to stabilize and perpetuate the inherently fragile political order of America's democracy. Reflecting on the state of manufacturing, commerce, and trade in Virginia and the U.S., Jefferson, in a daring break with all European economic theory, denied the "principle that every state should endeavour to manufacture for itself," and warned of its application to American contexts. Whereas Europe had advanced to the manufacturing stage "of necessity not of choice" to support its large populations due to the lack of available land, the U.S. had an "an immensity of land courting the industry of the husbandman."

Therefore, it was exempt from the laws of economic development; instead of having to advance from the simple agrarian state to a more complex industrial order, the U.S. could afford to perpetuate the agrarian economy and thereby escape the social problems and corruption that were inevitably connected to an industrial economy. "Those who labour in the earth," Jefferson explained, "are the chosen people of God," and as such, they were a "peculiar deposit for substantial and genuine virtue." History offered no example of an agrarian people becoming corrupt in its morals.

In Jefferson's way of thinking, virtue was political through and through. Virtue meant responsible self-government on behalf of the common good, it meant the ability to abstract from one's own particular interests and ambitions on behalf of the general interest. Thus, virtuous people would serve as guardians of America's political order, would make individual sacrifices to defend the liberty of all, and would be immune to personal ambition. Most importantly, however, virtuous people would, in practicing self-government, always make sure that the very foundations of the political order were secured and perpetuated. Virtue was systematically produced by the agrarian way of life centering on land ownership, whereas industrial orders generated nothing but dependence, poverty, and corruption. In contrast to the independent yeoman farmer, industrial workers were dependent in the broadest sense; they were not only economically dependent but also intellectually unfree. "Dependance," Jefferson wrote, "begets subservience and venality," and "suffocates the germ of virtue." This made the working-class poor "fit tools for the designs of ambition" that eventually would destroy liberty. He advised: "While we have land to labour then, let us never wish to see our citizens occupied at a work-bench, or twirling a distaff. Carpenters, masons, smiths, are wanting in husbandry: but, for the general operations of manufacture, let our work-shops remain in Europe." Only this would secure the "happiness and permanence of government" in the U.S. Agrarianism thus would help to perpetuate the political experiment in liberty and democracy started by the American Revolution—and America's exceptionalism with it. However, the political economy of agrarianism relied on the imagined endlessness of the land supply. The question of what would happen to America's exceptionality when all land in the U.S. was cultivated, settled, and owned was not really debated by Benjamin Franklin, Thomas Jefferson, and other champions of agrarianism in the Early Republic.

The agrarian myth found its visual manifestation in the landscape paintings of Thomas Cole, Asher B. Durand, Frederic Edwin Church, and other artists of the Hudson River school. These artists represented the American land as pastoral landscapes, that is, as landscapes in which wilderness had been transformed into farmland, orchards, and gardens. In this pastoral state, wilderness had largely been tamed while men and women were still in tune with nature. A beautiful example of such a landscape is Thomas Cole's oil painting *View from Mount Holyoke, Northampton, Massachusetts, after a Thunderstorm*, executed in 1836. Also termed *The Oxbow*, this painting offers a view from an elevated position into the vast pastoral scenery of the Connecticut River Valley. It shows the river bending in a valley dotted with farms, peaceful in golden light. The river separates the two halves of the scene, which has a thick, undeveloped and supposedly untouched forest representing wilderness on its left, while the right half, dominated by the majestic curve of the river, depicts an agricultural landscape where farmers in a happy balance of agricultural simplicity live virtuous lives without want but also without greed. This division corresponds to a darkness-and-light opposition that relates darkness to wilderness and light to civilization. The storm has passed and still hovers over the wilderness, while the viewer can look into the infinite light shining over the agricultural area. The scene visualizes the meeting ground of wilderness and civilization, with the painter looking from an elevated position in the forest into the pastoral landscape of abundance before him.

While this painting could be read as praising the achievements of America's yeoman farmers, in fact, it carried a paradoxical tension of triumph and nostalgia. On the one hand, Cole's pastoral landscapes of abundance celebrated the settlers' victory over wilderness as the basis of an agrarian economy that perpetuated the American experiment in liberty, self-determination, and self-government. On the other, it represented a sense of nostalgia growing from a deep skepticism about progress destroying the very nature that was the source of America's morality and virtue. For Cole and the other painters of the Hudson River school, the first settlers were both builders of a civilization and destroyers of a nature that defined America's exceptionality in contradistinction to Europe. Sooner or later, these paintings suggested, the agrarian state would be replaced by an industrial one—and what this would mean for America was anything but clear.

Many writers, artists, and intellectuals in the first half of the nineteenth century shared this sense of uneasiness about progress. The mass of settlers moving westward during the tumultuous U.S. expansion in that period was hardly touched by it. They tended to perceive the American land, not primarily as landscape in the aesthetic sense, but as territory waiting for them to develop it. Millions of settlers dreamed of getting rich in the thick forests and on the fertile soils of the North American West. Their hopes were based on the economic opportunities of the

Thomas Cole, *View from Mount Holyoke, Northampton, Massachusetts, after a Thunderstorm—The Oxbow*, oil on canvas, 1836. The Metropolitan Museum of Art, New York. http//:www.metmuseum.org

American land as they were celebrated in newspaper ads and immigrant manuals; travel accounts, poems, and novels; and paintings, prints, and other visual material.

One of the most enthusiastic celebrations of the U.S. as a farmers' heaven flowed from Gottfried Duden's pen. Duden was a German writer who investigated the U.S. as a possible destination for German emigrants after the Napoleonic Wars. He arrived in Missouri in 1824, purchased land about fifty miles west of St. Louis, and worked it for three years before he returned to Germany. He wrote about his experiences in his *Bericht über eine Reise nach den westlichen Staaten Nordamerika's und einem mehrjährigen Aufenthalt am Missouri* (Report about a Journey to the Western States of North America and a Stay in Missouri Lasting Several Years), which was published in 1829 and widely read.

The report offered a description of Missouri as a farmers' heaven in the most glowing of colors. Duden raved about the easy availability of enormously fertile land, abundance of minerals, low cost of living, and high wages in America. He wrote about the incredible ease of caring for livestock that seemingly did not involve any work at all. The farmer, Duden suggested, had to do nothing but let the cattle roam freely in the woods, where the animals would take care of themselves for the day and return punctually in the evening for milking, without any ever getting lost. Even setting up a farm in the woods of Missouri, while it did involve some work, was not a very hard and strenuous task, the way Duden represented it. The farmer would chop down some trees, set fire to the others, and then leave it to wind to tear the trees down—with the wind making sure that the falling trees did not damage the log cabin.

Landscapes of agricultural abundance continued to be a central element in concepts of American Exceptionalism for the rest of the nineteenth century. However, as the country entered a period of rapid industrialization after the Civil War, the idea of natural abundance took on a new meaning. Without replacing the agrarian myth, landscapes of abundance were now also framed in terms of the natural resources needed to fuel America's mindboggling industrial growth.

In a piece titled *Triumphant Democracy*, industrial magnate Andrew Carnegie in 1886 highlighted the substantial transformation and fast-paced growth of the U.S. over the last fifty years. Recollecting the U.S. transition from an agricultural to an industrial order, Carnegie saw the "old nations of the earth" creeping on "at a snail's pace," while the U.S. was thundering "past with the rush of the express." Within just a century, the U.S. had "reached the foremost rank among nations," and was "destined soon to out-distance all others in the race." In terms of population, wealth, agricultural production, and manufacturing, Carnegie lost no time in pointing out, America was already leading the "civilized world." Asking for the "causes which have led to the rapid growth and aggrandizement" of the U.S. during the last fifty years, Carnegie identified three factors as the most important ones. He traced America's exceptional growth, first, to the hegemony of Anglo-Saxon culture; second, to the U.S. political institutions founded upon liberal values; and third, to the "the topographical and climatic conditions" in America.

This fascination with America's industrial growth extended to Europeans like Max Goldberger as well. In his 1911 analysis of America's industrial economy *Das Land der unbegrenzten Möglichkeiten: Beobachtungen über das Wirtschaftsleben der Vereinigten Staaten von Amerika* (The Land of Unlimited Opportunities: Observations on the American

Business Life), he spent a whole chapter reflecting on the country's rich endowment of natural resources as one major factor behind America's economic strength. He depicted the American land as a "Zaubergarten" (magic garden) with wonderfully rich soils and a surplus of minerals that left the visitor standing in awe and wonderment. Listing the country's deposits of iron ore, coal, oil, copper, lead, mercury, and zinc, Goldberger concluded that America's mineral resources were so gigantic that the U.S. could easily win the economic race against the other industrial nations of the world from one day to the next.

LANDSCAPES OF WILDERNESS

Before there were landscapes of abundance, there were landscapes of wilderness, and they played their own role in the conceptual history of American Exceptionalism. By wilderness, I mean uncultivated and otherwise undeveloped land in an immense and largely unknown area, where men are absent and wild animals are present. *Wilderness* thus describes a world alien to man and a place yet untouched by human civilization. As such, wilderness has a double reality. On the one hand, there is the physical reality of natural environments in North America: its thick primeval forests, prairies, deserts, and other treeless lands, and its many craggy mountainous areas. On the other hand, wilderness is also a symbolic reality, which grows from the decision of individuals and social groups to imagine nature as untouched and unaltered. Wilderness, as both a physical and a symbolic reality, and a material fact and human imagination, was of towering importance for the intellectual history of American Exceptionalism. "Wilderness was the basic ingredient of American civilization," Roderick Nash wrote in his seminal study *Wilderness and the American Mind*. "From the raw materials of the physical wilderness Americans built a civilization; with the idea or symbol of wilderness they sought to give that civilization identity and meaning."

While wilderness figured prominently in concepts of American Exceptionalism, it did so in two different ways: first, as hostile, inhospitable, mysterious, and dangerous nature and, second, as beautiful and friendly scenery that was capable of elevating and delighting the viewer because it was a mirror of God's greatness and the providential blessing

He bestowed on the U.S. However, this latter appreciation of America's nature as a source of the sublime only came to the fore in the nineteenth century, when the real wilderness was vanishing rapidly on the continent; for most of U.S. history, the majority of settlers viewed wilderness as hostile and alien to man. It hemmed them in, narrowed their vision, and concealed many real and imagined dangers. Fearing and hating wilderness, settlers strove to destroy it in order to guarantee security, comfort, prosperity, and the enjoyment of life's pleasures.

The tradition of perceiving North America's natural environments as hostile wilderness started with William Bradford and the Pilgrims who came to America on the *Mayflower* and founded Plymouth Plantation in 1620. In his journal, *Of Plymouth Plantation*, Bradford, a signatory to the Mayflower Compact and longtime governor of the colony, recollected the moment of the Pilgrims' arrival in New England. He described how they joyfully thanked God for having brought them safely over the "vast and furios ocean," only to find themselves confronted with a howling and desolate wilderness, which Bradford represented as a nonhuman world completely untouched by civilization. Nobody was there to welcome them, Bradford wrote; there were no "inns to entertain or refresh their weatherbeaten bodies; no houses or much less towns to repair to, to seek for succor."

Ten years after the Pilgrims, the Congregationalists led by John Winthrop started to settle in Massachusetts. They, too, perceived of New England's nature as wilderness, but for them, *wilderness* not only referred to the physical realities of North American nature; it also had a religious and figurative meaning. Wilderness was not only a natural state but also a moral state insofar as it was seen as the habitat of the devil and sin. It was both an existential threat and a moral temptation through which one could either strengthen or lose one's faith in God. Cultivating wilderness, therefore, was equal to moralizing natural environments and the people that lived in them. Carving a garden from wilderness not only meant controlling nature and checking its threats but also bringing a spiritual light into darkness and redeeming the world from its moral wilderness. This was the famous "Errand into the Wilderness" that the Puritans saw themselves engaged in. For them, North America's wilderness had been spied out by God as the Promised Land for a chosen people with an agenda to create an ideal Christian society. Mastering New England's exceptional wilderness, in this way of thinking, only added to the sense of chosenness among the Congregationalists.

The Puritan perception of North American nature became the basis for heroic tales about civilizing wilderness, which, however, were increasingly divorced from their original religious meaning and reformulated in the secular terms of progress, reason, and prosperity. Wilderness continued to be seen as a moral threat, to be sure, but this no longer revolved around problems of salvation and doom in the next world. Rather, the moral threat that wilderness posed in the secularized narratives of progress went right to the very humanity of civilized men and women. Accordingly, a life in North America's wilderness could lead to their reverting to savagery, thereby losing the state of civilization and sociability they had had before.

In the third of his *Letters from an American Farmer*, John Hector St. John de Crèvecœur in 1782 detailed American life "near the great woods, near the last inhabited districts," and he went on tell his readers that there was "something in the proximity of the woods" that had strong effects on the people living there. Their behavior, as Crèvecœur saw it, was "regulated by the wildness of the neighbourhood." The settlers had come there to farm and raise livestock only to see the deer eating up their grain, the wolves destroying their sheep, the bears killing their hogs, and the foxes catching their poultry. "This surrounding hostility," Crèvecœur elaborated, "immediately puts the gun into their hands." Saying "farewell to the plough," the farmers became hunters. In Crèvecœur's eyes, this meant reverting to a lower and inferior state of human existence. The return to hunting marked the end of both agriculture and social organization. Hunting, Crèvecœur wrote, rendered the settlers "ferocious, gloomy, and unsocial." Hunters did not want any neighbors, whom they despised as potential competitors for the kill, and they began to "neglect their tillage." The first settlers in the woods, Crèvecœur concluded, were "our bad people," people who were "half cultivators and half hunters" with the "worst of them" being "those who have degenerated altogether into the hunting state."

The American Indians were seen as an integral part of the wilderness that Crèvecœur and others depicted. Already, Bradford in *Of Plymouth Plantation* had written about the "wild beasts and wild men" that the Pilgrims saw themselves confronted with, and the secular narratives of progress continued to dehumanize the American Indians by seeing them as part of the essentially nonhuman sphere of wilderness. This way of thinking justified the destruction of the American Indians for the sake of progress, as became manifest in President Andrew Jackson's "Message to Congress on Indian Removal" of December 6, 1830. In it, Jackson supported the removal of the Five Civilized Tribes from the states of Georgia, Tennessee, Alabama, Mississippi, and North Carolina to federal territory west of the Mississippi River. These tribes—the Chickasaw, Choctaw, Muscogee-Creek, Seminole, and Cherokee—were large in number and had adopted agriculture. This, however, did not matter much to Jackson, who in his address talked about the tribes as a "few savage hunters" occupying "large tracts of country" who needed to be removed to clear the land for "a dense and civilized population." Jackson argued that the expansion of European American civilization was an unstoppable historical process that saw "waves of population and civilization [...] rolling to the westward," letting the American Indians "mel[t] away to make room for the whites." At the heart of Jackson's justification of Indian removal was the idea that wilderness, which he considered Indians to be an integral part of, needed to be destroyed to promote progress in the widest sense. Interestingly enough, he added an aesthetic dimension to his argument, suggesting that wilderness was ugly, while civilization was seen as beautiful and its manifestations as an 'embellishment' of the natural landscape. "What good man," Jackson asked, "would prefer a country covered with forests and ranged by a few thousand savages to our extensive Republic, studded with cities, towns, and prosperous farms embellished with all the improvements which art can devise or industry execute, occupied by more than 12,000,000 happy people, and filled with all the blessings of liberty, civilization and religion?"

In Jackson's way of thinking, cultivating wilderness became a morality play in which wilderness was the villain and the settlers were the heroes. Survival in the wilderness became an indicator of success. The transformation of wilderness into civilization and the material prosperity resulting from it were the rewards for sacrifices made and temptations resisted. The settlers' triumph over an exceptionally wild North American wilderness thus gave evidence of both the enormous magnitude of their accomplishments and their exceptional moral steadfastness.

The idea of a heroic conquest of wilderness to spread the American way of life found its visual representation in John Gast's *American Progress*. At its center, the painting shows a beautiful young woman with long

John Gast, *American Progress*, oil on canvas, 1872. Autry Museum of the American West, Los Angeles. http//:www.TheAutry.org

and wavy hair allegorically representing progress. She is clad in a white dress blowing in the wind, and on her forehead, we can see what George Crofutt, an engraver and distributor of Gast's painting, called the "Star of Empire." As she is angelically flying aboveground from east to west, she brings settlers, farmers, miners, and people of other trades with her, while the bison, other wild animals, and the American Indians—all of them located on the left margin of the majestic painting—are retreating. They are literally on their way out of the picture.

Furthermore, progress is visually represented in terms of a dualism of black and white, darkness and light. While, from the viewer's perspective, the right margin of the painting is in the broadest daylight, its left margin is all dark. The advance of Euro-American civilization thus literally brings light into darkness and order into chaos, forcing the American Indians, some of whom are disbelievingly looking back, toward the darkness at the left. Behind the feminine figure, suspending a telegraph cable as she moves along, one can see railroads connecting the western parts with a city on a large river in the upper right quadrant of the painting. The telegraph and the railroads represent the revolution of transportation and communication the nineteenth century experienced, and they also stand for the commercial links between the agrarian landscapes of the American West and the industrial towns of the East. The viewer can observe quite a few smoking smokestacks in the city, and there are many ships on the river conveying produce and goods to the national and overseas markets.

John Gast's *American Progress* nicely sums up what this chapter has elaborated on so far: The wilderness condition was an important factor shaping concepts of American Exceptionalism insofar as the exceptional hostility and dangerousness of America's wilderness defined the exceptionality of settlers' achievement in conquering, taming, and controlling it. This perception of wilderness was inseparably intertwined with an imperialist gaze that conceived of the American continent as an empty space waiting to be settled by Euro-American settler societies. It let Americans imagine themselves as the masters of an immense, allegedly unused domain, who battled with nature solely, in the end, to master it.

LANDSCAPES OF BEAUTY

Beginning in the late eighteenth century and coming to the fore in the nineteenth, writers, artists, philosophers, railroad managers, and other Americans discovered the continent's supposedly untouched and pristine nature in its aesthetic value as a source of beauty and a path to the Divine. This altered the ways in which wilderness figured in ideas of American Exceptionalism substantially, and the literary movements of Romanticism and American transcendentalism contributed significantly to this transformation.

The nature writing of James Fenimore Cooper, Ralph Waldo Emerson, Henry David Thoreau, or Walt Whitman no longer viewed wilderness as a sinful and hostile wasteland. Instead, they interpreted wilderness as a majestic and marvelous space revealing the well-ordered complexity, harmony, and balance of the natural world as a divine creation. Framed in terms of grandeur and beauty, wilderness became a mirror of God's greatness. From there, it was only a small step to the idea of the sublime, which suggested that wilderness was a medium through which God communicated directly with mankind.

This pattern emerged in the eighteenth century, when Enlightenment philosophy, fascinated by the orderedness of the world, began to identify order with beauty. An early manifestation of this new way of aestheticizing America's natural environments was "Query V" of Thomas Jefferson's *Notes on the State of Virginia*, in which he elaborated on Virginia's Natural Bridge. Introducing it as "the most sublime of nature's works," Jefferson narrated how he climbed the steep arch of that bridge to have a look into the abyss and over the countryside. Recalling how, when creeping to the parapet, he involuntarily fell on his hands and feet to peep over it, he described this as a sublime moment of shocking insight into the beautiful orderedness of nature that was beyond words. "Looking down from this height about a minute, gave me a violent head ach. [. . .] It is impossible for the emotions arising from the sublime, to be felt beyond what they are here: so beautiful an arch, so elevated, so light, and springing as it were up to heaven, the rapture of the spectator is really indescribable!"

In writing that, Jefferson was deeply indebted to an Enlightenment deism that accepted the world as a divine creation but denied that God continued to intervene in worldly affairs after He had completed His work. Nineteenth-century American transcendentalism, however, introduced an outspokenly religious dynamic to the thinking about wilderness insofar as it reflected wilderness both as the medium of an active Christian God and as a source of Christian religiosity. The transcendentalist persuasion emerged in the second third of the nineteenth century, coinciding with the new cultural nationalism of the American Renaissance that wanted to create a decidedly American culture to become culturally independent of Europe. In this context, North America's wilderness began to figure as a unique source of an Americanness that had no counterpart in the Old World.

Postulating the existence of a higher world of spiritual truth behind the lower world of material things and physical reality, Ralph Waldo Emerson, Henry David Thoreau, and other writers of American transcendentalism saw nature as a medium connecting both worlds. While their bodies rooted human beings in the natural world, their capacity for imagination and intuition gave them the potential to transcend this condition and connect with the spiritual sphere. This had important implications for the meaning of American wilderness, which was now seen to reveal the presence of the Divine and higher moral truth in its purest form. Wilderness, therefore, seemed to enable the most direct and least blunted vision of the Divine. Here, man alienated by urban civilization and the complexity of life in the more developed areas of the U.S. could reconnect with God and reach an awareness of himself as an integral part of His creation. Man and nature thus became symbols of universal truths—and the American wilderness offered a unique environment to experience them.

With his essay "Nature," published in 1836, Emerson created the manifesto of American transcendentalism. In it, Emerson reflected on the experience of harmony with nature and the Divine creation emerging from a retreat from society into the solitude of the forests. Arguing that "in the woods," which he saw as "plantations of God," man would "return to reason and faith," Emerson reflected on the sublime moment of insight into the Divine order of the world and his own personal place in it. This moment of insight transcended all "mean egotism" and connected the individual with God, Emerson wrote. "I become a transparent eye-ball," he exclaimed about this transient moment of insight. "I am nothing; I see all; the currents of the Universal Being circulate through me; I am part or particle of God." This experience of the sublime was only to be had in the solitude of the woods. "In the wilderness, I find something more dear and connate than in streets or villages."

Wilderness, for Emerson, was immortal beauty that could be seen and felt but not intellectually grasped. He delighted in "the simple perception of natural forms," and characterized nature as that "perfectness and harmony" that is beauty. This beauty could be experienced both in the "totality of nature" and in every single natural object insofar as it mirrored the perfection of the whole. "Nothing is quite beautiful alone: nothing but is beautiful in the whole. A single object is only so far beautiful as it suggests this universal grace," Emerson suggested. Wilderness thus paved the way to the experience of beauty, which for Emerson was equal to the experience of moral truth and the Divine. "God is the all-fair," Emerson wrote, and he continued: "Truth, and goodness, and beauty, are but different faces of the same All."

While Emerson's nature writings had an implicit exceptionalist tone to them, Henry David Thoreau was one to enthusiastically celebrate America's wilderness as a cultural and moral source of American Exceptionalism. While his writings echoed Emerson's in many respects, Thoreau added a strong nonconformist and individualist dynamic that saw wilderness as enabling the most radical forms of individual freedom and self-determination. From 1845 to 1847, Thoreau lived a simple, frugal, and self-reliant life in a log cabin he built all by himself at Walden Pond, a mile outside of Concord, earning his living through manual labor. He wrote about his wilderness experiences in *Walden, or Life in the Woods*, published in 1854, in which he celebrated wilderness and the experience of the sublime as nobody before him had.

Thoreau's enthusiasm for wild nature went hand in hand with a deep dislike of civilization that, in his eyes, alienated man from nature, truth, and God. Civilized man, in Thoreau's view, was weak, dull, and unfree. Rejecting all materialistic pursuits, Thoreau opted for "voluntary poverty," when he decided to live at Walden Pond. Civilization for him was smallness, narrowness, futility, vanity, and transience that enslaved individuals, forced them into a vain and futile hunt for material goods, and alienated them from the eternal truths of the world. Wilderness, in contrast, was greatness, width, eternity, truth, and freedom. All good things, Thoreau argued, were wild and free, which made wilderness necessary to keep man vital, true to his own nature, and connected to the Divine. Looking, as Emerson did, at nature through an aesthetic prism, Thoreau wrote in one passage of *Walden* that a lake was "the landscape's most beautiful and expressive feature. It is earth's eye; looking into which the beholder measures the depth of his own nature." Bathing in the pond thus became "a religious exercise, and one of the best things which I did."

For Thoreau, this experience of the sublime was only to be had under American skies. In contrast to Europe, which was all cultivated and civilized, and therefore sterile, corrupt, and on a decline, America had wilderness in abundance, which was an endless reservoir of U.S. moral and cultural superiority. With that, the U.S. even surpassed biblical places, Thoreau suggested in his *Journal*, where he stated that "Adam in paradise was not so favorably situated on the whole as is the backwoodsman in America." In celebrating American wilderness in such a way, Thoreau was also celebrating the American core values of individual liberty, self-reliance, and self-determination. Even more than Emerson, Thoreau tied the sublimity of America's wilderness to notions of American Exceptionalism.

This rhetoric of the sublime in connection with wilderness was not confined to the circles of intellectual elites. It quickly became a standard way of understanding the meaning of America's natural wonders accepted by many. In countless statements, visitors to Niagara Falls, Yellowstone National Park, or other scenic highlights celebrated what they saw in words of religious awe and rapture. A case in point is U.S. president John Quincy Adams, who traveled to Niagara Falls in 1843 at the age of seventy-five. Pointing to his old age and the fact that he had never been to the falls before, in a speech delivered in Buffalo a couple of days after the visit, he said: "But now I have seen it! Yes, I have seen it in all its sublimity and glory—and I have never witnessed a scene its equal." He went on to elaborate on the "deep impression which will last with my life—a feeling overpowering, and which takes away the power of speech by its grandeur and sublimity."

Concepts of American Exceptionalism centering on landscapes of the sublime took on a visual form in the works of Albert Bierstadt and other painters of the trans-Mississippi West in the second half of the nineteenth century. Convinced that this region made the U.S. unique among nations, and determined to capture the landscapes in big panoramas, Bierstadt joined several expeditions that took him to the Rocky Mountains and California in 1859 and 1863.

His panorama paintings of the American West represented an Edenic, untouched nature in majestic grandeur on immense canvases. Most famous are his depictions of Yosemite Valley like, for example, his 1867 *The Domes of the Yosemite*, a monumental oil painting capturing the sublime splendor of the landscape. It featured a view of the Domes from midway up Yosemite Falls near Columbia Rock. From this elevated position, the viewer looks down into a misty valley framed by the craggy granite domes of Yosemite Valley. In the right foreground, Yosemite Falls, dramatically lit by a few rays of the sun, is gushing its masses of water into the Merced River. The sky is full of fantastically illuminated clouds, and the whole scene is structured with a dramatic composition of light and dark. Like most of Bierstadt's Yosemite scenes, the pristine beauty of the wilderness in *The Domes of the Yosemite* shows no trace of human beings; it represents a nonhuman world of natural splendor that aims to overwhelm the viewer with its sheer sublimity. Yosemite Valley's sublime splendor surpassed by far anything known

Albert Bierstadt, *The Domes of the Yosemite*, oil on canvas, 1867. St. Johnsbury Athenaeum, St. Johnsbury, Vermont. http//:www.stjathenaeum.org

from Europe, where there simply was no scenery whose grandeur could for one moment be held comparable with that of the Sierra Nevada in the Yosemite District.

This new appreciation of wilderness fueled the rise of a conservationist movement that deliberately wanted to preserve wilderness as a source of American Exceptionalism, and this movement led to the creation of today's vast system of national parks, preserves, recreation areas, rivers, lakeshores, and seashores that is unique to the U.S. There were many actors, interests, and motivations involved in the creation of the U.S. National Park System. Some advocates of wilderness protection wanted to regulate the exploitation of timber, minerals, and other natural resources on behalf of economic sustainability. Others, especially the large railroad companies and hotel businesses, saw national parks as a chance to make money with tourism. Again, others wanted to protect wildlife and control hunting to keep a hunting ground area intact. Only preservationists like John Muir and his friends of the Sierra Club saw the protection of America's nature as an end in itself because it helped preserve a source of American identity. National parks thus were sites where Americans could experience, themselves, an exceptional nation at a time when, due to industrialization and urbanization, it actually became increasingly more like Europe.

Theodore Roosevelt's speech dedicating the Grand Canyon as a National Monument on May 6, 1903, may serve as a case in point. Identifying the Grand Canyon "a natural wonder which [...] is in kind absolutely unparalleled throughout the rest of the world," he asked his countrymen "to keep this great wonder of nature as it now is." He demanded that the site be unaltered by any kind of building in order not "to mar the wonderful grandeur, the sublimity, the great loneliness and beauty of the Canyon. Leave it as it is. You can not improve on it." All that Americans should do was to keep it for the generations to come "as one of the great sights which every American if he can travel at all should see." In preserving wilderness, Americans were also preserving their exceptionality.

However, this concept of wilderness was in a way an invention that centered on the idea of untouched nature unaltered by human intervention. For John Muir, Theodore Roosevelt, and other preservationists, nature was pristine only as long as it was a nonhuman world, which is why in many cases the creation of a national park was actually preceded by efforts to remove the American Indians from the designated wilderness areas. Furthermore, the only nature that the preservationist thought worth preserving was exceptionally beautiful and picturesque natural areas like Niagara Falls, the Grand Canyon, or Yosemite National Park.

In the twentieth century, the nineteenth-century tradition of sublime landscape paintings found continuity in the landscape photography of Ansel Adams and others. Adams's highly popular black-and-white photographs of Yosemite National Park and other natural wonders of the American West transformed nature into subtle compositions of light and shadow, lines and structures, surfaces and shapes. As a member of the Group f/64, an association of largely West Coast photographers championing a small aperture setting (f/64) that enabled a sharp focus, Adams developed his own Zone System, which centered on sharp contrasts of black and white, and used all zones of gray to create subtly toned photographs of lakes, rivers, and waterfalls, mountains and stones, forests and trees, and clouds and other atmospheric phenomena. Intending to reveal the hidden beauty of nature, Adams's sharp-focused photography uncovered more than the naked eye could see, rendering details with a greater reality than the viewer was conscious of.

The theme of the American sublime also had a technological variant. With the U.S. transition from an agrarian to an industrial society, Americans began to invest technology with sublimity. Next to natural wonders like Niagara Falls or the Grand Canyon, great public works and mechanical triumphs like canals and bridges, steamboats, railroads, telegraph lines, skyscrapers, factories, and power stations became icons of America's greatness. These icons amalgamating natural, technological, and religious elements into a new aesthetic created new technological landscapes of the sublime.

A case in point is Charles Sheeler's painting *American Landscape*, executed in 1930. Based on his six-week stay at the Ford Motor Company's River Rouge plant, Sheeler's canvas shows a factory complex neatly constructed along a dead canal that, being completely mechanized, impersonal, and abstract, holds no nature at all. It is a manmade landscape of silos, smokestacks, large structures, railroads, loading machinery, and heaps of raw material dominated by sharp lines and geometrical structures. Reflecting the machinery and structures in terms of grandeur, beauty, and also poetry, Sheeler's painting represented the factory complex in categories of the sublime. This aesthetic of what David Nye has called the "technological sublime" sees bridges, railroads, or skyscrapers as manifestations of man's conquest of natural obstacles and his control of time and space. Technology was evidence of the superiority of American civilization and a manifestation of American Exceptionalism. Tellingly enough, George B. McClellan, the mayor of New York City, speaking to foreign guests at the Hudson-Fulton celebration in 1909, praised the emerging New York skyscraper skyline as a "city that is set on a hill." With that, the mayor suggested that New York had finally become what the Puritans had wished for in colonial America at the beginning of the seventeenth century.

This chapter has shown that the nature-related narratives of American Exceptionalism emerged from the interplay of three different kinds of geographies, the physical, the social, and the moral. The physical geography featured the abundance, wilderness, beauty, and grandeur of North America's natural environments. This was inherently connected to a social geography that saw American landscapes as inhabited by self-reliant, hard-working, and free individuals who were relentlessly working to tame, control, and transform the natural environments of

Charles Sheeler, *American Landscape*, oil on canvas, 1930. MoMA, New York. http//:www.moma.org

the American land. This American land was associated with the moral values of virtue and innocence, simplicity and naturalness. In all of these narratives, Europe figured as the significant Other. Accordingly, in America there was an endless supply of fertile land just waiting to be cultivated by industrious settlers, while in Europe all land was owned and settled. While American landscapes represented the work of free and self-determined citizens enjoying all forms of social mobility, European landscapes visualized the traditions of feudalism and petrified social structures, enormous inequalities and dependencies, poverty and stagnation, and let's not forget, political authoritarianism. America appeared wild and woody, while Europe was tamed and cultivated, and while Americans supposedly had a direct and intimate connection with the land they lived on, Europeans were largely alienated from nature and thereby removed from the source of freshness and rejuvenation that kept America young, strong, and in flux.

2

The West and the South

Exceptional Regions and Regions of Exceptionalism

WHEN FREDERICK JACKSON TURNER SET OUT to define the Americanness of America in his trailblazing 1893 essay "The Significance of the Frontier in American History," he looked to the American West as the site of the frontier, where, in his view, the American way of life was born, and born again. Whatever we may think of Turner's frontier thesis today, it takes us right into the regional dimensions of American Exceptionalism, which can be viewed from two different angles: On the one hand, certain regions, for example the West, can be seen as unique and specific to U.S. history. On the other hand, there have always been regions in the U.S. whose sense of regional identity was carried by an exceptionalism of its own. Think of California as *America's America*, or of the Southwest as *Mexamerica*, or of the Midwest as the alleged true heartland of the U.S. Historically speaking, New England was actually the first region postulating to have its own brand of exceptionalism. This began in the colonial period, which we will deal with extensively in the next chapter. This chapter will look at the American West and the American South to highlight the regional dynamics of American Exceptionalism.

THE AMERICAN WEST AND THE PROBLEM OF AMERICAN EXCEPTIONALISM

The American West was key to ideas of American Exceptionalism from early on, although the exact location of the American West is hard to define because the West itself moved constantly westward in the course of U.S. history. Prior to 1890, the American West was the site of the frontier, and as such, it was a region of transition where farmland was carved from *wilderness*, to the effect that the frontier condition vanished at every given place in the course of time, only to reemerge in the less developed areas further west until it reached the Pacific. In 1890, the superintendent of the U.S. Census Bureau declared the North American continent to have been settled to a degree that a frontier line could not be said to exist. With this official statement, the American West ceased to be identical to the frontier.

The significance of the American West as the site of the frontier for notions of American Exceptionalism can hardly be overestimated. Although countries like Canada, Mexico, Australia, or Russia also had settlement frontiers, in none of them did a myth emerge that saw the frontier as the source of national uniqueness. Before there was the myth, however, there was the reality of violently removing the American Indians, chopping down trees and clearing fields, carving farms from the thick woods, building log cabins and fences, founding villages and cities, building societies, and establishing government and other institutions in places where, in the European American imagination, none of this had existed before. This dynamic cultivation of the North American land fascinated contemporaries from early on, and in the eighteenth century it was increasingly being discussed as a marker of American exceptionality.

In the third of his *Letters from an American Farmer*, written in 1782, John Hector St. John de Crèvecœur traced the colonial society from the sea to the woods. Hypothetically traveling west from the Atlantic coast to the woodsy frontier regions of the backcountry, Crèvecœur likened this travel in space to travel in time. He described his journey from east to west as a trip through the different stages of human development. This journey took him from the most advanced stage of statehood, society, economy, and culture on the Atlantic seashore all the way to the primitive stage of hunting and gathering on the frontier line of settlement.

Crèvecœur's representation of life on the frontier was altogether negative and bleak, as already shown in chapter 1. Settlers on the frontier appeared to be left all to themselves. There were only a few and very loose social ties in this group of hedonistic egoists who basically tried to make do on a day-to-day basis. Beyond the reach of the government, and lacking all moral codes, Crèvecœur saw the pioneers as living primitive lives of lazy inactivity, mutual distrust, and envy. Dominated by nature instead of controlling it, they had given up agriculture to become hunters, which for Crèvecœur was also the reason of their moral deficiency.

The importance of this representation of frontier life for the argument of this chapter is that it was deeply indebted to the philosophy of the Enlightenment and how it imagined historical change. Anchored in the idea of progress, the Enlightenment saw the history of mankind developing in a clear succession of stages. According to this model, the first stage was hunting and gathering, the second was agriculture, and the third was industrial and urban civilization characterized by social complexity, economic differentiation, cultural richness, and moral refinement. In this thinking, the only function for the pioneers in an area was to pave the way for the transition to the next higher stage of human development. The first settlers, morally deficient as they were, started a project that would be completed by a new and better type of settler coming after them. The pioneers on the frontier would sooner or later make room for a "more industrious people," Crèvecœur explained, describing how they would finish what the first settlers had begun by converting "that hitherto barbarous country into a fine, fertile, well-regulated district. Such is our progress; such is the march of the Europeans toward the interior parts of this continent."

Although Crèvecœur did not mythologize the frontier in any way, its very existence made North America distinct in two ways: First, it offered freedom and the promise of abundance. Second, it provided the unique opportunity to observe society in the making. Whereas in Europe and other parts of the world, the beginnings of human civilization lay in the darkness of prehistoric times and could not be dated, in America one could literally see the beginning of history by going to the frontier.

A similar idea of travel in space as travel in time was articulated by Thomas Jefferson in a letter to William Ludlow of September 6, 1824. Reflecting on the "progress of society from its rudest state to that it has now attained," Jefferson suggested that a "philosophic observer," that is, a champion of Enlightenment ideas, should begin a "journey from the savages of the Rocky Mountains, Eastwardly towards our sea-coast," which would be "equivalent to a survey, in time of the progress of man from the infancy of nation to the present day." While this only seems to be summarizing Crèvecœur once more, it is important to stress that Jefferson's reflections were not just bloodless intellectual abstractions. His remarks were anchored in the changes he himself experienced during his lifetime. His is a theory of progress saturated with biographical experience. "I am 81. years of age," Jefferson wrote, "born where I now live, in the first range of mountains in [the] interior of our country. [A]nd I have observed this march of civilisation advancing from the sea coast, passing over us like a cloud of light, increasing our kno[w]ledge and improving our condition insomuch as that we are at this time more advanced in civilisation here than the seaports were when I was a boy."

In the nineteenth century, the frontier experience came to define America's national identity in contradistinction to Europe even more fully. It became manifest in novels and travel accounts, letters and diaries, paintings and prints. The fascination with the frontier West as the source of U.S. national identity was at the heart of James Fenimore Cooper's five Leatherstocking Tales—*The Pioneers* (1823), *The Last of the Mohicans* (1826), *The Prairie* (1827), *The Pathfinder* (1840), and *The Deerslayer* (1841)—that created the genre of the frontier novel.

Convinced, like so many writers after him, that America lacked the historical depth and traditions needed to create great literature, Cooper saw the settlement frontier providing the kind of subjects that a genuinely American novel could be built around. Constructing the frontier as a meeting ground of wilderness and civilization, Cooper interpreted it as the site of a heroic struggle for the westward expansion of Euro-American civilization. Although he was a moral critic of this very process, exposing the environmental, human, and also moral costs of westward expansion in his books, Cooper constructed the frontier as a distinctly American space providing unique experiences that defined America's national character.

Europeans were fascinated by the American frontier as well, and some of them went to see for themselves. When Alexis de Tocqueville visited the U.S. in the 1830s on an official mission investigating American prisons, he unhesitatingly took the opportunity, when it arose, to travel to the frontier regions of Michigan Territory. Deeply convinced that one of the primary causes of America's astonishing growth and prosperity was its vast area of unoccupied lands, Tocqueville, in his travel essay *Quinze Jours dans le Désert* (A Fortnight in the Wilderness), stated that the U.S. was the only country in the world where one could observe the beginnings of society. Like Crèvecœur and Jefferson before him, Tocqueville was convinced that traveling to the western frontier offered the chance to encounter "the encapsulation of the history of the whole human race" between a few degrees of longitude, and like Cooper, he reflected the pioneer as a new and decidedly American kind of man to whom "the future of the New World belongs." Tracing the restless temper of the Americans that so fascinated him to the frontier experience, Tocqueville felt that settlers moving westward cast off their European habits and institutions to become Americans.

At the same time, Tocqueville reflected the frontier as a safety valve for social problems in the settled areas of the east. The possibility of buying cheap land in the interior prevented real misery from occurring in the east, he argued, and those who were not content with their situation in the settled areas had the chance to better their lot by going west. The very existence of the frontier was thus a guarantee of order and interior tranquility in the U.S., which contrasted sharply with the situation in Europe, where Tocqueville had experienced the turmoil, disruption, and violence of two French revolutions, and where early industrialization was causing all kinds of hardships and social unrest.

All of these ideas and myths about the frontier were firmly in place when Frederick Jackson Turner sat down to write his famous essay "The Significance of the Frontier in American History" in 1893. It developed a full-fledged frontier thesis of American Exceptionalism with an unprecedented stringency and clarity. Born on November 14, 1861, in Portage, Wisconsin, Turner was the first truly famous historian of the U.S., whose influence on American historiography can hardly be overestimated. He earned his PhD in history from Johns Hopkins University in 1890, where his German-inspired professors had familiarized him with the Germanic germ theory of history. It suggested that America's political values, habits, and institutions were determined by the innate racial attributes of the Americans as members of the Germanic race, and it influenced Turner's frontier thesis to a significant degree.

Ironically, Turner theorized the significance of the frontier at a historical moment when the frontier itself had officially been declared closed by the U.S. Census Bureau in 1890. Taking this as his point of departure, Turner declared the "first period of American history" to have ended, a period that began "four centuries" ago with the arrival of Columbus and whose inner unity was defined by the existence of the frontier. "Up to our own day," Turner elaborated, "American history has been in a large degree the history of the colonization of the Great West. The existence of an area of free land, its continuous recession, and the advance of American settlement westward, explain American development." U.S. history was thus structured by the continuous "progress out of the primitive economic and political conditions of the frontier into the complexity of city life," with the peculiarity of America being that this process began anew time and again in the westernmost settlement areas. This had the effect of U.S. society "continually beginning over again on the frontier." The frontier thus witnessed a "perennial rebirth" of American values, practices, and institutions that accounted for the "fluidity of American life." Where Crèvecœur diagnosed a loss of humanity and the degeneration into associability, Turner saw the creation of a rugged and liberty-loving individualism that had "from the beginning promoted democracy" on the frontier.

Certainly, Turner's essay, which found the sources of American Exceptionalism on the frontier, is the strongest and most systematic reflection of the frontier as a moving space, a process and—most importantly—a myth. At the same time, however, his essay can be read as an articulation of uncertainty and doubt as to whether America would be able to maintain its uniqueness. The end of the frontier, in Turner's theorization, marked the potential end of American Exceptionalism and the beginning of a new process through which America could easily become like Europe.

This feeling of uncertainty surfaced in the preface to *The Frontier in American History*, a collection of Turner's essays published in 1920. At a time when the U.S. had developed into an industrial giant and a world power, Turner argued that only the future could reveal "how much of the courageous, creative American spirit, and how large a part of the historic American ideals" would be carried over into the post-frontier age, into "that new age which is replacing the era of free lands and of measurable isolation by consolidated and complex industrial development and by increasing resemblances and connections between the New World and the Old."

Turner's frontier thesis arguably is the single most important interpretive frame of U.S. history. It triggered hundreds, even thousands of books about the American West, and it also became influential in popular culture, where the Western genre was strongly influenced by Turner's interpretation of the frontier. This brings to mind Owen Wister's popular novel *The Virginian* or the countless classic Western movies of the 1930s, 1940s, and 1950s, starring John Wayne, Gary Cooper, or Robert Mitchum. John Ford's movies *Stagecoach* and *The Searchers*, especially, are prototypical manifestations of the frontier exceptionalism that carried much of the heroic Western genre celebrating westward expansion as the unerring fulfillment of a God-given mission to expand Euro-American civilization across the continent and to enlarge the sphere of freedom and democracy.

Yet the West of the twentieth-century Western genre was no longer the water-rich and densely forested frontier of Cooper's Leatherstocking Tales. Rather, it was in the drier states of Arizona, Utah, Nevada, New Mexico, Texas, and parts of California. The majestic and monumental, yet harsh and austere, landscape of the American Southwest allowed only a certain character type to survive there, one that was an independent, self-reliant, and rugged individualist operating on the basis of honor, justice, and courage. These skills, qualities, and values of the Western hero, which made him morally superior to others, were closely tied to the grandiose yet hostile natural environments of the Southwest, with which the cowboy hero experienced an almost "mystical affinity," as Deborah L. Madsen writes in her book *American Exceptionalism*.

Until roughly the middle of the twentieth century, the frontier thesis was widely accepted by U.S. historians. Then, a generation of scholars coming of age in the 1950s and 1960s began to lay the foundations for a new critical regionalism that questioned the frontier myth under the auspices of a New Western History. It is primarily associated with the work of historian Patricia Nelson Limerick, who highlighted the primitiveness, deprivations, and violence of frontier life; featured the human and environmental costs of westward expansion; and deconstructed the exceptionalist ideology carrying Turner's frontier thesis, arguing that Turner's writings were the manifestation of a nationalistic and ethnocentric ideology that justified U.S. imperialist westward expansion. Furthermore, Turner was charged with heroizing the achievements of white, male, European American pioneers, while largely ignoring the presence of women, African Americans, Asian Americans, and other ethnic groups on the frontier.

Most importantly, however, Turner's frontier thesis was identified as having at its core both a unitary model of the frontier and a unitary model of American culture that was essentially white, Anglo-Saxon, and Protestant. Highlighting the many frontiers in North America, New Western History pointed out that there were farming, cattle, and mining frontiers in nineteenth-century America, and that there was not only a U.S. frontier in North America but also Spanish, Canadian, and Russian ones.

While all of this contributed to deconstructing the myth of the frontier as the source of American Exceptionalism, the most important intellectual innovation wrought by New Western History is the conceptualization of the frontier not as a line separating *wilderness* from *civilization* but as a borderland and contact zone, where several different cultures met, mingled, interacted, and exchanged ideas and knowledge, goods and objects, practices and people. The results of these multidirectional processes of cultural transfer and exchange were specific borderland cultures that were neither fully European American nor American Indian, African American, or Latin American, but a bit of it all. Thus, instead of repeatedly reproducing a unitary *American* culture, the frontier actually produced several new borderland cultures with multiple cultural influences and strands in regionally specific mixtures. The American West is thus no longer reflected as the cradle of an essentially white, Anglo-Saxon, and Protestant Americanness, but rather as a place of a linguistic, religious, ethnic, and cultural diversity unsurpassed by any other region of the U.S. As a space of cultural exchange and transfer, where European American, American Indian, African American, and Latino cultures interacted to forge hybrid borderland societies and cultures, the frontier regions of the American West may still appear as an exceptional space of American history—but the exceptionalism connected to it celebrates the U.S. as a land of diversity and plurality.

SOUTHERN EXCEPTIONALISM

Southern Exceptionalism is anchored in the idea that the South is a distinct and exceptional region within the U.S., a *Mythic Land Apart*, as the title of a collected volume edited by John David Smith and Thomas

H. Appleton Jr. suggested. The notion of Southern exceptionalism has two sides, and both are relevant to the conceptual history of American Exceptionalism.

The first way to view it is from the perspective of white Southerners, who imagined the South as having a unique and distinct civilization that was sharply different from the rest of the U.S. Seen from this angle, the notion of Southern exceptionalism appears as a Southern identity narrative anchored in the racist ideology of white supremacy. It laid the basis for a separatist Southern nationalism coming to full fruition with the secession of eleven southern states from the Union in 1860–1861, and it served to justify white racial control through Reconstruction and Jim Crow all the way to the gated communities of today's South.

The other way to look at Southern exceptionalism is to understand it as a construction from the outside that sees the South as the conservative exception to the widely shared liberal consensus in the U.S. In this interpretation, the notion of Southern exceptionalism is functional for cementing liberal myths about the U.S., and it blinds us to the pervasive racism penetrating the fabric of American life in every part of the country. The Northern and Western narratives of Southern exceptionalism confine racist discrimination to the South alone.

There is a general agreement among historians that the South, for long parts of its history indeed, was distinct from other regions in the U.S., with Wilbur J. Cash, in his 1941 book *The Mind of the South*, going as far as to argue that the South was "another land" inhabited by what was "not quite a nation within a nation, but the next thing to it." Yet there is the question of how to define the region in the first place. Does the South comprise those fifteen states that were slaveholding in 1861, or is it defined only by the eleven states that seceded from the Union to form the Confederate States of America? Other scholars have distinguished an upper South from a lower South, pointing to the very different economies in these two subregions on the eve of the Civil War, and their very different development after 1865. Still others have elaborated on a cultural South of very fuzzy boundaries, with some identifying the cultural South with the Mississippi delta, and others seeing the cultural South shading into the North as far as Chicago and Harlem in New York. In all, therefore, we have to take multiple Souths into consideration when it comes to Suthern exceptionalism.

Still, there are factors that can be drawn on to make a point for Southern distinctness throughout the centuries, and these factors can be found in the fields of demography, economy, politics, and history. In terms of demography, the South was always the U.S. region with the highest concentration of blacks and, prior to 1945, the least ethnic and cultural diversity. While, due to mass immigration from Europe and Asia, the North and the West underwent tumultuous processes of ethnic and cultural diversification between 1830 and 1945, the South, which did not receive a large share of immigrants from abroad, remained an essentially biracial society of blacks and whites.

Southern identity was built on slavery, King Cotton, and Jim Crow. While the history of Southern society is a history of racial separation, discrimination, and conflict drawing on the ideology of white supremacy, it is also a history of blacks and Protestant whites of British descent living together and very closely interacting with one another. The history of Southern culture is one of blacks and whites imitating each other, borrowing from one another, and mutually influencing each other. It is a history of multidirectional cultural exchange and transfer that created the two cultures of the black and the white South, which were separate and yet inseparably intertwined at the same time. Above all, both were variations of a shared Southern culture that was distinct from the rest of the U.S.

Slavery developed into a factor of Southern exceptionality only after 1800, when it became a regional phenomenon unique to the South. On the eve of the American Revolution, all of the thirteen colonies that declared independence had slavery. Then, however, the revolutionary ideology of natural rights liberalism shattered the ideological foundations of slavery, and an abolitionist movement began to form in the North. By 1804, slavery had been largely abolished in the northern states, although the roads to abolition were multiple, winding, and in some cases very long. Still, while the northern states ended the system of chattel slavery in the first half of the nineteenth century, the South not only held on to the institution but actually expanded it dramatically when cotton became king after 1820.

After the Civil War, the South continued to stand in the long shadow of slavery and the plantation system. White supremacy remained the underlying foundation of Southern exceptionalism and the "backbone of southern political unity," as V. O. Key Jr. wrote in his classic 1949 study *Southern Politics in State and Nation*. The Southern economy stayed essentially agrarian in a period when the U.S. underwent a process of rapid and disruptive industrialization that, by the eve of World War I, had turned the country into the strongest and most productive industrial economy in the world. The industrialization of the U.S. Northeast kept the economy of the South in an essentially colonial state insofar as it cemented the South's role as a provider of raw materials for the industrial centers, and as a market for the finished goods produced there.

This constellation accounts for the fact that the economic history of the South from 1865 to 1945 is one of backwardness, poverty, and want, which stood in sharp contrast to the cyclical economic growth, affluence, and plenty that the industrialized and urbanized Northeast experienced in that same period. Prior to 1945, the overall standard of living in the South was significantly lower than in other regions of the U.S. Observers at home and abroad celebrating the economic miracles of production, efficiency, and affluence of American capitalism in the nineteenth and twentieth centuries were obviously not looking at the U.S. South. President Franklin D. Roosevelt, however, had no illusions about the region, when in a 1938 speech given at a conference sponsored by the National Emergency Council, he declared the South to be "the Nation's No. 1 economic problem."

Social and economic life in the postbellum South continued to be structured by sharp inequalities that perpetuated the class and race distinctions of the antebellum era. The distribution of property originating in the plantation economy remained intact. Land ownership continued to be concentrated in the hands of white planters, while former slaves—and a significant share of poor whites—became tenants and sharecroppers working land they did not own for a share of the crop. This system soon brought them into a cycle of debt that tied sharecroppers to the land and made them permanently poor; sharecropping thus cemented the connection between poverty and blackness that is still visible today.

The economic discrimination against blacks in the South was soon complemented by the Jim Crow system of legal segregation that came to full fruition between 1880 and 1920. Unwilling to accept the social and political equality of freedmen guaranteed by the Thirteenth, Fourteenth, and Fifteenth Amendments to the U.S. Constitution, Southern legislatures sought to maintain prewar racial hierarchies by passing a host of laws that disenfranchised blacks and segregated one public place and facility after the other. In 1896, the Supreme Court, with its *Plessy v. Ferguson* ruling, declared the system of segregation constitutional as long as the segregated facilities were formally of equal standards. From then on, de jure segregation combined with de facto segregation to define Southern distinctness and exceptionality within the U.S.

One major factor reinforcing both Southern distinctness and segregation was religion. The post–Civil War South developed into a stronghold of Protestant, fundamentalist Christianity. Derided as the "Bible Belt" by liberal northern critics like Henry Louis Mencken, the South is still the region with the strongest commitment to biblical literalism and evangelical Protestantism. Southern churches were important institutions sustaining both a sense of regional distinctness and racial separation. In the Reconstruction period, freedmen and freedwomen voluntarily withdrew from white churches to create their own congregations as spheres of black autonomy and self-determination. To this day, the great majority of Southern congregations are still completely black or white, more or less by mutual consent, as Charles P. Roland has argued in his 1975 study *The Improbable Era: The South since World War II*. Thus, the hour from eleven to twelve on Sunday morning has been the most segregated time of the week in the South.

Politically speaking, the South also formed a distinct entity within the U.S. for much of the nineteenth and twentieth centuries. Already during the American Revolution, the southern states emerged as a clearly identifiable political camp whose unity was forged by slavery interests. Unwilling to abolish the institution of slavery during a revolution based on the ideas of individual liberty, inalienable rights, and egalitarianism, the southern states in the Constitutional Convention pushed for recognition of the slave population in the national censuses, as became manifest in the infamous Three-Fifths Compromise, according to which five blacks were to be counted as three whites in national censuses. In the Early Republic, when the U.S. embarked on its course of dynamic westward expansion, southern states strove to prevent any regulation that closed the western territories to slavery, and when abolitionist forces and voices became increasingly stronger after 1830, the southern states were knit together ever more tightly in their defense of the institution of slavery as the core of a Southern way of life. With the demise of the national party system of Democrats and Whigs over the slavery question in the 1850s, and the foundation of the Republican Party as the antislavery party of the North in 1854, the Democratic Party changed from a national party to a regional party of the "Solid South," and this one-party electoral system politically defined southern exceptionality prior to the 1960s.

While one can thus indeed identify several factors defining the uniqueness and distinctness of the South as a region within the U.S., Southern exceptionalism is much more an imagined reality than an objective fact. As an imagined reality, the idea of Southern exceptionalism was the result of both Southern self-descriptions—that is, Southerners imagining themselves as exceptional—and descriptions of the South from the outside.

White Southerners did not develop a group identity based on a common culture, shared interests, and a sense of historical distinctness prior to 1820. Then, however, a Southern nationalism with separatist potential emerged at the confluence of the states' rights theory, the region's growing economic dependence on slavery, the rapid westward expansion of the U.S., and a rising Southern nervousness about the abolitionist agitation against slavery that rapidly gained national prominence in the 1830s. Southern nationalism thus was essentially defensive in nature; it proclaimed a superior Southern civilization standing in stark contrast to northern "Yankee culture," and in need of being defended against northern aggressions aiming at the complete destruction of slavery and the whole Southern way of life based on it. Southern whites thus used Southern exceptionalism to defend themselves against outside critics, who, not being insiders to Southern society and culture, supposedly could never understand the racial dynamics and the allegedly unique history of the South. However, Southern nationalism was not only about protecting Southern civilization where it already existed. It also claimed the right to expand slavery into the hitherto unorganized western territories.

Southern nationalism was forged in a series of political crises. The first was the conflict over the admission of Missouri as a slave state in 1819 that ended with the famous Missouri Compromise of March 6, 1820. The second crisis, which forced the southern states to articulate their interests and to close ranks around the emerging theory of states' rights, was the

Nullification Controversy over the right of Congress to legislate tariffs protecting U.S. infant industries in the North against European competition. When Congress passed such a law in 1828, Southerners were ferociously opposed to it, calling it a "Tariff of Abominations." In that year, John C. Calhoun published a pamphlet, *South Carolina Exposition and Protest*, in which he argued that the tariff was unconstitutional because it favored the North at the expense of the South. As the federal government had overstepped its authority with this law, Calhoun wrote, the states had the right to nullify it. Yet Calhoun was not only worried about constitutional matters when he made his points. The underlying subtext was racism and slavery. As William Freehling has argued in his still authoritative study *Prelude to Civil War: The Nullification Controversy in South Carolina, 1816–1836*, published in 1966, beneath the legal argument lay Southern planters' fears that a hostile Northern majority would abolish slavery in the U.S.

This fear was not completely uncalled for. In the 1830s, the abolitionist critique of slavery as a moral vice and a contradiction to the U.S. liberal founding ideology gained momentum all over the Union, with the important effect that opposition to slavery now became a national movement. This nationalization of the abolitionist cause reached a climax with Harriet Beecher Stowe's 1852 bestselling sentimental novel *Uncle Tom's Cabin*. It portrayed blacks as full human beings endowed with intelligence, capable of truly Christian sentiment, and longing for freedom and self-determination. This depiction of African Americans undermined the very legitimacy of slavery. At the same time, the 1840s witnessed the strongest expansionary push since the Louisiana Purchase of 1803, so that by 1848 the U.S. had reached the Pacific. The great mass of unorganized territory in the trans-Mississippi West intensified the ongoing debates about states' rights and the westward expansion of slavery to an unprecedented degree.

Faced with a growing and increasingly militant national opposition to slavery, white Southerners developed a defensive bunker mentality. Sectionalism became stronger, Southern challenges to federal authority became ever more emotional, and slavery was now aggressively and self-consciously defended as a "Positive Good" and core of the Southern way of life that allegedly was superior to the northern order on all accounts.

The intellectual ideologization of the Southern way of life came to full fruition in the writings of George Fitzhugh, who published works such as *Sociology for the South, or the Failure of Free Society* in 1854 and *Cannibals All! or, Slaves Without Masters* in 1857. His argument was anchored in the sharp distinction of Southern "slave society" and Northern "free society." While he glorified Southern slave society as an ideal social order, Fitzhugh criticized the emerging industrial society in the North, with its ideologies of free labor and free competition, as a failure based on wrong philosophical premises.

Fitzhugh's defense of slavery drew on the racist dogma of black inferiority. He represented blacks as people of childlike immaturity, who were neither morally nor intellectually fit for self-government and self-determination. Set free, Fitzhugh argued, blacks would be outwitted and outcompeted in the free market by the racially superior whites. Unable to provide for themselves, blacks would have to live in dire circumstances, becoming a burden on society. Under slavery, however, blacks lived comfortable lives impossible for them to achieve in a free society, according to Fitzhugh. The proclaimed racial inferiority of blacks thus justified their enslavement, while the abolition of slavery appeared to be an act of irresponsibility that sprang from the Northern abolitionists' sheer ignorance of blacks.

Slavery was, however, not only good for blacks in Fitzhugh's view, it was also good for whites insofar as it enabled them to develop and maintain their full humanity as independent, self-determined, and superior beings. Fitzhugh saw the free-labor ideology of the North as reducing whites to menial jobs and wage slavery. This, in his racist mind, was scandalous, as it undermined the dogma of white supremacy. At the same time, Fitzhugh felt, as he wrote in *A Sociology for the South*, that the industrial capitalism emerging in the North was degrading the humanity of whites because it reduced them to purely utilitarian and materialistic pursuits that made them low, vulgar, and insensitive to "genius, taste and art."

Another strand of the Southern proslavery argument was religious in nature. It drew on the Bible to suggest that slavery was God's will. Fitzhugh devotes a whole chapter, "Scriptural Authority for Slavery," to this in his *Sociology for the South*; one of the most popular Christian defenses of slavery was *A Brief Examination of Scripture Testimony on the Institution of Slavery* by Reverend Thornton Stringfellow, published in 1850. In it, the Baptist minister closely read the Bible to demonstrate that "slavery was instituted by Jehovah himself," and that Jesus Christ had recognized the institution of slavery as "lawful among men." Accordingly, Southern society was much more in keeping with God's word than the Northern one, which was based on the seemingly false premise of universal liberty.

In all, therefore, slavery and its defense became the key element of a Southern nationalism emerging as a response to northern abolitionism in the antebellum period. It drew heavily on exceptionalist ideas. Southern nationalism not only stressed the distinctness, uniqueness, and superiority of Southern civilization in comparison to the North; it also suggested that a way of life that revolved around slavery exempted the South from the social ills, problems, and disruptions of the dawning industrial age. Southern society was represented as a harmonious, stable, and prosperous society held together by benevolence and paternalism. This ethos, centering on the figure of the father, saw social formations structured by rigorous hierarchies of power, authority, and command, which, however, were softened by the emotional bonds of mutual affection between husband and wife, parents and children, masters and slaves. "Slavery without domestic affection would be a curse," wrote Fitzhugh in *A Sociology for the South*, "and so would marriage and parental authority."

The patriarchal society that Southerners celebrated as superior and exceptional was a society of family relations in which the powerful, the rich, the independent, and the educated—all of them white—protected and cared for the weak, the poor, the dependent, and the uneducated in exchange for obedience, work, and support. In contrast, the emerging industrial society appeared as harsh, heartless, and without any compassion for the poor. Free labor, white Southerners argued, was actually slavery without being called such. It was a system of "wage slavery" that was actually more oppressive and crueler than the chattel slavery of the South. The wage laborers of the North were worse off than the slaves, southern defenders of slavery argued, as they were only provided for when they could work, while slaves in the South were also cared for when they could not work, for example during childhood, old age, or sickness. Free laborers in the North, wrote Fitzhugh in *A Sociology for the South*, were excluded from the "holy and charmed circle" of paternalistic care. "Shelterless, naked and hungry," the wage laborer was "exposed to the bleak winds, the cold rains, and hot sun of heaven, with none that love him, none that care for him."

Paternalistic, elite compassion for the weak and needy amid affluence and wealth, therefore, was what made Southern society, in the eyes of white Southerners, a unique phenomenon in the emerging industrial world. The "greatest strength of the South," argued Senator James Henry Hammond of South Carolina in a speech delivered in the U.S. Congress on March 4, 1858, arose from "the harmony of her political and social institutions." This harmony gave Southern society "an extent of political freedom, combined with entire security, such as no other people ever enjoyed upon the face of the earth." Southern society, for him, was the "best in the world."

Southern exceptionalism was also based on an economic nationalism that stressed the rich endowment of natural resources of the southern land as economic assets. "No people on earth—none that ever lived—are, or were so well supplied by nature with all the resources from which may be derived wealth, power, and prosperity, as those of the slaveholding section of the United States," remarked Georgia's Joseph A. Turner in 1860. Other arguments for Southern exceptionalism featured the world's dependence on Southern cotton. Senator Hammond, in his above-mentioned speech, stressed that a Southern embargo on cotton would "bring the whole world to our [Southern] feet," as industrial production in Europe and the U.S. would come to a grinding halt. "England would topple headlong," he exclaimed, "and carry the whole civilized world with her, save the South."

In the end, Southern nationalists suggested that defending slavery meant defending the ideals of the American Revolution and American Exceptionalism with it. They discussed the Southern slave society as an instrument to perpetuate the revolutionary promise of self-determination and affluence because slavery guaranteed freedom and autonomy to all whites—that very liberty that Southern nationalists saw threatened and undermined by white "wage slavery" in the North. In *South Carolina Exposition and Protest*, Calhoun argued that by holding the propertyless, dependent laboring class (that is, the slaves) in bondage, slavery was a way to prevent conflicts between capital and labor from destroying the U.S. republic.

Against this backdrop, secession could appear as a righteous step of resistance to defend the ideals of the American Revolution against a federal government that had seemingly become destructive of preserving the Southern slaveholders' right to "life, liberty, and the pursuit of happiness." References to the American Revolution were heard everywhere in the South after the election of Abraham Lincoln to the presidency on November 6, 1860. Anticipating Lincoln's victory, the *Charleston Mercury* commented three days before the actual election date that Lincoln's election to the presidency made the "extinction of slavery" imminent. The time for action, therefore, had come, "now or never." It was time for the southern states to set "the ball of revolution [. . .] in motion" and create a Southern confederacy. In a letter to his father, Charles C. Jones of Liberty County, Georgia, wrote on April 17, 1861, that the South should "redeem the tomb of Washington from the dominion of that [Northern] fanatical rule." In *Our Danger and Our Duty*, published in 1862, Presbyterian minister James Henley Thornwell argued that Southerners were only "upholding the great principles which our fathers bequeathed us," and promised that they would "perpetuate and diffuse the very liberty for which Washington bled, and which the heroes of the Revolution achieved."

The Great Seal of the Confederate States of America provided a visual form for this framing of the conflict. It showed a full-length portrait of George Washington in his revolutionary uniform, mounted on a white horse at the center of a circle. The equestrian portrait referred to Washington as a military hero and personification of the American Revolution, as white Southerners understood it. It suggested that the U.S. had been founded in and through war, and that it would take another war to defend the values of the American Revolution against the encroachments of a despotic central government, now located in Washington, DC, not London. On the seal, the equestrian portrait of George Washington was surrounded by a wreath composed of the principal agricultural products of the Confederacy: cotton, tobacco, sugar cane, corn, wheat, and rice. This made visual the connection between agrarianism and republicanism and the superior morality that supposedly came of it. The motto *Deo vindice*, displayed at the bottom margin of the seal, claimed that the Southern cause was protected and supported by God.

With the secession of eleven states from the Union in 1860–1861, a separatist Southern nationalism reached its apex. For Southerners, the war to defend their Southern way of life was a war not only to defend their right to be left alone and live according to their notions of happiness.

It was also a war to defend their reading of the American Revolution against an alternative interpretation of it originating in the North.

The Confederacy's defeat in the Civil War did not bring an end to the sense of Southern exceptionalism. Quite the contrary, it was resuscitated under the auspices of the "lost cause" culture emerging already during the Reconstruction period and fully developing afterward. Faced with the enormous losses and destructions wrought by a war fought for a failed and utterly discredited political cause, Southerners invented a highly romanticized Old South as an idyllic place free of conflict, hardship, and want. Accordingly, the Old South was a chivalric and preindustrial world inhabited by the last knights and their fair ladies of a paternalistic society knit together by family networks, close kinship ties, and deep emotional bonds between men and women, husbands and wives, parents and children, and—most importantly—masters and slaves. This plantation myth of moonlight, cotton fields, and magnolias that imagined the South as a land of feminine belles and honor-driven, gallant cavaliers and as a world of caring masters and happy-go-lucky Sambos emerged quickly after the *real* slavery South had vanished. It came to full fruition in Margaret Mitchell's epic historical novel *Gone with the Wind*, published to great success in 1936. Mitchell's melancholic representation of the Old South was reinforced three years later by the hugely successful technicolor motion picture featuring Clark Gable as Rhett Butler and Vivien Leigh as Scarlett O'Hara, which, to this very day, is one of the most successful movies of all time. The epigraph to the movie, penned by novelist, journalist, and screenwriter Ben Hecht, described the Old South as a "pretty world" that was no more "than a dream remembered," and a "civilization gone with the wind."

The post–Civil War sense of Southern distinctness continued to be based on the ostentatious embrace of an agrarian ideal that militantly rejected the economic and social order of industrial modernity. In the 1930s, this Southern stance was theorized by a group of Southern writers and intellectuals based at Vanderbilt University, who called themselves the "Southern Agrarians." Under the informal lead of John Crowe Ransom, in 1930 they published the collected volume *I'll Take My Stand: The South and the Agrarian Tradition* as a manifesto defending Southern distinctness. Radically criticizing the urban and industrial modernity of the North as a destruction of Southern (and eventually also American) culture, tradition, and heritage, the contributions to this book supported, as it said in the introduction, "a Southern way of life against what may be called the American or prevailing way." Postulating an unbridgeable distinction of "Agrarian versus Industrial," the contributors to *I'll Take My Stand* celebrated agriculture as "the leading vocation, whether for wealth, for pleasure, or for prestige," and as "a form of labor that is pursued with intelligence and leisure," which became the "model" to which others would and should aspire. "The theory of agrarianism," the Southern Agrarians claimed, "is that the culture of the soil is the best and most sensitive of vocations, and that therefore it should have the economic preference and enlist the maximum number of workers."

More important for white Southerners' sense of distinctness than the agrarian ideal, however, was their unbroken adherence to the ideology of white supremacy. With the Jim Crow system replacing slavery as the anchor of Southern identity, white racists all over the South defended legal discrimination against blacks as their forefathers had defended slavery. In George Wallace's inaugural address as newly elected governor of Alabama, delivered January 14, 1963, this sentiment found its purest manifestation when he countered the attempts of the federal government to enforce the desegregation of public schools and other institutions in Alabama with the famous phrase: "In the name of the greatest people that have ever trod this earth, I draw the line in the dust and toss the gauntlet before the feet of tyranny, and I say segregation now, segregation tomorrow, segregation forever."

The debate about Southern exceptionalism, however, was not only in the South. Outside observers also constructed the notion of Southern exceptionalism related to American Exceptionalism insofar as it represented the South as an exception to the liberal consensus of the U.S. This view defined white supremacy, racism, slavery, and Jim Crow segregation not as a possibility of American democracy but as an aberration of it.

Already, the first prophet of a liberal American Exceptionalism, John Hector St. John de Crèvecœur, in his *Letters from an American Farmer*, described Charleston and its slavery society as an exception to the rule in many ways. While he represented New England and especially the Mid-Atlantic region as a homogenous middle-class world of independent family farmers that was superior to European societies, he depicted the slavery society of South Carolina as inhumane, contrary to Christian values, and generally a moral scandal. To illustrate the horrors of slavery, Crèvecœur included an episode that narrates how he found a black slave suspended in a cage, where he was left to die as punishment for his murder of an overseer. By the time Crèvecœur reached him, the black man was so weak already that insects and birds of prey were picking at him. Describing this as "agonizing torture" and "shocking spectacle," Crèvecœur admitted that he could not "endure to spend more time in the south" for the very cruelty of its slavery.

In the first half of the nineteenth century, a growing number of travelers from Europe and the U.S. went to the South to learn about plantation society and its slavery system, among them Thomas Ashe, John Melish, James Kirke Paulding, Alexis de Tocqueville, Charles Dickens, Harriet Martineau, Frederica Bremer, and Frederick Law Olmsted, to name but a few. In one way or another, all of these outside observers were puzzled by the existence of slavery in a land of freedom. To explain this paradox, many of them supported the notion of the South as a distinct region with its own way of life that did not fit in with American ways. In the most important analysis of antebellum American democracy, Alexis de Tocqueville argued that the institution of slavery, exercising "a huge influence over the characters, laws, and the entire future development of the South," was the prime factor defining Southern distinctness. Slavery, he wrote, "brings dishonor to work; it introduces idleness into society together with ignorance and pride, poverty, and indulgence." Contrasting the "industrial zone" of the North with the "agrarian one" of the South, Tocqueville diagnosed an "amazing difference between the commercial capabilities of men from the South and those from the North." Whereas, for him, the industrial growth and economic development of the North was the result of entrepreneurial energies unleashed by free labor and free-market competition, he traced the economic backwardness of the South to the institution of slavery. Slavery, he wrote, numbed the entrepreneurial spirit and institutionalized idleness and insolence among both slaves *and* masters. In sum, he argued "that almost all the observable differences in character between northerners and southerners have their roots in slavery."

In quite similar terms, voices from the North echoed the idea of an unbridgeable political, social, economic, and cultural antagonism between North and South, with the South appearing as an exception to the American rule of egalitarianism, liberalism, democracy, and free-market capitalism. The South, said the Transcendentalist and reforming minister of the Unitarian church Theodore Parker, was "the foe to Northern Industry—to our mines, our manufactures, and our commerce. [. . .] She is the foe to our institutions—to our democratic politics in the State, our democratic culture in the school, our democratic work in the community, our democratic equality in the family."

In a similar vein, the eminent Republican William H. Seward, in a speech delivered in Oswego, New York, on November 3, 1856, claimed that the institution of slavery had negative effects on both blacks and whites, undermining the "intelligence, vigor, and energy" of both races. It produced "an exhausted soil, old and decaying towns, wretchedly-neglected roads," as well as "an absence of enterprise and improvement," which is why it was "incompatible with all [. . .] the elements of the security, welfare, and greatness of nations." The U.S. for him was not one but two nations, a situation that could not long endure, as the U.S. would "become either entirely a slaveholding nation, or entirely a free-labor nation" in the near or distant future. Abraham Lincoln picked up on this theme in his famous acceptance speech for the Republican Party's nomination for president on June 16, 1858, at the Illinois state capitol; he said: "A house divided against itself cannot stand. I believe this government cannot endure, permanently half slave and half free. I do not expect the Union to be dissolved—I do not expect the house to fall—but I do expect it will cease to be divided. It will become all one thing or all the other."

Even after the North and South were reunited after the Civil War, outside views continued to see the South as a distinct entity that stood in sharp contrast to the liberal culture of the U.S. When the Swedish economist, sociologist, and politician Gunnar Myrdal reflected on the situation of U.S. blacks in 1944, he framed this in terms of an "American Dilemma." This dilemma was defined by the paradoxical clash of legal segregation and racist discrimination against blacks in a country founded on a liberal and egalitarian American creed. This dilemma was even deepened, Myrdal argued, by the fact that the U.S. was then in the middle of fighting a cruel and costly war to defend its liberal and democratic values against totalitarian and racist aggressions in Europe and Asia. While Myrdal was fully aware that the "Negro problem" was an all-American one, he felt that it was more pronounced in the South. Southern society, he claimed, was a distinct and closed one with its own mind and view of things. Myrdal wrote: "The South is divergent from the rest of the country not only in having the bulk of the Negro population within its region but also in a number of other traits and circumstances—all, as we shall find, directly or indirectly connected with the Negro problem."

Myrdal explained Southern distinctness by describing the slow-paced social change in the region, its economic backwardness and poverty, and the continuing strength of the "tradition of aristocracy." In this constellation, he argued, the "main way to get and remain rich in the South has been to exploit the Negroes and other weaker people, rather than to work diligently, make oneself indispensable, and have brilliant ideas." Therefore, he claimed, the "Negro problem" had "nowhere in the North the importance it has in the South."

Ideas and metaphors of the South as some sort of an island within the U.S. reached a peak during the civil rights era of the 1950s and 1960s, when civil rights activists imagined the South as a land apart. For many civil rights workers, journalists, lawyers, and filmmakers, Mississippi was the most Southern place on earth, completely out of step with the rest of the country. In 1964, the Southern historian James W. Silver, who at that time was teaching at the University of Mississippi, published his book *Mississippi: The Closed Society*, in which he argued that Mississippi's violent resistance to desegregation was in line the with fire-eating radicalism of the antebellum secessionists, and he reflected that this was a manifestation of a totalitarian tradition in a closed society. A year later, folk singer Phil Ochs released his song "Here's to the State of Mississippi," in which he represented Mississippi as a violent place of institutionalized crime, suggesting that it should find itself "another country to be part of." These ideas and metaphors of Mississippi as a distinctive place set apart from the rest of the nation still resonated in Alan Parker's 1988 movie *Mississippi Burning*, which was loosely based on the FBI's investigation into the murder of three civil rights workers participating in the drive to register African American voters during the so-called Mississippi Freedom Summer of 1964. It is, however, important to stress that Northern notions of Southern exceptionalism were functional for forging a fragile liberal consensus in the North and the West, without which the civil rights legislation of the 1960s would never have come to pass.

In all, therefore, Southern exceptionalism was imagined at the crossroads of two intersecting intellectual processes: first, a Southern self-description that constructed the notion of a distinct Southern civilization standing in direct opposition to the rest of the U.S., especially the Yankee North; and second, a liberal American Exceptionalism defined by what has been called the American creed of egalitarianism, individualism, liberty, and self-determination. This latter strand portrayed the South as an exception to the American rule and helped sustain myths of a liberal American Exceptionalism. It also helped protect white racial innocence insofar as the outside view on Southern exceptionalism blinded U.S. citizens to the realities of discriminatory racism in the North and the West. This racism manifested itself in a widespread de facto segregation that did not require laws to discriminate against blacks. The ideology of American Exceptionalism, wrote Matthew D. Lassiter and Joseph Crespino in their edited volume *The Myth of Southern Exceptionalism*, "can survive only through the constant renewal of southern exceptionalism." It seems to require the imagination of a distinct South "as oppositional region to remain intact." To deconstruct narratives of Southern exceptionalism, therefore, can appear as "a necessary step in overcoming the mythology of American exceptionalism, transforming the American Dilemma into a truly national ordeal, and traversing regional boundaries to rewrite the American past on its own terms and in full historical perspective."

This chapter has approached the spatial dynamics of American Exceptionalism from a regional perspective. Dealing with the frontier West and the South as distinct, if not unique, regions in U.S. history, we have traced the powerful impact that they had on the conceptual history of American Exceptionalism. We have seen how, especially in reading Frederick Jackson Turner, the frontier as a westward moving place and process was mythologized into the single source of America's Americanness. Yet the chapter has also demonstrated how exactly this view was disputed by the scholars of New Western History, who not only deconstructed the frontier thesis but reflected the frontier West as a site of what one could call a negative American Exceptionalism. In their view, the American West was a site of genocide, environmental destruction, capitalist exploitation, and imperial domination. Whether it was celebrated or condemned, the American West as the site of the frontier in one way or another was an important factor in the conceptual history of American Exceptionalism.

The same holds true for the South, although the regional dynamics there were quite different. The South developed its own distinct way of life and sense of identity that made it exceptional within the U.S. The construction of a distinct South fed into the conceptual history of American Exceptionalism in two ways. On the one hand, it produced a regional identity based on the notion of a Southern exceptionalism that justified white supremacy and white racial control throughout the course of Southern history. On the other, it set the South apart from the rest of the U.S., declaring it to be an exception to the American way of life centering on ideas of liberty, equal opportunity, democracy, and free-market capitalism. This liberal version of American Exceptionalism fed on the idea of Southern exceptionalism insofar as it defined the South as something that the U.S. was *not*, to the effect that racism appeared solely as a feature of the Southern way of life, which, of course, it was not.

3

Cities upon Hills

The Colonial Foundations of American Exceptionalism

AMERICAN EXCEPTIONALISM WAS PLANTED into colonial soils. It came to North America with John Winthrop and the Congregationalists who famously sought to create a "city upon a hill" in the thick woods of Massachusetts. However, the Puritans were not the only ones striving to realize an ideal society in colonial British North America. Many European groups, from the Puritans in New England to the Quakers, Mennonites, and Moravians in the Mid-Atlantic colonies, and the poor in the more secular experiment in Georgia, migrated to colonial North America to create planned societies from scratch, which were held to be ideal and a model to the world. Colonial British North America was a place to make European dreams of a good society come true.

THE PURITAN PROJECT

The term *Puritans* refers to a very diverse lot of English Protestants united in their dissent from the Anglican Church. Convinced that the Protestant Reformation in England had not gone far enough, and charging the Anglican Church with still being too Catholic in dogma, liturgy, and beliefs, Puritans criticized a church that claimed to be Protestant but in their eyes was not. Furthermore, Puritans held that the Anglican Church was too closely tied to secular authorities and worldly pursuits that alienated it from God. England's dissenting Protestants, therefore, worked to purify the Anglican Church of all its remaining *Catholic* elements and to disentangle the mingle-mangle of church and state. This, for them, paved the way for a truly Christian commonwealth based solely on the precepts of the Bible.

The Puritans were Calvinists; their doctrine was deeply rooted in the ideas of original sin, predetermination, and the problem of salvation connected to this doctrine. In the Puritan way of thinking, mankind had entered into a state of total depravity after Adam's fall and had been living in sin ever since. The only hope was salvation in the next world, which, however, was anything but certain, and more importantly, beyond human agency and control. The Calvinist doctrine of predetermination suggested that an omniscient, powerful but enigmatic God had predetermined the course of the world and the fate of the individual believer. This doctrine divorced the problem of salvation completely from an individual believer's conduct, deeds, and morality. Predetermination suggested that a gloriously powerful God, whose works escaped human rationality, would redeem individuals independent of what they had done in this world. Instead of being able to work for God's grace, all a believer could do was read the Bible, live a God-fearing life, be pious—and see what happened after death. This state of perpetual uncertainty posed a heavy psychological burden on every individual believer—and from it grew the tension between the sense of chosenness and the possibility of failure that is so characteristic of American Exceptionalism's intellectual history.

In the seventeenth century, some English Puritans—but by no means all of them—decided to emigrate to North America to live their faith and build societies exclusively based on God's word. The reasons for the Puritan migration to North America were quite complex. The most obvious was the wish to escape religious persecution. In 1604, King James I declared that Puritanism agreed with monarchy as much as God agreed with the devil, and with the ascension of Charles I to the throne in 1625, the simmering crisis escalated. Together with the Anglican clergyman William Laud, whom he elevated to bishop in 1628 and to archbishop in 1633, King Charles I clamped down hard on the Puritans: Ministers were dismissed, laypeople taken to court, and Puritan tracts and pamphlets strictly censored.

Religious persecution alone, however, cannot fully explain why some Puritan groups left England for America. Just as important was a deep-seated feeling of crisis among themselves. Looking at the world in terms of an eternal struggle between good and evil, a growing number of Puritans increasingly became convinced that in England, this struggle threatened to be decided in favor of evil. They perceived the situation in England as perpetuating a life in sin. By silently acquiescing to it, Puritans saw themselves sharing England's sinfulness and becoming guilty before God. Although as Calvinists, they believed in predetermination and understood all human history to be divinely foreordained, Puritans were doers who would not passively accept their circumstances, waiting for the next life—and one way of doing something about their situation was to leave England.

In the eyes of those Puritans who set sail for North America, God had chosen New England for them as a providential place that offered the chance to embark on a holy experiment that could recreate the original, pure, and simple church of Jesus Christ. In building this religious society, the Puritans would finally fulfill the promise of the Protestant Reformation, which had seemingly been betrayed by the Anglican Church, and purify their own faith by ridding it of everything that was not in keeping with the Christian doctrine as laid down in the Bible.

In the history of the U.S., the two most important Puritan groups were the Pilgrims and the Congregationalists. While the Pilgrims were the first to settle in New England, crossing the Atlantic on the *Mayflower* and founding Plymouth Plantation in 1620, they were rather unimportant to the conceptual history of American Exceptionalism. This has to do with them being separatists from the Anglican Church who were convinced that England was beyond repair and that nothing could be done about Europe's sinfulness. By emigrating to North America, the Pilgrims literally turned their backs on the Old World to live a God-abiding life in the forests of New England. Wanting to be left to themselves, the Pilgrims wasted few thoughts on the reformation of England, let alone mankind. Their mindset did not invite an exceptionalist thinking. This was different for the Congregationalists, who came to North America ten years after the Pilgrims.

In contrast to the Pilgrims, the Congregationalists were reformers who wanted to change the Anglican Church from within. They believed that they could turn it into the true Christian church by cleansing it of its Catholic remnants, and for John Winthrop and his friends, this reform project started in New England. For the Congregationalists, emigration to North America, therefore, did not mark a complete break with Europe but the beginning of Christianity's rejuvenation that would sooner or later leap back to Europe. This became the basis for a sense of exceptionalism centering on the image of a "city upon a hill," as it was formulated by John Winthrop in his sermon "A Model of Christian Charity," which he delivered onboard the ship *Arbella* during the Atlantic passage.

In this sermon, Winthrop described his vision of an ideal Christian commonwealth as a hierarchically ordered society bound together by a shared faith, brotherly love, solidarity, and mutual responsibility. Following the usual pattern of a Puritan sermon, Winthrop substantiated his argument with numerous passages from the Bible, and then came to the application of his biblical interpretations to the situation he saw his own group involved in. "Thus stands the cause between God and us," Winthrop exclaimed, establishing a direct relationship between God and the Puritans, who appeared as the chosen people of God. Winthrop saw God and his people connected by a contractual relationship, whose purpose was the creation of a society solely based on God's word as revealed in the Bible. "[W]e are entered into covenant with Him for this work," Winthrop said; he suggested that their safe arrival in New England, still in the future when he was preaching these words, would be a sign that God had "ratified this covenant and sealed our commission." In return, He would "expect a strict performance of the articles contained in it." Should they "neglect the observation of these articles" and dissemble with their God, Winthrop argued, "the Lord will surely break out in wrath against us, be revenged of such a perjured people, and make us know the price of the breach of such a covenant."

The only way to "avoid this shipwreck," Winthrop suggested, was to follow the Bible strictly and "be knit together in this work as one man." Should their settlement grow and prosper, this would be a sign of God's continued support. "We shall find that the God of Israel is among us," Winthrop explained, "when ten of us shall be able to resist a thousand of our enemies; when He shall make us a praise and glory [so] that men shall say of succeeding plantations, 'The Lord make it like that of New England.'" With these words, Winthrop stated his intention to turn the Puritan settlement in North America into a model for the rest of the Christian world.

Having said this, Winthrop uttered the famous words: "[F]or we must consider that we shall be as a city upon a hill, the eyes of all people are upon us. So that if we shall deal falsely with our God in this work we have undertaken, and so cause Him to withdraw His present help from us, we shall be made a story and a by-word through the world."

The sense of chosenness and mission was obvious in Winthrop's sermon. What should be pointed out, however, is that it was connected to strong obligations and responsibilities, and that the possibility of failure was inseparably tied to it. While he envisioned the Puritan settlement project in New England as a model society, where the reform of Christianity would originate, Winthrop was also convinced that the Puritans stood under enormous pressure to actually make this Christian utopia happen. Should they fail to realize it, they would be but "a story and a by-word through the world." In Winthrop's reading, therefore, the Congregationalists were either in for a "city upon a hill" or "a story and a by-word" in the history of mankind.

This possibility of failure created a distinct set of anxieties that are as specific to the concept of American Exceptionalism as is the missionary zeal to make the world over. Bound to God by a contract, the Congregationalists, as the chosen people, were, on the one hand, under God's special protection but, on the other, stood under a special obligation to justify His trust. Only if they realized and consolidated a Christian commonwealth would the covenant continue; if they failed in this endeavor, the Puritans would have broken the treaty, God would abandon them, and His revenge would be horrible.

On the Puritan mental map, North America thus occupied a special place; a place that was exceptional insofar as it offered the one and only chance to recover the original, pure, and simple church of Jesus Christ and establish a way of life based on the Bible as the only manifestation of the pure Christian doctrine. In Massachusetts, and only in Massachusetts, could they begin their work of purifying their own faith, ridding it of everything deemed not in keeping with God's word, and thus finally completing the promise of the Protestant Reformation that had gone so utterly wrong in England and continental Europe. In New England, the Puritans hoped to build the appropriate social and ecclesiastical structures providing the opportunity to live a pious life and foster the Divine plan—with no guarantee that this pious life would actually materialize.

For the Congregationalists, New England figured as the New Canaan, and they saw themselves as successors of the biblical Israelites. Typology was the intellectual operation that allowed John Winthrop and his friends to think that way. The typological way of thinking, which had a long tradition going all the way back to antiquity, looked for parallels between the Old and the New Testaments to demonstrate from scripture that the New Testament indeed fulfilled the prophesies of the Old. The Puritans expanded this theological way of thinking to include parallels between biblical events and their own situation in the early modern world. Interestingly, the Congregationalists imagined New England as the New Canaan even before they got there. They thus anticipated North America as the Promised Land while still in England.

John Cotton used this formulation in his farewell sermon, "God's Promise to His Plantation," which he gave at Southampton, England, as the Winthrop fleet was about to set sail for the Atlantic crossing. Interpreting 2 Samuel 7:10, which reads, "Moreover, I will appoint a Place for my people Israel, and I will PLANT them, that they may dwell in a place of their OWN, and MOVE NO MORE," Cotton pointed out that God personally had promised the Israelites a land for them to live in. While all peoples lived in places provided to them by God, Cotton argued, the Israelites were a special case because they were actually given a land by God's personal promise. While others took the land by His providence, Cotton explained, "God's people take the Land by Promise," and this "Land of Promise" was Canaan. What Canaan was to the Israelites, the New Canaan in North America was to the Congregationalists: a land given to them by divine decree.

The concept of a New Canaan defined how the Puritans perceived the natural environments of New England. The differences in perceptions between the Pilgrim Fathers around William Bradford and John Winthrop's Congregationalists are telling, however. Bradford, in his *Of Plymouth Plantation*, describing New England's natural environment as a desolate and hostile wilderness full of "wild beasts and wild men," was rather shocked. The New England he described ran counter to the biblical descriptions of the Promised Land. It was not the land of milk and honey offering rest after their weary travels but rather a howling wilderness that offered but little solace. Bradford and other Pilgrims thus flatly denied any likeness between New England and Canaan.

In contrast to the Pilgrims, Winthrop and his followers did perceive New England as the New Canaan; their social experiment was thus tied to the geographical site of New England. This is anything but self-explanatory, as the "city upon a hill" could actually stand on any hill. The Puritan reform of Christianity was a universal project that, originally, was not tied to any particular place. It only became so in the course of time. In 1629, Winthrop had still argued that the geographical location of the new church was irrelevant. By 1640, however, the project of building a "city upon a hill" could only take place in New England as a unique site of salvation history.

It is important to note that in its time, the rhetoric of the New Canaan also served as a defense against the charge of desertion brought forth against the Congregationalist emigrants by their fellow Puritans staying behind in England. In a time when they were actually most needed to fight the moral decay in their homeland, so the charge went, Winthrop and his friends had left the country, taking the seemingly easy way out. By arguing that New England was the New Canaan directly promised to them by God Himself, the emigrating Congregationalists were also clearing their consciences.

Yet, the sense of chosenness and mission posed enormous psychological and emotional challenges to the New England Congregationalists, especially because they were utterly aware that their social experiment could fail, and the possibility of failure indeed was omnipresent. It started with the physical challenges of survival in New England's harsh and uninviting environment, continued with the worldly temptations of thriving settlements, and climaxed in the eternal battle between God and Satan the Puritans saw themselves facing. New England's Puritans considered themselves under constant surveillance, with both God and Satan watching them, and fighting for their souls. Should they fail in this spiritual struggle, they would not only fail for themselves but would betray the hopes of the entire Christian world.

From this mindset emerged the fear of declension, which Winthrop had envisioned as the possibility of the Puritans "dissembling" with their God to embrace worldly pleasures. Declension, however, was not only a fear; it was also an experience resulting from the deep transformations that New England underwent during the seventeenth and eighteenth centuries. The history of colonial New England was shaped by

Puritanism, to be sure, but its history is also one of declining Puritan influence as New England became more populous, more diverse, more prosperous, and also more secular. After 1660, New England's population grew rapidly to more than 115,000 people by 1710. Twenty years later, the population had grown to 215,000, reaching 450,000 in 1760. This population growth was almost exclusively the result of natural reproduction. Along with it came the rapid expansion of settlement from the Atlantic coastline into the inland areas. This settlement process was largely borne by young men and women who did not stand a chance of inheriting land in the settled areas and so migrated west in search of land. As New England's society became more mobile, parental authority eroded, and the formerly tight-knit community structures became weaker.

The second motor of change in colonial New England was its rapidly growing prosperity. As port cities along the Atlantic coast, such as Boston or Salem, developed into prosperous mercantile hubs and centers of the trades and crafts, many new economic opportunities outside of farming arose. A rising spirit of enterprise surfaced that led to a gradual polarization of wealth, created a new commercial elite, and fostered forms of social stratification and distinction. Realities in colonial New England increasingly contrasted sharply with the egalitarian and collectivist visions of the first Congregationalist settlers. As a consequence, the religious foundations of life in New England eroded, especially in the towns and cities, but not as much in the countryside. The younger generations lost the original settlers' sense of mission and its urgency. The clergy's authority and status, prestige, and influence declined, and the rich merchants emerged as the new urban elite in an increasingly diversified society. A growing number of New Englanders, rejecting the values of their parents, began to embrace ideas of individualism and began to pursue their notions of happiness in this world. These deep social and political transformations defined the basis for jeremiad narratives anchored in the image of an "Errand into the Wilderness."

The jeremiad is a rhetorical device of divine threat and warning centering on the fear of backsliding and leaving the path of righteousness in the embrace of worldly pleasures. Revolving around the terms *afflictions* and *punishment*, the jeremiad was all about warning the community of the dangers of neglecting their mission to build a model Christian commonwealth. The jeremiad, Madsen writes in *American*

Exceptionalism, in suggesting "that God's chosen people are subject to particular suffering by virtue of their exceptional destiny, provided a powerful explanation for the many kinds of affliction that befell the colony: famine, disease, Indian attack, and so on, all could be explained as the signs of God's displeasure as He sought to keep His people to the path of righteousness."

The jeremiad found a paradigmatic articulation in Samuel Danforth's election sermon "A Brief Recognition of New England's Errand into the Wilderness," preached and published in 1670. Addressed to the assembled delegates on the occasion of the election of Massachusetts General Court officers, Danforth's sermon was an eloquent and extended meditation on Matthew 11:7–9, "What went ye out into the wilderness to see?" In this passage, Jesus reflects on how John the Baptist retreated into the solitude of the desert to prepare the path for the Messiah; how the Israelites, as the chosen people of God, went to see him; and how they lost their connection to God during this "Errand into the Wilderness."

Danforth used this biblical passage to ask his fellow Congregationalists whether they had not also "in a great measure forgotten" their own "Errand into the Wilderness." Reminding them that they had left England for the "waste and howling Wilderness" of New England to establish a truly Christian commonwealth based on the precepts of the Bible "without humane Mixtures and Impositions," Danforth invited his audience to "consider whether our ancient and primitive affections to the Lord Jesus, his glorious Gospel, his pure and Spiritual Worship and the Order of his House, remain, abide and continue firm, constant, entire and inviolate."

Demanding that his contemporaries remember the early years of the Puritan settlements and compare them with the present time, Danforth asked "whether it was not then better with us, then it is now." Framing his historical comparison in a model of declension, Danforth saw the enthusiasm, dedication, and rigor of the original settlers having waned significantly. Instead of sticking strictly to the Gospel and striving to create the Christian commonwealth of brotherly love envisioned by John Winthrop, the Puritan settlers in New England, like the biblical Israelites, had succumbed to worldly pleasures, caring more about their personal well-being in this world than about God and the next world. "Pride, Contention, Worldliness, Covetousness, Luxury, Drunkenness and Uncleanness," Danforth argued, "break in like a flood upon us, and good men grow cold in their love to God and to one another."

Reflecting on the troublesome developments, hardships, and setbacks the Puritans experienced—bad harvests, American Indian attacks, diseases, and thunderstorms—as "afflictions," Danforth interpreted these incidents as Divine punishment for a growing "unbelief" among the Puritans. "Afflictions" were both a sign of God's wrath and a manifestation of His ultimate favor and caring love for His chosen people, whom He punishes to return them to the right path. Using them as a tool to reform the whole of Christianity, God lashed out in punishment against the New England Congregationalists to make them renew their faith and commitment to their common cause.

Danforth's sermon was anchored in a paradoxical tension amid a sense of chosenness, an awareness of responsibility, and the anxiety of failure that was directly related to the city-upon-a-hill exceptionalism standing at the cradle of the Puritan project in New England. The jeremiad organized a perspective on the world through which the Puritan settlers in New England interpreted their colonial experiences in categories of declension, which, in turn, created great uncertainties about their own exceptionality.

OTHER RELIGIOUS GROUPS, OTHER RELIGIOUS QUESTS

Although the New England Puritans were crucial for the conceptual history of American Exceptionalism, they were by no means the only ones pursuing social and religious experiments in colonial British North America. Rather, the Atlantic coast was dotted with religious groups busy creating their own utopian societies, that is, societies that were held to be ideal and that could not be realized in Europe, where an alliance of thrones and established churches enforced orthodoxy, prevented diversity, persecuted religious dissenters, and thereby, in the view of the dissenters, alienated Christian believers from their God.

In New England, Roger Williams founded Rhode Island in 1636 as the first colony built on the principle of religious freedom from a spirit of dissenting Protestantism that turned against the Congregationalists in Massachusetts. Through their dogmatic rigor and militant orthodoxy,

Williams was convinced, the Congregationalists of Massachusetts had betrayed the promise of a new Christian beginning in the New World. For Williams, who was a Puritan minister himself, religious freedom was the condition of possibility for the thorough reformation of the world. He was convinced that if the Christian God's word was only preached *correctly* in a society free to choose, everybody would necessarily have to see the truth of the Gospel and embrace the Christian faith as he understood it. As this was not the case in Massachusetts, Rogers went on to start his own religious experiment in Rhode Island.

The hub of religious diversity in colonial British North America, however, was Pennsylvania, which was started by the Quakers under the leadership of William Penn in 1681. The Quakers were another group in the diverse spectrum of England's dissenting Protestantism. Plain in dress, speech, and behavior, the Quakers believed that Christ had already returned to reign, that He was among them, and that the end of the world and the Lord's terrible day of reckoning and punishment were near. The Society of Friends, as the Quakers called themselves, scorned all secular and clerical authority, served in no armies, paid no taxes, took no oaths, and did not doff their hats to anybody because the Christian God for them was the only entity deserving their respect. Denouncing all worship but their own as false, the Quakers were the most zealous missionaries and, as such, a potentially disruptive force wherever they went.

It is hardly surprising, therefore, that they were persecuted not only in England but also in the North American colonies, where they had been present since the mid-1650s. The harshest persecution occurred in Massachusetts, where returning Quaker missionaries, who had been banished from the colony, faced the death penalty. As time progressed, however, persecution became less intense, so that by the 1670s, every colony from New Hampshire to South Carolina had Quaker congregations.

Still, the Quakers' situation in both England and North America remained strained, which is why William Penn, offspring of a wealthy English family in the service of the Crown and real estate entrepreneur, sought to secure a colony to create a society planned in accordance with Quaker ideals. Fortunately, King Charles II was so heavily in debt with the Penn family that, in 1681, he granted to William Penn a large piece of land on North America's Mid-Atlantic coast to settle the financial claims.

Penn lost no time in establishing the colony of Pennsylvania as a holy commonwealth created from scratch—and free from the pressure of European circumstances and corruption—to serve as a model to others. Although the history of Pennsylvania's founding was a thoroughly secular affair, Penn understood it to be a manifestation of God's providence. Reflecting on the recently granted colonial charter in a letter to his fellow Quaker James Harrison, Penn wrote on August 25, 1681, that he had "eyed the Lord in the obtaining" of the charter. Owing the colonial charter to God's "hand and power," Penn felt the obligation to prove that he "may not be unworthy of his love." To "answer his kind providence, and serve his truth and people," Penn wanted to set up Pennsylvania as an "example [. . .] to the nations." In North America, "though not here" in Europe, there was "room" for "such a holy experiment." In this letter, the pattern of chosenness, mission, and failure surfaced in a Quaker variant.

Like Winthrop in Massachusetts, Penn sought to construct a new type of community in the woods of Pennsylvania. The colony's capital, Philadelphia, which means "city of brotherly love," carried Penn's utopian program in its name. In addition, the various "Frames of Government" drafted between 1682 and 1701 as well as the brochure "Some Account of the Province of Pennsylvania," which Penn published in 1681 to attract settlers from all over Europe, guaranteed freedom of worship to all those professing some key beliefs of the Christian faith, and a large degree of political freedom.

While the Quakers set the tone of the colony and maintained political dominance well into the eighteenth century, Pennsylvania was the religiously most diverse place in colonial British North America. It was especially a haven for Pietistic splinter groups from Germany, whence the Mennonites, Dunkers, and Moravians immigrated. They had all been severely persecuted in Europe, wanted to live in communities organized solely on the basis of their religious beliefs and convictions, and saw colonial North America as the place to go to.

Finally, in the context of colonial British North America as a religiously diverse place and a site of social experiments based on the precepts of the Bible, one should not forget Lord Baltimore and his colony, Maryland, founded by royal charter as an asylum for England's persecuted Roman Catholics in 1632. The spirit of dissent so important to the religious history of colonial British North America and the history of American Exceptionalism took a Roman Catholic turn in Maryland, which, along with Rhode Island, pioneered the principle of religious tolerance. Although the colony never became the place of refuge for England's Roman Catholics it was intended to be (thirty-five years after its founding, only 10 percent of Maryland's settler population professed this faith), it is still remarkable that Maryland was started as an experiment in practical Roman Catholic tolerance.

This short overview shows that many religious dissenters from Europe viewed North America as the place to translate religious ideas into concrete realities; it offered the exceptional—even unique—opportunity to make a new beginning and start the world over, and this planted exceptionalist persuasions and mindsets deeply into the soils of colonial British North America. All of the religious groups discussed above shared a providential view of history and their own place in it, and so they were all too ready to believe that their religious experiments in the North American wilderness were the Lord's doing, and that this was but the beginning of a thorough and sustainable reform of Christianity as such. In their view, the rejuvenation of Christianity started in the remote colonial periphery of the Old World and would one day return to the European center, where they had all had worked, suffered, and sacrificed for their religious convictions before. America's exceptionality was thus defined against a standard of normalcy represented by Europe. American Exceptionalism breathed the spirit of exile and dissent.

All religiously dissenting emigrants to North America were convinced that their religious experiments would be impossible to conduct in Europe, and subscribing to a providential view of history, many of them believed that God had literally reserved the North American colonies for them and their projects. While many Congregationalists saw New England as the New Canaan, William Penn was convinced that God had provided him with the "room" in North America for the Quaker experiment. Like Penn, many other colonial dwellers were convinced that God's spirit was making itself felt in an unusual way and that God had a special destiny in store for America.

With religious freedom explicitly guaranteed in Rhode Island, Maryland, and Pennsylvania, and with de facto religious tolerance existing in other colonies, colonial British North America was a place of unprecedented religious diversity, and this, in turn, became a marker defining the exceptionality of America. In the eyes of many a contemporary, religious tolerance was not only the source of peace and harmony but also the cause of colonial British North America's spectacular growth and prosperity.

In "Query XVII" of his *Notes on the State of Virginia*, Thomas Jefferson wrote in 1781 that Pennsylvania and New York had done away with established churches altogether to embrace the principle of religious tolerance. Calling this an unheard of experiment that many people doubted in the beginning, Jefferson pointed out that the experiment proved successful "beyond conception." Both states flourished "infinitely," religion was "well supported," and all religious groups were working to "preserve peace and order." The crime rate in Pennsylvania and New York was not higher than that of Virginia, which still adhered to an established church, and both states were "not more disturbed with religious dissensions" than Virginia. "On the contrary," Jefferson explained, "their harmony is unparalleled, and can be ascribed to nothing but their unbounded tolerance, because there is no other circumstance in which they differ from every nation on earth."

One year later, John Hector St. John de Crèvecœur, in the third of his *Letters from an American Farmer*, explained how the violent conflicts between religious groups and denominations of Europe gradually petered out in the North American colonies *because* of the religious tolerance guaranteed there. As soon as every religious group had the right to live its religion free from political interference and other disturbances, Crèvecœur argued, they would all embrace the idea of tolerance and engage in the culture of live and let live. The potential of religious persecution born from the missionary zeal inherent to all religions, which proved so destructive in the contexts of Europe, would first cool down and eventually be extinguished completely.

THE PHILANTHROPIC PROJECT IN GEORGIA

Not all social experiments in colonial British North America were religious in nature. Georgia, founded in 1732 as the last of the British colonies on the Atlantic coast, was set up as a secular project of social reform deeply indebted to the traditions of English philanthropy. It was masterminded by James Edward Oglethorpe and a group of like-minded men who wanted to solve England's problems of unemployment, poverty, and the social ills connected to them: immorality, misery, alcoholism, violence, and crime.

Like so many eighteenth-century social reformers, Oglethorpe, a well-educated member of the English gentry with high standing, considerable landed property, and quite a lot of political influence, was convinced that poverty was the result of idleness, a lack of discipline, and other character defects. In light of this diagnosis, Oglethorpe and his philanthropic friends wanted to make the poor self-supporting by changing their morals; they saw work as the best educational instrument to teach the poor the discipline, ethics, and morals necessary for an affluent and stable life in middle-class respectability. This produced the idea of founding a labor colony in North America, where England's poor and unemployed would get a second chance. At the same time, a labor colony overseas offered the chance to expel deviant, criminal, and unwanted people to a place outside of England.

The immediate impulse for the founding of Georgia resulted from Oglethorpe's work as head of a committee to investigate the English debtor-prison system. By February 25, 1729, when he was made chairman of the committee, Oglethorpe, an elected member of Parliament since 1722, had made himself a name as an expert on social issues. Having served on forty-two different committees dealing with issues of the unprivileged class, Oglethorpe was well familiar with the plight of England's debtors, poor, and needy. He saw that, once released from debtors' prison, the ex-convicts were stigmatized, unable to find work, and in for a life of perpetual poverty. A labor colony in North America offering the outcasts of England's society the opportunity to start over appeared as a sustainable solution to the problem.

In July 1730, Oglethorpe joined forces with other prison reformers and several Protestant ministers to draft a petition for a debtor colony to the southwest of South Carolina. It was presented to the Privy Council on September 17, 1730, and on June 9, 1732, King George II finally issued the charter for Georgia. In it, the king mentioned that many of his subjects "through misfortunes and want of employment" were living in poverty, unable "to provide a maintenance for themselves and families."

If these subjects had had the means to pay for the Atlantic passage and the "other expences, incident to new settlements, they would be glad to settle in any of our provinces in America" to gain a "comfortable subsistence" by cultivating North American land "at present waste and desolate." While the royal charter also stated that the colony was to serve as a military buffer protecting the Carolinas from attacks by the French, Spanish, and American Indians, it should be stressed that the philanthropic impulse behind the founding of Georgia was very strong.

The charter created the body Trustees for Establishing the Colony of Georgia, nominated James Oglethorpe and nineteen other high-standing gentlemen as its members, and put them in charge of running the colony for a period of twenty-one years, after which the grant would revert to the Crown. Operating through the Common Council of the Trustees, situated in London, Oglethorpe and his friends worked to realize their social vision of an all-white, hardworking, property-owning, and morally sound society of farmers, traders, and merchants of the *middling sorts*. They nominated Oglethorpe as their publicity agent, and in this capacity he initiated a promotional campaign that advertised the new colony as a "land of Liberty and Plenty," offering England's poor the chance to become landowners without long servitude to pay for their passage. In Georgia, with its fertile soils, rivers teeming with fish, and woods full of game animals free for everybody to hunt, they would be able to live a life of affluence and comfort.

This promotional campaign met with a lot of interest, and hundreds wanted to be sent to the new colony by the trustees. After a careful selection process, 114 pioneer settlers, under Oglethorpe's leadership, left England on November 17, 1732, arriving in Georgia in January 1733. Other English emigrants soon followed, as did Protestant exiles from Salzburg; Scottish Highland families; and settlers from Switzerland, Germany, and France.

The well-meaning philanthropy of the trustees and their serious wish to solve a grave social problem was carried by a moral rigor that was translated into a benevolent dictatorship over the colony. Claiming to know what was good for the settlers, the trustees did everything for them without doing anything with them. This became manifest in the *Trustees' Rules for the New Colony of Georgia, 1735*, which defined the regulations and conditions for the handpicked settlers of Georgia. They listed watch coats, muskets with bayonets, hatchets, hoes, hammers, spades, and other items to be given to every settler at the trustees' expense. In addition, the trustees would pay for transportation and the first year of supplies ranging from beef or pork, rice, peas, cheese, and butter to vinegar, salt, lamp oil, and soap for every family.

Furthermore, the *Trustees' Rules* ordered that for the first year from their landing, the settlers should work to clear the land, build houses and necessary defenses, and do "all other Works for the common Good and public Weal[th]" of Georgia "according to such Plan and Directions as shall be given." Starting the second year, the settlers would settle, inhabit, and cultivate the land allotted to them and their heirs by the trustees. The maximum land grant for an immigrant at the expense of the trustees was set at fifty acres. Lots of this size were believed to be large enough to provide sustenance for a family and some surplus production for sale at regional and overseas markets. At the same time, the parcel would be small enough to prevent large estates and fortunes from emerging, which would divide society into rich and poor, producing the kind of dependencies and vicious cycles of poverty and debt that the philanthropic project of Georgia was originally set up to overcome.

Everyone receiving land was expected to clear, fence, and cultivate it. Should they fail to do so in a period of ten years, the land fell back to the trustees. All lots were to be "preserved separate and undivided," and they could not be united. All land was entailed to males, so if there was no male heir, the land reverted to the trustees; alienation by landholders was forbidden without the trustees' permission. Land tenure, therefore, was seen as a prime instrument to realize a model society that had eliminated the causes of poverty and social misery. While defense considerations also played a role in this land policy—it was a way to keep the colony densely populated with farmers who would be soldiers in times of war—the social vision carrying the Georgia project was just as important a reason for this highly restrictive land policy.

Another important measure in realizing the social vision was the trustees' ban on slavery in the colony. Although the settlers, soon after the founding of Georgia, began to demand that black slaves be allowed in the colony, the trustees prohibited this because they were convinced that slavery would make the settlers lazy. This would undermine the very reform project of Georgia that, to a very large extent, rested on the conviction that laziness was the prime cause of moral deficiency and the poverty that came from it. In this same vein, the trustees also forbade the consumption of rum altogether, and put heavy restrictions on beer and wine.

Overall, therefore, Oglethorpe and his philanthropic friends envisioned their project in Georgia as a chance to create a planned society from scratch. An Enlightenment optimism about rationality and its capacity to solve social problems through rigorous planning was at the heart of what Phinizy Spalding, in her essay on Oglethorpe in the collected volume *Forty Years of Diversity: Essays on Colonial Georgia*, called a "secular Zion" that would also serve as a model for England. Georgia was thus a secular equivalent to the religious project of the Puritans in Massachusetts. Oglethorpe and the trustees, wrote Spalding,

> may have looked to America in the same way the early Puritans had viewed the New World: as a stage upon which to erect a model for the Zion they wished England to become. [. . .] The drunkenness, vice, and corruption that were so readily apparent particularly in London, would be purged; the established church would be cleansed; the province would provide a haven for the unemployed and the ambitious small merchants and shopkeepers who could remake their lives in America. [. . .] Prosperity for Georgia, then, also meant prosperity and improvement for the mother country.

When it was founded, Georgia indeed was a land of the most extravagant hopes—hopes that did not materialize. Settlement was slow and sluggish. The work of clearing the land was hard, and not very much profit could be reaped from agricultural pursuits. Life in Georgia was harsh and primitive, the climate was hostile, the American Indians were anything but welcoming, and starting in 1739, there was constant warfare with the French, the Spanish, and their American Indian allies. Many settlers died of exhaustion, of disease, or due to war. Those who survived all too often went hungry and stayed poor. Many left Georgia for South Carolina and other colonies that seemed to offer better opportunities.

In sum, the educational experiment in Georgia did not get off the ground, and the trustees' moral rigor had a lot to do with it. Carried by an illusion of simplicity that traced England's social problems to the deficient morality of the poor, the trustees' policies were out of sync with both the realities of life in colonial British North America and the human nature of the settlers. The benevolent educational dictatorship of the trustees gave rise to local discontent that targeted the very basis of Georgia's social experiment. The settlers wanted to own their land without any restrictions, and they wanted to be able to pass it on to their children as they liked. Furthermore, they wanted to have slaves, and they wanted to drink alcohol.

In the 1740s, the philanthropic enthusiasm of the trustees began to wane. In 1743, Oglethorpe left Georgia for good and returned to England, and with his departure, Georgia was robbed of its prime mover. At the same time, the relentless pressure from the settlers eventually obliged the trustees to modify their regulations on land, labor, and liquor to the degree that, by 1752, when their rule over Georgia was drawing to a close, nothing of their initial plan was still in place. Georgia had become like many other colonies in British North America. On June 25, 1752, a full year before the date originally set by the royal charter of 1732, the trustees surrendered their charter to the Crown; two years later, the first royal governor arrived to administer Georgia as a Crown colony. The philanthropic experiment that had added another facet to colonial British North America as a site for the creation of utopian societies was over.

The conceptual history of American Exceptionalism begins in the colonial period. It was to a very large extent driven by the utopian longings of European reformers who conceived of colonial British North America as a place to create ideal societies from scratch that could serve as a model to others. In North America, there seemingly was nothing to hinder successfully conducting the social experiments of the Puritans, Quakers, Mennonites, or philanthropists, nothing that needed to be destroyed before one could start building something new. Such utopian European hopes were built on the notion that North America was an empty space and a virgin land, which, of course, it was not. American Indians had been living there for ages, and they had changed the land.

With the exception of Georgia, all of the social experiments in colonial British North America were religious in nature and heavily structured and shaped by the culture of England's dissenting Protestantism. For the dissenting Protestants, the Bible was not only a religious text but also a manual of social engineering. Although started with religious fervor and great enthusiasm, the social experiments in Massachusetts, Pennsylvania, and other colonies lost momentum in the course of the seventeenth and eighteenth centuries. The dynamic growth of colonial British North America and its overall affluence, the massive influx of new settlers who cared more about owning land than pleasing God, and the growing diversity wrought by constant migration took a lot of utopian wind out of the reform projects' sails. By 1750, the time for utopian experiments on colonial grounds was largely over. The exceptionalist persuasions and mindsets to which the colonial projects in Massachusetts, Rhode Island, Pennsylvania, Maryland, and Georgia had given birth, however, continued to circulate in colonial British North America.

4

Sacred Fire of Liberty

The American Revolution and the Transformation of American Exceptionalism

On April 30, 1789, in the first ever inaugural address of an American president, George Washington spoke of "the sacred fire of liberty" kindled by the American Revolution and in need of constant care and protection. He also spoke of "the Republican model of Government," whose destiny would be decided in the U.S. For Washington, America's political order built on natural rights, popular sovereignty, and limited government was an "experiment entrusted to the hands of the American people." With these words, the first U.S. president politicized narratives of American Exceptionalism already circulating in the colonies, and he tied them to the American Revolution and both the state and the nation created by it. This intellectual transformation of American Exceptionalism lies at the core of this chapter's argument, which identifies the American Revolution as the point from which the combination of natural-rights liberalism and a future-oriented rhetoric of progress became a central feature in concepts of American Exceptionalism that traced the uniqueness of the U.S. to its revolutionary founding act.

It was not only Americans, however, who were thinking about the exceptionality of their union and their nation. The transformation of American Exceptionalism at the turn of the nineteenth century had a transnational dimension, insofar as European observers, in what Robert R. Palmer identified as the "the age of democratic revolution" in his book of that same name, began to wonder about how to relate the American to the succeeding French Revolution; the conclusions they reached were prone to cement the uniqueness of the American Revolution in rather surprising ways.

FOUNDING AN EXCEPTIONAL STATE AND NATION

Twenty-five years before Washington's inauguration, virtually nobody in the thirteen British colonies along the Atlantic coast would have dreamed of revolution. "What do We mean by the revolution?" John Adams asked his fellow revolutionary Thomas Jefferson in a letter of August 24, 1815; he went on: "The War? That was no part of the Revolution. It was only an Effect and Consequence of it. The Revolution was in the Minds of the People, and this was effected, from 1760 to 1775, in the course of fifteen Years before a drop of blood was drawn at Lexington." This "Revolution in the Minds of the People" was essentially a matter of identity. Driven by the events and experiences of the fifteen years from 1760 to 1775, a growing number of the American colonists ceased to think of themselves as Englishmen in America and embraced the idea of being Americans. This went hand in hand with the conviction that the newly imagined community of Americans should declare its independence, put government as such on a new footing, and begin governing itself.

When the Treaty of Paris that concluded the French and Indian War was signed on February 10, 1763, American colonists were proud to be Englishmen. They enjoyed their rights and liberties as subjects of the king of England, and they felt attracted to the mother country's imperial might, which that had just increased enormously. The French and Indian War left England the master of North America, and the colonists had contributed significantly to winning this final military conflict in a long imperial struggle for the continent between England and France that had started in the 1680s. In February 1763, England stood triumphant, and a majority of American colonists were proud to share some of its glory.

This era of good feelings did not last long. Shortly after the war, England began to reorganize its colonial rule, ending a long period of what Edmund Burke once called "salutary neglect." Prior to 1763, England had left the American colonists pretty much to themselves, granting them great autonomy in terms of self-government and a high degree of mobility. This policy was salutary for both sides insofar as the colonies prospered, and the mother country did not have to shoulder the heavy financial and administrative burdens of colonial rule.

In 1763, England changed course. The French and Indian War had cost a lot of money. England was broke, and given the vast territorial acquisitions in North America from the Peace of Paris, its rule over the American colonies was in dire need of reorganization. In this situation, London embarked on a new imperial policy that aimed at tightening England's grip on its colonies and having the colonists contribute more to the costs of their own defense and administration. There is no room here to go into the details of the policy measures to raise revenue in the colonies. Suffice it to say that the colonists were up in arms against this new imperial policy. Drawing on the privileges of their colonial charters and the unwritten "Rights of Englishmen," they argued that they could only be taxed by parliaments in which they were represented. Therefore, they would accept taxation by the locally elected colonial assemblies, but not by the British Parliament in faraway London. From the colonists' perspective, the tax laws passed there were a blatant violation of the British constitution and a threat to the liberty they believed they enjoyed as Englishmen. A growing number of colonists increasingly became convinced that the mother country's new colonial policy did not accept them as Englishmen in America but, rather, reduced them to second-class subjects of the Crown.

Initially, the colonial protest was conservative in nature. The American colonists claimed to be defending the ancient Rights of Englishmen and the unwritten British constitution against the aggressions of the mother country. Not only did they argue with the past to legitimate their protest, they also wanted to preserve the world they had known until 1763, defending it against the changes introduced by the royal government in London. The longer the conflict lasted, however, the more the debate over taxes turned into a debate over legitimate rule, to the effect that, by 1774, American colonists were increasingly unwilling to accept British rule as such. Two years later, on July 4, 1776, they declared independence and founded the United States of America.

The Declaration of Independence and the developments leading to it mark the turn to revolution, which is defined by three overlapping developments. First, while they had been primarily reacting to acts and actions originating in England since 1763, the colonists now began to set the agenda, putting Great Britain on the defensive. Second, the colonists established their protest on a new intellectual basis. Having drawn on the particular Rights of Englishmen so far, the leaders of the colonial protest now moved to embrace the natural rights of man. This was a movement away from the particularism and uniqueness of the British constitution and toward the universalism of the Enlightenment, which suggested that people had inalienable rights as human beings, and not as Englishmen, Frenchmen, or Germans. Third, there was a shift in the temporal semantics of the political agenda: Prior to 1774, the colonial protests had been preoccupied with the past; now the protests turned toward the future. Instead of wanting to preserve the world before 1763, the protesters began to think of themselves as harbingers of a change that laid the basis for a better future.

This revolutionary turn during 1774 to 1776 had far-reaching effects for the concept of American Exceptionalism. It was Thomas Paine who reformulated it in his bestselling pamphlet *Common Sense*, published in January 1776 by Robert Bell in Philadelphia. Born on February 9, 1737, in the English Midlands, Paine was pretty much a drifter, working and failing in several professions before he came to Philadelphia in 1774. Paine arrived just in time to witness the rapid escalation of the conflict between England and its colonies. After the Boston Tea Party of December 16, 1773, England had clamped down hard on Massachusetts, which triggered a huge wave of solidarity among all of the colonies, producing a unity among them that had not been there before. Tensions were rapidly rising, and the colonists openly defied England's authority and effectively started to govern themselves. The likelihood of a military confrontation increased. On April 19, 1775, the "shot heard round the world" was fired during the military skirmishes at Lexington and Concord that marked the beginning of the Revolutionary War. Still, hardly anyone in colonial British North America dared to think of independence even then.

On January 10, 1776, Paine's *Common Sense* crashed onto the scene. The pamphlet, which is said to have sold as many as 120,000 copies in the first three months, was an urgent plea for immediate independence. To convince his numerous readers, Paine redefined the nature of the conflict between the colonies and the mother country. For him, it was no longer a conflict between Englishmen unfolding in the frame of the British constitution but a conflict of two competing and mutually exclusive political systems: monarchy versus democracy. Identifying monarchy and hereditary succession as "evil," Paine argued that only a political order anchored in self-government and majority rule was in keeping with human nature. This is why for Paine the "cause of America" was "in a great measure the cause of all mankind."

Drawing on this diagnosis, Paine urgently called for immediate American independence, which, for him, was three things in one: First, it was a means to keep the thirteen colonies united. Second, it was a way to preserve America "uncontaminated by European corruption," and third, it laid the basis for the creation of an ideal state and society based on the political values of the Enlightenment. "Should an independancy be brought about," Paine concluded in an appendix contained in the second edition of *Common Sense*, published in Philadelphia on February 14, 1776, "we have every opportunity and every encouragement before us, to form the noblest purest constitution on the face of the earth. [...] The birthday of a new world is at hand."

Independence from Great Britain thus promised a better world, but to make this promise come true, the Americans had to make the right political decision in the here and now. Paine constructed the situation that he saw himself and his contemporaries acting in as a "peculiar time, which never happens to a nation but once, viz. the time of forming itself into a government." Should the colonists "neglect the present favorable and inviting period," should they forfeit the chance of making the world over, Paine argued, they "must charge the consequence to [them]selves." The failure to live up to the historical moment, in Paine's view, would not only have consequences for the American colonists but also for the whole of mankind, whose future fate was determined by what the colonists did or did not do.

In all, therefore, Paine's argument moved in an intellectual frame that we already know from John Winthrop and his idea of a "city upon a hill." Yet Paine divorced the vision of an ideal society to be created in America from all preoccupation with salvation in the next world. Instead, he tied it to the future, which he conceptualized as a temporal space that was not controlled by God but could actually be shaped by human beings and what they did or did not do in the present. The future that Paine envisioned was to be a republican one. Only political and social systems based on widespread self-government were manifestations of a purely secular *progress* leading to a future that was, in Paine's view, better than the present.

Paine's *Common Sense* pushed the political mood in the American colonies toward independence, and on July 4, 1776, this step was finally taken. The Declaration of Independence is the seminal document of U.S. history, and it is a revolutionary document in and of itself insofar as it defined a set of political and social ideas upon which a future state and society were to be built. The document made natural-rights liberalism America's founding ideology, and this ideology revolved around four key concepts.

The first concept is that of natural rights, the idea that "all men are created equal," and that they are endowed with "certain unalienable Rights," among which "Life, Liberty, and the pursuit of Happiness" figure prominently. One had these rights as a human being, not because one was an Englishman or a member of some other group or polity, for that matter. The natural rights that the Declaration of Independence spoke of were universal rights, not particular ones; they were individual rights, not collective ones. This individualism went hand in hand with a radical egalitarianism anchored in the idea that all men are born free and equal, which is why they all enjoy the same rights.

The second key concept written into the Declaration of Independence was a liberal theory of state, according to which the protection of rights was the sole purpose of government and the only criterion for the legitimate use of political power. Government thus was not an end in itself but the means to an end, and states did not have a life of their own, divorced from the general welfare of the population. They had a function only insofar as they established and guaranteed the frame in which individuals could live freely and make the best of the opportunities they encountered. In protecting individual rights, the liberal state also protected every individual's equality of opportunity.

The third key concept was popular sovereignty. The "Governments . . . instituted among Men," so the Declaration of Independence stated, received their "just powers from the consent of the governed." This concept bound government and society to one another. The separation of state and society known from European absolutism was overcome by identifying the "consent of the governed" as the source of all the government's "just powers." Instead of putting individuals and the whole of society in the service of an abstract state that somehow had a life of its own, the Declaration of Independence put the state in the service of society, and more precisely in the service of individual liberty and happiness.

The fourth and final key concept was the right of the people to perennial revolution. "[W]henever," the Declaration of Independence stated, "any Form of Government becomes destructive of these ends" (i.e., whenever a government no longer protected individual liberty), "it is the Right of the People to alter or to abolish it." In the further course of its argument, it even spoke of the "duty" of the people "to throw off such Government." Together with Thomas Paine's *Common Sense*, the Declaration of Independence can be seen as a masterpiece of a radical Enlightenment that unconditionally embraced universal values to justify independence and absolutely refused to invoke English tradition, precedents, and history. It was this unconditional human-rights universalism in combination with the doctrine of fundamental equality that defined the political radicalism of the American Revolution.

The Declaration of Independence had far-reaching consequences for the concept of American Exceptionalism insofar as it tied it to the political and social project of America's democracy. The old Puritan "Errand into the Wilderness" that would purify the Christian church and create a perfect society piously working for salvation in the next world was redefined to mean the creation of a society of free and equal individuals who were self-reliantly pursuing their notions of happiness in this world. In this, they were protected by a secular state that guaranteed its citizens their individual rights and worked to ensure equality of opportunity. America's exceptionality now lay in the fact that the ideological foundations for a civil society based on natural rights, self-determination, and self-government had been laid; this made the U.S. potentially a "land of opportunity" where everybody could rise from rags to riches through his their own work, talent, and skills. Yet such a society did not yet exist anywhere at the end of the eighteenth century. It still needed to be built. This is the point where we should briefly touch on Benjamin Franklin and his autobiography, which we will come back to in greater detail in chapter 8.

As is well known, Franklin's autobiography tells the success story of a rise from rags to riches in colonial and revolutionary North America. What is less well known, however, is that it is even more a story about moral self-perfection. Affluence, for Franklin, was not an end in itself but, rather, only the means to an end, and that was a life dedicated to public improvement and public service. Franklin's often-cited core values—education, industry, frugality, and moral conduct—are, therefore, not primarily the way to wealth but the way to a morality needed in a society built on individual freedom and self-determination. In Franklin's view, his own project of moral self-perfection was but the starting point for the thorough reform of society as such, in which eventually all individuals would act as he had done in his lifetime. A society of free and self-determined individuals acting voluntarily on the principles of sincerity and justice, moderation and humility, and industry and frugality in dedication to public improvement would be a republican society of stable social relationships, a society without fraud, broken promises, and other disruptive forms of social conduct. Not primarily wanting to turn his readers into millionaires but to educate them into "useful Citizen[s]," Franklin aimed at defining the normative ideal of republican conduct that would turn America's revolutionary experiment of liberty into a success, not just for Americans but for the whole of mankind. Citizens acting like Franklin would help keep the "sacred fire of liberty" burning in the U.S., and American Exceptionalism with it.

THE U.S. CONSTITUTION AS A HISTORICAL NOVELTY

The political order born from the Declaration of Independence was a historical novelty. Written constitutions creating a government from scratch were unheard of. All European states had evolved over time. Their origins lay in the darkness of the past. Nobody knew how they had been founded, and who had done it. Their sole claim to legitimacy was the fact that they had seemingly been there forever. The governments of Europe could not really produce founding documents; even the famed British Constitution was unwritten. The revolutionary Americans were the first to actually create a government originating in a written document that, declaring itself to be the supreme law of the land, organized the political system and its decision-making procedures.

While the U.S. Constitution, being a written document founding a political order, was without precedent at the end of the eighteenth century, the order it created was outright spectacular in the eyes of many a contemporary in the Atlantic world. Prior to 1787, the world had not seen a liberal, parliamentary democracy in an extended federal republic that was bound to expand even further, and that—in all of its parts—was based on the principle of popular sovereignty. Seen from the perspective of what was conventional wisdom at the end of the eighteenth century, the U.S. seemed like a daring but weird experiment in liberty and self-government, which hardly anyone believed would last long. This only increased both the burden of responsibility and the fear of failure among U.S. political actors, who felt that it was for the Americans to prove that a political order based on individual liberty and self-government could persist, thrive, and prosper while the whole world was watching.

Constitution making appeared to be the key to the problem, which is why the years from 1776 to 1787–1788 witnessed an exciting period of debating, drafting, and ratifying constitutions in the U.S. This process moved on two planes, that is, the state and federal levels; to grasp its full excitement, one has to see that constitution making in revolutionary America was an attempt to translate the political principles of the Declaration of Independence into a political order that would perpetuate the American Revolution.

On the state level, the process of constitution making led to thirteen rather different ways of creating republican orders. On the federal level, the U.S. Constitution of 1787 was already the second attempt to cast the ideas of 1776 into an institutional mold. America's first national constitution was the Articles of Confederation, passed by the Continental Congress in 1777 and ratified by 1781.

The Articles of Confederation constituted a confederacy, a "firm league of friendship" among sovereign states. Sovereignty thus continued to reside in the states, which only delegated a limited set of expressly defined powers to the national government. Under this order, the central government was weak, while the states were strong. This construction was a manifestation of the conviction held by many revolutionaries that one had to decentralize power if one wanted to protect individual liberty.

A second feature of America's first constitution was its parliamentary radicalism. The Articles provided for a national government consisting of only one chamber, whose delegates were elected by the state legislatures. This arrangement was carried by the widely shared belief that parliaments, and not the executive, were the best bulwark of liberty. The events of the American Revolution had not only discredited monarchy but also executive power as such. While revolutionary Americans were generally suspicious of central governments, they were outright afraid of the executive as the stepping-stone to monarchy, tyranny, and despotism.

With the national government consisting of only a unicameral parliament, the Articles did not provide for a separation of powers; there was neither an independent executive branch nor a separate judicial branch. All government functions were handled by the Confederation Congress, in which all states interacted on the basis of absolute equality. Each state had one vote, no matter how large or small or how populous.

Compared to the Articles of Confederation, which in many respects followed the well-known model of a league among sovereign states, the U.S. Constitution of 1787 was a much greater historical novelty. Transforming the confederacy into a federal union, the Constitution created a state made of states that were subordinate to a newly established national government in which all political sovereignty resided. Under the Articles, the states had retained all the sovereignty rights not expressly delegated to the national government; under the Constitution, it was the other way around. Furthermore, while the Articles was a treaty among sovereign states, the Constitution invoked the "we" of the American people as the author and sovereign of the political order constituted by it.

The Constitution, with its innovative forms of representation, its complex system of checks and balances, and its double separation of powers—horizontally on the federal level between the executive, legislative, and judicial branches, and vertically between the federal and the state governments—was unique in its time. Representative democracy and federalism were inventions of the delegates to the Constitutional Convention in session in the hot Philadelphia summer of 1787. The concept of an extended republic based on self-government and widespread popular participation in the decision-making process was a radical break with the European history and theory of republicanism, which held that self-governed republics could only exist in small political entities like cities or small states such as Switzerland or the Netherlands but never in a large and growing state like the U.S. Many, therefore, expected that the U.S., in wanting to realize self-government in an extended republic, would, in the distant or not so distant future, either fall apart into several smaller republics or develop into a monarchy or some other form of authoritarian government that would destroy individual liberty altogether. To substantiate their argument, contemporaries could point to the ancient Roman republic, which collapsed as it expanded around the Mediterranean, resulting in the monarchic reign of the Caesars replacing the republican order of old.

The historical novelty of America's constitutions added to the sense of exceptionalism in revolutionary America, and it is important to understand that exceptionalist narratives were tied to both the Articles of Confederation *and* the Constitution. The ratification debate of 1787–1788 can serve as a case in point.

The draft of the Constitution signed on September 17, 1787, by thirty-nine delegates to the Constitutional Convention and handed over to the American people for ratification was a highly controversial and contested document that instantaneously unleashed a fierce political battle of epic dimensions between the Federalists and the Anti-Federalists. The Federalists were all for ratifying the Constitution, spreading their views and arguments in the famous *Federalist Papers* penned by Alexander Hamilton, John Jay, and James Madison. In sum, the Federalists argued that the creation of a federal republic and the centralization of power that went with it were the only ways to protect and perpetuate the ideals of the American Revolution.

The Anti-Federalists, however, thought otherwise. In their view, the proposed Constitution would destroy liberty and American Exceptionalism with it. They were afraid of a strong central government that robbed the states of important governmental functions and bore the potential of tyranny. To substantiate their opinion, the Anti-Federalists pointed to the absence of a bill of rights in the original draft of the Constitution. They also shared the widespread skepticism about extended republics, and they argued that the representative democracy envisioned by the Constitution would alienate the elected representatives from their electorate, remove political decision making from the popular will, and promote the emergence of a quasi-aristocratic caste of politicians corrupting liberty. For the Anti-Federalists, therefore, the decentralized, state-centered system of government created by the Articles of Confederation marked the ideal translation of revolutionary principles into a political order. Thus, while both the Federalists and the Anti-Federalists wanted the same thing— the protection and perpetuation of America's revolutionary experiment in liberty and self-government—they walked very different political paths to achieving this goal.

Although the Constitution was ratified in the end, the Anti-Federalist mindset did not vanish after 1788. Rather, it remained a potent force in the Early Republic, resurfacing in the states' rights theory as it became manifest in the Kentucky and Virginia Resolutions of 1798–1799, the Nullification Controversy of 1832–1833 and—most importantly—in the secession of the Southern states in 1860–1861. The states' rights theory was deeply indebted to the Anti-Federalist critique of the Constitution and developed into a central element of Southern nationalism and its interpretation of American Exceptionalism, as discussed in chapter 2.

In contrast to the Anti-Federalists and states' rights theorists, the Federalists of the Early Republic did everything they could to connect American Exceptionalism to the federal union. In this context, there is no way of getting around George Washington, who (as victorious commander in chief of the Continental Army, president of the Constitutional Convention, and first U.S. president) personified the American Revolution like none other, with the sole exception of Benjamin Franklin. Acting as the interpreter in chief of America's revolutionary history and fully aware of the symbolic weight of his biography and persona, George Washington used much of his political influence and charismatic power to install the Constitution as the consequential institutionalization of the "Spirit of '76" manifest in the Declaration of Independence. In his magisterial study *George Washington and American Constitutionalism*, Glenn A. Phelps argued that, in the end, Americans were for the Constitution because George Washington was for it, and Washington himself, indeed, did his best to establish the connection between the federal union and the revolutionary heritage.

In his Farewell Address of 1796, he urged his countrymen to stay united behind the federal union, which, in Washington's view, was of "immense value" to the "collective and individual happiness" of the Americans. Identifying the federal union as "a main pillar in the edifice" of America's independence, peace, and prosperity, Washington demanded that his countrymen think of it as "the palladium of your political safety and prosperity" and as "a main prop" of their liberty, so that in preserving the union, they would also safeguard their liberty and what they fought for in the American Revolution.

This federalist narrative, which linked American Exceptionalism to the Constitution as the adequate translation of the political principles laid down in the Declaration of Independence, found its visual manifestation in John J. Barralet's highly popular image *Apotheosis of Washington*. Published untitled in 1800, only months after Washington's death on December 14, 1799, it showed Washington's ascension to heaven as an immortal demigod. On the print, one can see Father Time, a bearded old man with angelic wings, raising Washington's body from the tomb and handing it over to a female angel, who conducts the first American president to heaven. The angel, holding Washington's right arm in her left hand and pointing the index finger of her right hand toward the skies, is situated in a broad beam of light breaking through heavy clouds, while the rest of the scene is in darkness.

A group of earthly mourners surrounds Washington's tomb, which carries the inscription "Sacred to the Memory of Washington." In the lower right corner of the image, an American Indian is desperate over Washington's death. To his left, we can see a female figure allegorically representing America weeping over Washington's armor and holding a staff surmounted by a Cap of Liberty. To her left is the national eagle with shield, olive branch, and an *E Pluribus Unum* ribbon representing the American republic and Washington's service to it. The eagle looks directly at the apotheosis scene, while America and the American Indian are turning their heads away. At the center left of the engraving three women, reminiscent of biblical figures, represent the virtues of faith, hope, and charity.

This image democratized the baroque tradition of apotheosis scenes that showed European monarchs ascending to heaven. Here, a secular hero of the American Revolution and democratically elected head of state replaced the absolute monarchs of the Old World. Associating the death of Washington with Christ's ascension, the print not only glorified George Washington but also gave a religious aura to the political order that Washington, as the personification of the American Revolution and father of the country, had helped found. In doing all of this, Barralet's print made visual the connection between American Exceptionalism and the federal union that Washington had identified as the bulwark of American liberty in his Farewell Address.

John J. Barralet, *Apotheosis of Washington*, engraving and etching, ca. 1800. The Metropolitan Museum of Art, New York. http//:www.metmuseum.org

Overall, therefore, Federalist interpretations of the American Revolution understood the Declaration of Independence and U.S. Constitution to be related documents of the same historical process, and suggested that preserving the federal union meant preserving the values of the American Revolution and American Exceptionalism. Their opponents from the camp of Anti-Federalists and states' rights theorists disputed exactly this connection and interpreted the centralization of power under the U.S. Constitution as a break with the "Spirit of '76."

THE AMERICAN REVOLUTION IN THE AGE OF ATLANTIC REVOLUTIONS

So far, this chapter has examined the meaning of the American Revolution for the transformation of American Exceptionalism from a purely national perspective. Yet there was a transnational dimension to these developments insofar as America's real or supposed exceptionality was also defined by what happened in Europe at the time. In building on the same liberal ideology proclaimed in the Declaration of Independence, the French Revolution seemed to continue the American Revolution in Europe, as did the bourgeois revolutions of 1830 and 1848–1849. From the perspective of 1789, 1830, or 1848, therefore, the American Revolution could appear as the first in a series of Atlantic revolutions that aimed at realizing liberal democracies all over Europe.

However, the revolutionary experiences in Europe, featuring class warfare, violent counterreactions by feudal forces, extended warfare all over Europe, and the eventual collapse of the revolutionary liberal democracies, appeared to be so different from those of the U.S. at the end of the eighteenth century that contemporaries began to wonder whether the American model could be transferred to Europe at all. This debate reinforced American Exceptionalism in a rather surprising way: European conservatives, and a significant number of liberals as well, reached the conclusion that America was possible only in America—and that it could not be transferred to Europe for being so exceptional. The famous controversy between Edmund Burke and Thomas Paine over the legitimacy of the French Revolution was a first manifestation of this intellectual development, which reached its climax with French aristocrat Alexis de Tocqueville's enormously influential analysis *Democracy in America*, published in the 1830s. Tocqueville was the first to use the term *exceptional* in connection with the U.S.

The French Revolution triggered heated political controversies all over Europe that tackled the most fundamental political questions. This revolution debate began with a massive attack on the French Revolution by Edmund Burke, who in his *Reflections on the Revolution in France* (1790) set out to fend off all revolutionary aspirations in England by declaring monarchy and hereditary rule; aristocracy and landed property; and the established church, its clergy, and its material wealth as the only legitimate way to organize state and society. This provoked scores of radical writers to reply with critiques of monarchy and aristocracy, and to suggest alternative models ranging from republicanism and agrarian socialism to anarchy. Thomas Paine, the pamphleteer of the American Revolution, turned out to be Burke's main antagonist in this dispute.

In his *Reflections*, Burke interpreted the French Revolution, already in its early stage, as an illegitimate act of usurpation that destroyed the existing order on the behalf of abstract universal rights, which for him did not exist. The result of this, therefore, was bloodshed, turbulent disorder, and political chaos happening in a constitutional void. Burke rejected the idea that political orders could be created from scratch. In his eyes, states and societies were legitimate because they had been there for ages. They had grown over time and were validated by their history. "The very idea of the fabrication of a new government," Burke wrote, was enough to fill him "with disgust and horror," because he wished "to derive all we possess as an INHERITANCE FROM OUR FOREFATHERS."

Burke's constitutional thinking corresponded to his theory of society. His sociology was not anchored in the idea of free and autonomous individuals defined in their rights. Rather, Burke understood society to be made of groups, and the relationships between them were based on differences and distinctions, not on equality. The liberal concept of natural rights, for him, was a doctrine of dangerous "levelling" that destroyed all social hierarchies and cohesion. While Burke saw himself as a champion of "rational" or "regulated liberty," the universal rights of man for him were but "metaphysical abstraction[s]" and "monstrous fiction" that only produced wild, anarchic, and uncontrolled liberty that was utterly destructive, as events in France seemed to demonstrate.

While the debate that Burke triggered with his *Reflections* was first and foremost about the French Revolution and its universal claims, the participants—explicitly or implicitly—were also debating the American

Revolution, as becomes clear when one examines Thomas Paine's defense of the French Revolution in *The Rights of Man*, written on-site in France and published in 1791–1792. Paine's response to Burke's *Reflections* refuted the latter's argument point by point.

Where Burke had held high tradition and inheritance, Paine embraced the autonomy of the present, arguing that no living generation had any power to bind and control "posterity to the end of time." Rather, every living generation had the absolute right to create the world they wanted to live in. Rejecting the "authority of the dead," Paine wholeheartedly embraced "the rights and freedom of the living." Arguing for the existence of natural rights, in direct response to Burke's denial of them, Paine also stated that people indeed had the right to create a government of their own choosing and to regulate power by way of written constitutions.

When he refuted Burke's points, Paine felt that history was on his side. He saw himself living in an age of Atlantic revolutions that all aimed at realizing the same liberal ideas first formulated by the Declaration of Independence. He spoke of a "a spirit of political inquiry" beginning to "diffuse itself through the Nation at the time the dispute between England and the then colonies of America broke out," and he argued that the French and German soldiers who fought in the American Revolution brought the "cause of Liberty" back home with them so that the principles of freedom spread all over France. In *The Rights of Man*, Paine thus constructed an ideological link between the two revolutions, in America and France, that were allegedly both driven by an unstoppable quest for liberty. While Burke had argued that revolutionary change was illegitimate because it was disruptive and destroyed the foundations of an existing order, Paine suggested that only revolutionary change was legitimate because individual liberty, equality of opportunity, and self-government were only to be had if feudalism and monarchy were destroyed. Revolutions thus appeared to be a necessary stage in an unstoppable historical process that pushed for freedom, rationality, and humanity and that would only reach its end after all human beings had been set free.

This liberal thinking about history actually deprived the American Revolution of its exceptionality to a very large extent. The American Revolution was relevant only because the Atlantic Revolutions had started there; it was where liberty had first appeared, only to spread to Europe. Paine talked about "the woods and wildernesses of America," arguing that America, for being the less civilized, backward periphery to a European center, was the place where the Atlantic revolution could begin. Although Paine admitted that "America was the only spot in the political world where the principles of universal reformation could begin," no real exceptionality resulted from this, insofar as the American Revolution was but the first in a series of revolutions that were all headed toward the same goal. It was only the first manifestation of an anonymous process that happened with the necessity and regularity of a natural law. "Within the space of a few years we have seen two Revolutions, those of America and France," Paine explained to the readers of *The Rights of Man*, and he anticipated that "we may hereafter hope to see Revolutions, or changes in Governments, produced with the same quiet operation, by which any measure, determinable by reason and discussion, is accomplished."

European conservatives and a significant number of liberals thought otherwise. While they frequently admired the American Revolution as a legitimate and successful historical event, they saw the French Revolution standing in sharp contrast to it. Cutting all ideological ties between the American and French Revolutions, European conservatives and most of its liberals admired the American Revolution only as long as its principles stayed in America. In their view, the American way of life—and the liberal values it was built on—were too exceptional to be able to serve as a model for Europe.

The conviction that the U.S. was a unique political, social, economic, and cultural phenomenon possible only in America emerged during the French Revolution; the succeeding European revolutions of 1830 only cemented this view. In 1831, Tocqueville went to see for himself why America was so different. Born into the lower Catholic nobility of Normandy, which adamantly supported monarchy, Tocqueville's biography was structured by France's political history of the day. His family was persecuted during the reign of the Jacobins, and when the Bourbons were restored to the throne, Tocqueville's father was rewarded for his loyalty to the monarchy with important positions in the royal service. After attending the Lycée Fabert in Metz, Tocqueville studied law in Paris from 1823 to 1827, and then became an apprentice judge at the court of

Versailles. He still served in this capacity in 1830, when another revolution broke out in France. It led to the establishment of a constitutional monarchy under King Louis-Philippe, which Tocqueville despised. Faced with an open and uncertain professional future, Tocqueville suggested that he could go on an official mission to inspect U.S. prisons, and his request was granted.

While he did inspect some prisons during his nine-month trip to the U.S. in 1831, Tocqueville was much more interested in inspecting U.S. society, which for him was a fascinating phenomenon, as an egalitarian society built on individualism, equal rights, and self-government did not exist anywhere else in the world. It was a historical novelty, and in the eyes of many a European thinker, an impossibility. By traveling to the U.S., Tocqueville wanted to study such a society in operation, and he was determined to write an important book about it that would establish him as the leading expert on the U.S. This book materialized in the form of *Democracy in America*, published in two volumes in 1835 and 1840. It is to this very day the single most important analysis of the government, society, and culture of U.S. democracy.

Yet Tocqueville's fascination with American democracy was not self-centered. Rather, he was convinced that the U.S. was the *land of the future* that defined the direction that social and political developments would also take in Europe. By visiting, exploring, and analyzing U.S. society, Tocqueville wanted to find out about the future he anticipated for Europe—and whether he liked it or not.

There is no room here to go into a detailed analysis of Tocqueville's enormous tomes. Suffice it to say that his entire analysis unfolds as one attempt to solve the puzzle America presented to many a European observer, especially in light of their own revolutionary experiences. How could a political system based on popular sovereignty, majority rule, and the separation of political powers be stable? What held an egalitarian society without formal hierarchies together? What prevented free and self-determined individuals from becoming selfish and asocial? How was individual commitment to the public good established in a society in which everyone was pursuing their very individual notions of a good life? In short: What prevented chaos, anarchy, and the destruction of all social ties in a society built on individual rights, egalitarianism, and self-determination?

Against this backdrop, it is important to note that Tocqueville described the U.S. as a place where liberty, property, and religion were all highly honored; where democracy had been peacefully founded, consolidated, and expanded without disruptions, crises, eruptions of violence, and wars; and where ordered liberty and community spirit, widely shared prosperity, and bourgeois respectability existed. In all of this, the U.S. seemed to show that individual liberty and a democratic spirit did not necessarily have to produce instability and disorder.

In trying to explain why this was so, Tocqueville cited historical and geographical arguments; he concluded that the U.S. was so unique a phenomenon that it could not possibly serve as a model for Europeans. At one point in his book, he wrote: "Everything about Americans is unusual from their social condition to their laws; but what is more unusual still is the land that supports them." In another passage he summed up: "The American position is, therefore, entirely exceptional and it is quite possible that no democratic nation will ever be similarly placed. [. . .] Let us, therefore, stop viewing all democratic nations under the example of the American people and let us try to view them with their own characteristics."

This chapter has shown how the American Revolution changed the semantics of American Exceptionalism. It secularized and politicized the Puritan city-upon-a-hill exceptionalism, divorcing it from all preoccupation with salvation in the next world and tying it to pursuits of happiness in this world. While the old religious and providentialist layers of the concept continued to be present in the post-revolutionary rhetoric of American Exceptionalism, they were now enveloped by the secular values of natural rights, self-government, and progress, which formed the ideological coordinates of a good life in this world.

While the Revolution tied American Exceptionalism to the Declaration of Independence and the constitutions based on its values, the question of exactly which constitutional order was the ideal translation of these values was heavily disputed in revolutionary America and beyond. The constitutional seat of American Exceptionalism remained undefined; it was used to advocate both the centralization and the decentralization of political power.

The French and other revolutions in Europe between 1789 and 1848–1849 shed an altogether new, transatlantic light on the relation between American Exceptionalism and the American Revolution; the latter appeared as unique insofar as it was a seemingly successful revolution devoid of all the disruptions and destruction that the revolutions in Europe had wrought.

5

The American Way of Empire

Exceptionalism and U.S. Foreign Policy

AMERICAN EXCEPTIONALISM HAS PLAYED a crucial role in the formulation, justification, and pursuit of U.S. foreign policy since the 1790s. However, the concept was put to the use of very different, at times outright contradictory, foreign policy agendas. It provided the ideological fuel for the continental and global expansion of the U.S. under the auspices of Manifest Destiny and liberal internationalism, but it was also called on to support anti-expansionist policies. This ambivalence can be explained by the fact that U.S. foreign policy has always been a matter of identity. While U.S. foreign policy from its inception has been shaped and motivated by the energetic pursuit of wealth, power, and security, to be sure, it has equally been structured by the question of what kind of foreign policy befitted a country claiming to be exceptional.

THE REVOLUTIONARY FOUNDATIONS OF U.S. FOREIGN POLICY

The ideological foundations of U.S. foreign policy were laid down during the American Revolution, with independence being inseparably tied to high hopes of making the world over. This included putting the conduct of foreign policy, as such, on a new basis. In *Common Sense*, Thomas Paine in 1776 thus envisioned the independent America as a commercial republic peacefully trading goods with all nations of the world while refraining from getting involved in military conflicts in Europe and elsewhere. Pointing to North America's rich endowment of natural resources, the fertility of its land, and the remoteness of its geographical situation, Paine saw the U.S. role in the world as that of a producer of raw materials and foodstuffs and a buyer of manufactured goods from Europe. In his vision, therefore, the U.S. was a globally operating agrarian republic that used trade as a foreign policy tool to establish peaceful relations with other nations. "Besides what have we to do with setting the world at defiance?" he asked in *Common Sense*, and went on to explain: "Our plan is commerce, and that, well attended to, will secure us the peace and friendship of all Europe; because, it is the interest of all Europe to have America a FREE PORT. Her trade will always be a protection, and her barrenness of gold and silver secure her from invaders." At the same time, Paine urged Americans to pursue a policy of strict political neutrality in relation to European countries. "As Europe is our market for trade," he wrote, "we ought to form no partial connexion with any part of it. It is the true interest of America to steer clear of European contentions."

After *Common Sense*, the Declaration of Independence is the second foundational document of U.S. foreign policy. Not only did it create a new political actor in the international system by transforming colonies into sovereign states, but it also formulated an ideological basis upon which foreign policy agendas could be built. As such, the Declaration of Independence "constituted a manifesto of national identity that Americans would feel compelled to live up to in later years suffer charges of hypocrisy," as William Earl Weeks argued in his volume of the *New Cambridge History of American Foreign Relations*. The Declaration of Independence thus did its share in turning foreign policy into a matter of identity politics.

EXCEPTIONALISM AND NON-ENTANGLEMENT

The revolutionary foundation of the U.S. not only raised the question of what kind of foreign policy was capable of putting international relations, as such, on a new footing. It also posed the problem of how a state born from revolution should relate to subsequent revolutions based on liberal values. With the outbreak of the French Revolution in 1789, this question became virulent much sooner than any of the American founders could have anticipated.

The problem of how to react to the events in France, and especially to the wars of the French Revolution that began in 1792, produced the first deep political controversy in the young republic. It pitted the Jeffersonian Democrats around Thomas Jefferson and James Madison against the Federalists united behind Alexander Hamilton. Jefferson, Madison, and their political friends, filled with a liberal enthusiasm for the French Republic, argued that the U.S. should support France out of a spirit of republican solidarity to further the common cause of liberty. They pointed to the Franco-American Alliance of 1778, which had brought France to the side of the American revolutionaries, and felt that the U.S. had a moral, but also political, obligation to support France in her own freedom struggle.

The Federalist Party was adamantly opposed to this idealistic call for an interventionist policy in support of the cause of liberty overseas. Pointing to the military and economic weakness of the U.S., Hamilton felt that any U.S. intervention in the European wars would endanger its own experiment in liberty. In a realistic assessment of the U.S. weight in the international system, the Federalists were convinced that the U.S. had nothing to gain and everything to lose from an involvement in European affairs, especially since Great Britain emerged as the great antirevolutionary antagonist of France on the continent. A policy of formal neutrality that informally leaned toward the old mother country, therefore, was what the Federalist Party advocated.

Out of the context of this militant political controversy grew George Washington's Farewell Address of 1796, which defined non-entanglement in European affairs as the true course of U.S. foreign policy. Arguing that foreign policy issues encouraged factionalism and party strife at home, and that they opened the American door to foreign influence, Washington suggested that the U.S. should work to systematically expand its commercial relations with other countries while having with them "as little political connection as possible."

Convinced of America's exceptionality as he was, the first U.S. president argued that Europeans and Americans were living on different planets. "Europe has a set of primary interests," he stated, "which to us have none; or a very remote relation. Hence she must be engaged in frequent controversies, the causes of which are essentially foreign to our concerns." Separated from Europe by a vast ocean, which in Washington's understanding was both a geographic and moral barrier protecting America from European corruption, the U.S. could afford to refrain from an active and interventionist foreign policy in Europe, which would interweave the U.S. "destiny with that of any part of Europe," and entangle its "peace and prosperity in the toils of European ambition, rivalship, interest, humor or caprice." Why should Americans voluntarily give up the advantages resulting from their "detached and distant situation," Washington asked, only to conclude: "It is our true policy to steer clear of permanent alliances with any portion of the foreign world."

Washington's Farewell Address was the first programmatic statement on U.S. foreign policy. It was soon accompanied by a second one, the Monroe Doctrine of 1823, which was triggered by the Latin American revolutions taking place from 1808 to 1825. The events in the southern half of the hemisphere met with a lot of enthusiasm in the U.S., and leading politicians like Henry Clay demanded that Washington diplomatically recognize the newly independent states in Latin America. With some of the new states there explicitly embracing the U.S. Constitution, many U.S. citizens saw Latin America following the U.S. revolutionary lead. Yet many Americans also welcomed the events in Latin America for the economic opportunities opening up there.

When in 1823 it became clear that Latin American independence was inevitable, President James Monroe, in his seventh Annual Message to Congress of December 2, 1823, developed a set of principles for the conduct of U.S. hemispheric policy that carried a deep sense of exceptionalism. Like George Washington before him, Monroe was convinced that the federal union was the bulwark of liberty and independence, and the basis for U.S. future greatness, which is why he pursued a comprehensive strategy that aimed at consolidating the union, securing its right of expansion over the continent, and expanding its global commercial ties. To achieve these goals, Monroe explicitly claimed the entire hemisphere as a U.S. sphere of influence.

In his message to Congress, the fifth U.S. president defined three basic principles upon which European-American relationships were to be based from 1823 on. The first was the principle of non-colonization, according to which "the American continents, by the free and independent condition which they have assumed and maintain, are henceforth not to be considered as subjects for future colonization by any European powers." Second, Monroe promised that the U.S. would respect the integrity of all European colonies still existing in the hemisphere, but he left no doubt that the U.S. would consider any attempt by a European power to revoke the independence of the new Latin American states "as the manifestation of an unfriendly disposition toward the United States." The third foreign-policy principle Monroe defined was U.S. nonintervention in European affairs.

In all, therefore, the Monroe Doctrine breathed the spirit of American Exceptionalism. Anchored in the idea of a stark opposition between America and Europe in political and moral respects, it claimed that the political system of Europe was "essentially different [. . .] from that of America," which is why the U.S. would stay out of European struggles. "In the wars of the European powers in matters relating to themselves," Monroe said, the U.S. had "never taken any part, nor does it comport with our policy to do so." It would never "interfere in the internal concerns of any" European power.

With his message to Congress, President Monroe boldly asserted U.S. hemispheric dominance, this assertion having two sides. It was, on the one hand, carried by a sense of imperial mission that strove to turn the Western Hemisphere into a zone of liberty. On the other, it was driven by a certain sense of nervousness resulting from the alleged internal vulnerability of the U.S., which, as Jay Sexton writes in his *The Monroe Doctrine: Empire and Nation in Nineteenth-Century America*, seemed to require more "than just the safety of its borders—it required an entire hemispheric political system conducive to its political system and economic practices."

EXPANSION AND MANIFEST DESTINY

When President Monroe formulated his sweeping claim of hemispheric hegemony, the U.S. was in the middle of tumultuous territorial, demographic, economic, and infrastructural growth that was and remains "unprecedented in world political history," as D. W. Meinig wrote in volume 2 of his *The Shaping of America: A Geographical Perspective on 500 Years of History*, titled *Continental America, 1800–1867*. Growth had already been an outstanding feature of the colonial experience. What changed significantly in the early national period was its rapidity and scale and how it was explained: In post-revolutionary America, many were inclined to trace the spectacular growth of the U.S. to its liberal founding values. Accordingly, the U.S. was expanding *because* its order was based on individualism, liberty, self-determination, and a free-market economy, and with its expansion, it was also expanding the sphere of liberty in the world. In his first inaugural address, as the third president of the U.S., Thomas Jefferson said on March 4, 1801, that the U.S. possessed "a chosen country, with room enough for our descendants to the thousandth and thousandth generation," and he left no doubt that the seemingly endless landmass of the North American continent would be filled by American settlers one day. In expanding westward, the U.S. would thus create the "Empire of liberty" that Jefferson had already envisioned in a letter to George Rogers Clark on December 25, 1780.

This mindset laid the foundation for the expansionist ideology of Manifest Destiny that came to full fruition during the 1830–1840s. One of its most eloquent champions was John L. O'Sullivan, who, in two pieces written for the *United States Magazine and Democratic Review*, reflected on U.S. westward expansion as both an indicator of American Exceptionalism and a factor sustaining it. In "The Great Nation of Futurity," published in November 1839, O'Sullivan argued that U.S. history was following its own unique path and that it was exempt from all the actors, forces, and contexts defining Europe's historical development. Being a nation of many nations, founded on natural-rights liberalism, the U.S., according to O'Sullivan, was in a "disconnected position as regards any other nation," and it had only "little connection with the past history of any of them, and still less with all antiquity, its glories, or its crimes." The revolutionary founding of the U.S. marked "the beginning of a new history, the formation and progress of an untried political system." This novelty separated the U.S. from the past and connected it "with the future only," which is why the Americans were "destined to be THE GREAT NATION of futurity." From there, O'Sullivan went on to envision the future of the U.S. as one of endless and limitless progress toward the better. He saw the U.S. as embarked on a mission to create, consolidate, and spread "freedom of conscience, freedom of person, freedom of trade and business pursuits, universality of freedom and equality." Summarizing his reflections, he stated, "We are the nation of human progress," and he wondered, "who will, what can, set limits to our onward march? Providence is with us, and no earthly power can."

It is, however, important not to take statements like these at face value and see them as manifestations of timeless ideas somehow circulating in U.S. culture from its inception. For a conceptual history of American Exceptionalism, it is rewarding to reflect on O'Sullivan's text as an act of political argumentation directed against the critics of unlimited and unbridled expansion, of which there were quite a few. Their critique was to a very large extent driven by the fear of destroying American Exceptionalism through the rapid, tumultuous, and violent process of westward expansion. The anti-expansionist critique born from the spirit of exceptionalism revolved around three problems. First, some critics articulated doubts about the stability of an extended republic. Second, others saw expansion deepening the explosive problem of slavery. And third, again others were driven by racist fears of an erosion of white, Anglo-Saxon, and Protestant hegemony in a republic that threatened to become racially and culturally more mixed because of its expansion.

The fear of a territorial overstretch that would lead to the destruction of liberty informed much of the opposition to the Louisiana Purchase in 1803. During the ratification debates, voices, mostly from senators affiliated with Alexander Hamilton and the Federalist camp, argued that the massive extension of territory would eventually lead to the collapse of the Union. John Rutledge, a representative from South Carolina, wrote to Harrison Gray Otis on October 1, 1803, that the "purchase of a trackless world" was "a miserably calamitous business" that would necessarily "result in a disunion of these States." Generally, politicians like Henry Clay, Martin Van Buren, or Thomas Hart Benton felt that the nation's territorial expansion did not keep up with its inner consolidation and moral growth. They favored a slowdown of expansion to consolidate the situation in the new territories and states. On September 12, 1848, none other than Abraham Lincoln, in a speech at Worcester, Massachusetts, said that he did not "believe in enlarging our field, but in keeping our fences where they are and cultivating our present possession, making it a garden, improving the morals and education of the people."

Another strand of the anti-expansionist critique was defined by the slavery question raised by the rapid U.S. expansion, that is, whether to introduce slavery in the new states created in the hitherto unorganized western territories, and who should have a right to decide: the federal government, or the people living in the new states seeking admission to the union. President Monroe foresaw the looming battles over slavery as threatening the Union from early on. In a letter to Thomas Jefferson written in May 1820, he stated that it was "evident, that the further acquisition of territory, to the West and South, involves difficulties of an internal nature which menace the Union itself." Seen against this backdrop, the ideology of Manifest Destiny was born as an urgent call for further expansion in a time when expansion itself had become a contentious issue.

Things came to a head with the annexation of Texas in 1845. The Texas question had been on the agenda since 1836, when Texas, the northernmost state of Mexico, declared its independence. The Texas Revolution was, on the one hand, an act of resistance to the attempted centralization of power under the Mexican military dictator General Santa Anna. On the other, it was a political move to protect the institution of slavery, which an increasingly large contingent of U.S. citizens settling in Texas had introduced against the abolitionist inclinations of the Mexican government.

Upon reaching independence, Texas immediately moved to be annexed by the U.S., and already in August 1837, a proposal favoring annexation was laid before the U.S. Congress. It did not meet with much enthusiasm. Opposition was fierce, especially in the North, where many were appalled by the idea of another slave state in the Union. Abolitionists in New England classified the Texas Revolution as a slaveholders' uprising against a Mexican government willing to end slavery. Former U.S. president John Quincy Adams confessed his "solemn belief that the annexation of an independent foreign power to this government would, ipso facto, be a dissolution of this union," and that the U.S. would be "'DAMNED TO EVERLASTING FAME' by the reinstitution of that detested system of slavery." Faced with heavy critique at home and afraid of a war with Mexico, the Van Buren administration dropped the issue from its agenda.

The problem lingered on, however, and it became a major topic in the presidential election of 1844, which saw James K. Polk, the Democratic nominee, running as a determined annexationist, who not only wanted Texas but the whole of Oregon as well. His Whig opponent, Henry Clay, pursued an antislavery and anti-annexation agenda. Polk won the election in a narrow victory, and Texas was annexed in 1845, to strong opposition in both parties, Whig and Democrat. John Quincy

Adams argued that slavery was a disgrace undermining America's liberal founding credo, which is why it had no place in the union. Another former president, Martin Van Buren, also came out against annexation, classifying it as an act of aggression against Mexico that was driven by the "lust for power, with fraud and violence in the train." Both slavery and the annexation of Texas, for Van Buren, stained the honor of a nation that thought of itself as both historically and morally exceptional. On the Whig side, politicians like Henry Clay and Abraham Lincoln were adamantly opposed to admitting Texas to the Union.

In this situation, the Manifest Destiny ideology was born to silence all critics. "It is now time for the opposition to the Annexation of Texas to cease"—this was the opening line of John L. O'Sullivan's article "Annexation," published in the *United States Magazine and Democratic Review* in July 1845. In it, O'Sullivan declared the period of party strife over the Texas question to be over. It was time for "the common duty of Patriotism to the Country to succeed," since Texas was now part of the U.S., having taken its place "in the glorious blazon" of the U.S. "common nationality." Texas had come "within the dear and sacred designation of Our Country," and neither "our past party dissensions" nor any other nation "in a spirit of hostile interference against us" should thwart U.S. policy, hamper its power, limit its greatness, or check "the fulfillment of our manifest destiny to overspread the continent allotted by Providence for the free development of our yearly multiplying millions."

O'Sullivan saw expansion as means of spreading American values of freedom and self-determination over the continent to enlarge the "Empire of liberty" that Jefferson had envisioned at the end of the eighteenth century. Where the anti-annexationists argued that the annexation of Texas was an act of brutal aggression threatening to destroy America's exceptionalism, O'Sullivan saw expansion as the true fulfillment of this very exceptionalism. By expanding over the North American continent, Americans were perpetuating their great experiment of liberty, self-government, and federalism while at the same time curbing European imperial ambitions in North America.

The annexation of Texas was the prelude to the Mexican War (1846–1848), which has rightly been described as an imperial war fought for the large-scale conquest of territory. A true believer in the Manifest Destiny ideology, President Polk wanted to establish the U.S. as a Pacific power and further reduce the influence of European powers in North America. To reach his goals, Polk sought war with Mexico and got it by systematically escalating the unresolved boundary dispute over the Rio Grande between Texas and Mexico in the spring of 1846. The Mexican War was a glaring military success for the American side. It saw U.S. armed forces excelling at highly complex military operations involving swift advances, coordinated attacks over huge distances, and amphibious landing operations that by the fall of 1847 forced the Mexican government to seek peace negotiations.

In the U.S., the scenarios for the peace were as diverse as they were contradictory, and all of this is telling for the problem of American Exceptionalism insofar as it once again demonstrates how exceptionalist ideas were used to justify very different political agendas. The spectrum of possible peace scenarios discussed in the U.S. ranged from the demand to acquire the whole of Mexico to the complete rejection of all territorial acquisitions; in one way or another, American Exceptionalism was the subtext to them all.

A group of radical imperialists, such as Robert Stockton, Lewis Cass, and some editors of the northern penny press, demanded the annexation of all of Mexico to the U.S. as the fulfillment of the U.S. mission to spread out over the North American continent. This All Mexico option met with ferocious criticism, especially from Southern Democrats who feared that the U.S. would cease being an exclusively white, Anglo-American, and Protestant republic if millions of Mexicans were incorporated into the U.S. Rejecting the All Mexico option, John C. Calhoun, in his capacity as a senator from South Carolina, said: "Ours is the government of the white man." Fundamentally opposed to all schemes of territorial aggrandizement were the Whigs and their spokesman Abraham Lincoln. Arguing that the war had actually been started by the U.S. merely to satisfy a lust for power and territorial conquest, the Whigs felt that the U.S. was compromising its claim to moral superiority for pure ambition and the desire for military glory.

Faced with these starkly opposing views, the Polk administration pursued a middle-of-the-road approach that took territorial acquisitions for granted as a means to punish Mexico for its aggressions and to compensate the U.S. for its losses and war costs, but refrained from maximum demands. The Treaty of Guadalupe Hidalgo, which the Polk administration signed with Mexico on February 2, 1848, defined the Rio Grande as the U.S. boundary with Mexico and forced Mexico to cede what today is largely the U.S. Southwest. What is especially significant about the outcome of the Mexican War is that the U.S. decided against annexing the whole of Mexico. This epochal decision was built on the widely shared conviction that the mixed-race Mexican population, being seemingly incapable of self-government, would not only be a burden on the American system but might even cause the destruction of an extended republic that was supposedly made by and for white Anglo-Saxon Protestants.

IMPERIALISM, AMERICAN-STYLE

The years from 1865 to 1914 witnessed a massive overseas expansion of the U.S. during which a new imperial formation was created, which historian Walter LaFeber termed the "New Empire," in a book by the same name. It was a highly complex and multidimensional web of relationships, global in scope and involving different forms and degrees of control of regions outside of the U.S. This new American empire essentially was a market empire held together by the strongest and most efficient industrial economy of the world. It was created through bilateral trade agreements and U.S. direct investments in foreign countries, and it was protected by an increasingly large, efficient, and professional navy that the U.S. government systematically built up in this period.

Americans to this very day are uncomfortable with the term *imperialism* being applied to their country because it suggests aggressive expansion, conquest, and the brutal subjugation of other countries and peoples. In this view, imperialism was characteristic of autocracies and the great powers of Europe, but it could not, and should not, be applied to a country built on liberal founding ideals, democratic institutions, and a strong anticolonial tradition. "America has never been an empire," George W. Bush, then governor of Texas running for the presidency, said in a speech at the Ronald Reagan Presidential Library on November 19, 1999; he explained: "We may be the only great power in history that had the chance, and refused—preferring greatness to power and justice to glory." The denial of an American imperialism is, therefore, a prominent feature of the conceptual history of American Exceptionalism.

It will be helpful to clarify the meaning of *imperialism* before we continue the discussion. Wider definitions understand imperialism to be any attempt by a state to create an empire through expansion into foreign territory and the integration of it into its own political order. In this wide definition, imperialism can be applied to many countries and different historical epochs. The narrower definition of imperialism understands it to be a specific form of expansion taking place in a specific historical epoch. It ties imperialism to the age of industrialization and reserves it for the expansion of industrialized nation-states into economically less-developed regions of the world in the last third of the nineteenth and the first decades of the twentieth century. This period from roughly 1870 to 1914 witnessed a massive acceleration of the already ongoing process of industrialization in Great Britain, Germany, France, and, most importantly, the U.S., which all developed into fully matured industrial economies and societies. As these highly efficient industrial economies produced more than could possibly be consumed on the domestic market, and as these economies were increasingly dependent on access to raw materials of all sorts, the rationale for expansion changed significantly; it was no longer motivated by the quest for land and territorial aggrandizement but by the quest for overseas markets.

To talk about this kind of imperialism in connection with the U.S. makes sense because, after the Civil War, the U.S. systematically worked to expand its political and economic influence overseas. With that, the U.S. joined the group of imperialist powers rather late in the game, and it confined its imperialist energies to the two target regions Latin America and Asia. Africa, which was a major site of imperialist competition for Europe's great powers, was not on the radar of U.S. imperialists at the turn of the twentieth century. They felt that they had too much of a *race problem* at home already.

Be that as it may, the growing U.S. economic entanglements in Latin America and Asia created political interests in the course of time, so that the accelerating economic expansion led to highly complex political involvements with several countries there. Whereas in European imperialism, trade all too often followed the flag, in the case of U.S. imperialism, it was the other way around. Here, political interventions into other countries were largely the result of a growing economic involvement that had happened before.

To protect American trade and foreign direct investments, U.S. governments supported politicians and political parties in other countries friendly to U.S. interests, influenced elections, and used U.S. economic power to achieve political goals abroad. While American-style imperialism characteristically relied on these indirect forms of control, in the case of the Philippines, which was annexed as a colony after the Spanish-American War of 1898, and Cuba, over which the U.S. erected a protectorate under the auspices of the Platt Amendment, U.S. control was direct and strong.

U.S. overseas expansion was highly controversial at home. It caused ferocious arguments between imperialists and anti-imperialists—with both sides drawing on American Exceptionalism to justify their cause. While anti-imperialists charged imperialists with destroying America's exceptionality by acting like any other great power, the imperialists held that U.S. overseas expansion, and especially the colonial rule over the Philippines, actually rejuvenated American Exceptionalism.

The imperialist persuasion was built around a set of ideas, values, and arguments that stressed the economic opportunities resulting from overseas expansion; expanded the Manifest Destiny ideology to include the whole world; and justified U.S. colonial rule in the Philippines as a benevolent mission to educate and civilize a supposedly backward and inferior people. While this may appear as but a continuation of the expansionist rhetoric of the antebellum period, it is important to note that the imperialist persuasion around 1900 was inseparably tied to the nervousness, fears, and anxieties emerging from the industrial transformation of the U.S. The disruptive transition from an agrarian to an industrial order was experienced as a deep crisis by many middle-class Americans, who held that the effects of industrialization were prone to destroy America's exceptionality. Against this backdrop, imperial expansion could be presented as a way to preserve American Exceptionalism at home. This connection between a sense of crisis and the advocacy of overseas expansion can be traced in many pro-imperialist writings of the day, and most importantly in Frederick Jackson Turner's frontier thesis, in Josiah Strong's evangelical visions, and in Theodore Roosevelt's ideal of a strenuous life.

Although Turner's seminal essay "The Significance of the Frontier in American History" was primarily about the U.S. past, it was just as much about its present and the future. As we saw in chapter 2, Turner theorized that the frontier was the sole source and cause of American Exceptionalism at a historical moment, when the Census Bureau had declared this very frontier to have vanished. As is well known, Turner argued that the Americanness of America was born on the frontier, so the end of the frontier potentially marked the end of America's uniqueness. Turner's frontier thesis, therefore, can be read as articulating an unsettling uncertainty as to whether the U.S. would be able to maintain its exceptionality without a frontier. The author himself was explicit about this: In the preface to the 1920 edition of his collection of essays *The Frontier in American History*, Turner wrote that the "future alone" could "reveal how much of the courageous, creative American spirit, and how large a part of the historic American ideals are to be carried over into that new age which is replacing the era of free lands and of measurable isolation by consolidated and complex industrial development and by increasing resemblances and connections between the New World and the Old."

The foreign policy implications of the frontier thesis were immense. Turner himself, in an article titled "The Problem of the West" in the *Atlantic Monthly* in September 1896, saw U.S. overseas expansion in continuity with the continental expansion before 1890. Arguing that expansion had been "the dominant fact in American life" for the past three centuries, Turner showed himself convinced that "these energies of expansion" would continue to operate in the new era after the closing of the frontier. In his eyes, the then-current "demands for a vigorous foreign policy, for an interoceanic canal, for a revival of our power upon the seas, and for the extension of American influence to outlying islands and adjoining countries," were all "indications that the movement will continue." Fourteen years later, in his 1910 presidential address to the American Historical Association, Turner interpreted the U.S. involvement in Asia as the "logical outcome of the nation's march to the Pacific."

One person deeply influenced by Turner's frontier thesis was Josiah Strong, Protestant clergyman, organizer, widely read author, and activist of the Social Gospel movement. He supported missionary work all over the globe, and he believed that for being a superior race, Anglo-Saxons had a special duty to spread Protestant Christianity and *civilize* the *savage* peoples of the world. At the same time, Strong understood this missionary work as providing solutions for the problems at home as well.

Like so many of his contemporaries, Strong also perceived his own time as a time of crisis. He felt that the corporate reconstruction of American capitalism had produced a new form of "economic despotism" that concentrated money in the hands of a few who refused to share their wealth to improve the deplorable living conditions of the laborers. The industrial transformation of the U.S., as Strong saw it, endangered America's superior morality because wealth had become both the oppressor of the nation and a source of immorality. Most importantly, however, Strong was deeply unsettled by the closing of frontier. In his bestselling book *Our Country: Its Possible Future and Its Present*, written on behalf of the Home Missionary Society and with numerous editions after its first publication in 1885, Strong warned: "When the supply [of land] is exhausted, we shall enter upon a new era, and shall more rapidly approximate European conditions of life."

In light of this diagnosis, Strong recommended the search for a new frontier as the solution to the spiritual, economic, and political problems of his day, and this frontier, in his view, was to be a missionary frontier. After the American West had been conquered for Christ, Strong argued, the U.S. should work to spread Christ's word all over the world. Strong felt that the perpetuation of American Exceptionalism required an effort, and this effort should be the spreading of Protestant Christianity to overseas territories. Although Strong was convinced that Americans were a chosen people, he saw them no longer drifting "with safety to our destiny. We are shut up to a perilous alternative," he wrote, and explained that this alternative was either to act forcefully to Christianize the world or to accept the loss of America's exceptionality.

Theodore Roosevelt, who served in Cuba as one of the Rough Riders during the Spanish-American War of 1898 and would later become the twenty-sixth president, had a much more secular argument for the need for U.S. overseas expansion. On April 10, 1899, he delivered his speech "The Strenuous Life" at the Hamilton Club of Chicago, making a pro-imperialist argument that was inseparably connected to the sense of crisis resulting from the industrial transformation of America.

Roosevelt saw industrial America as "over-civilized," and out of touch with the primordial roots of its specific way of life that had made it strong, great, and powerful. In his view, shallow material pursuits had become ends in themselves in Gilded Age America, completely divorced from all higher goals in life. In his speech, Roosevelt depicted an America where everybody was hunting for the comfort, ease, and amenities offered by an advanced consumer culture. The effect of this shallow and self-referential materialism, according to Roosevelt, was that Americans had become disconnected from a "higher life," transcending the low and shallow commercial pursuits of the day. The over-civilized man of industrial America, Roosevelt argued, had "lost the great fighting, masterful virtues" that characterized life on the American frontier. All that industrial America seemingly held in stock was a life of weakness and softness that contrasted sharply with the strength, vitality, and harshness of life in the wilderness.

The gender dimension of this line of argument can hardly be overlooked: Roosevelt felt that over-civilized men had lost their masculinity; they were men emasculated by the "life of ease" in industrial-urban America. Roosevelt's "strenuous life" was a decidedly masculine life lived in the wilderness of the frontier, while life in industrial America was essentially feminine, with its very femininity destroying the masculinity upon which American Exceptionalism, in Roosevelt's reading, was built. Americans, Roosevelt argued, had lived strenuous lives for most of their history. This had made America great, strong, successful, and unique. The way to regain the strenuous life—and American masculinity with it—was overseas expansion. Roosevelt urged Americans to accept the responsibilities of an imperial power. "The twentieth century," he explained, "looms before us big with the fate of many nations. If we stand idly by, if we seek merely swollen, slothful ease and ignoble peace, if we shrink from the hard contests where men must win at hazard of their lives and at the risk of all they hold dear, then the bolder and stronger peoples will pass us by, and will win for themselves the domination of the world."

In this context, it is telling that Roosevelt, in his speech to the Hamilton Club, represented the Philippines as a new frontier, where righteous Americans as the spearheads of civilization were fighting a "wild" and "ignorant" "savage people" to spread liberty, self-government, and progress. U.S. imperialism in this reading was beneficial to both the colonizer and the colonized. Even in its colonialism, the U.S. appeared to be exceptional to American imperialists, who were keen on distinguishing American colonial rule from European colonialism.

When the U.S. annexed the Philippines as a colony in 1898, advocates of U.S. colonialism worked to represent U.S. rule as an inherently benevolent imperialism that aimed at developing the country and educating the indigenous population. Gradually assimilating the Filipinos to an American way of life would eventually put them in a position where they could govern themselves, so the argument went. The champions of an American-style imperialism thus represented U.S. rule in the Philippines as developmental and educational. It worked to improve a seemingly backward region, to educate and civilize its population, and, finally, to missionize the Filipinos—although they had been Catholic for centuries. The U.S. would only do all of this to abolish itself as an imperial power in the end. While in American eyes, European colonialism aimed at the permanent control of overseas territory, and was held to be brutal, exploitative, and oppressive, American imperialists thought of U.S colonial rule as temporary and transient. The "sole aim" of the American presence in the Philippines, stated Jacob Gould Schurman in a letter of March 12, 1900, to his friend Andrew Dickinson White, was "the welfare of the natives." Schurman was the head of a commission named after him and appointed by President William McKinley to investigate the situation in the archipelago in 1899, and his letter to White suggested that the U.S. was a fatherly teacher to the Filipinos, who appeared as childlike pupils, with Americans claiming to know what was best for them.

The only problem was that the Filipinos did not want to accept U.S. authority and tutelage. In 1899, a Filipino independence movement led by Emilio Aguinaldo started a war against the U.S. that lasted for three bloody years. Faced with this resistance to their rule, America's self-declared benevolent imperialists saw the Filipinos as misbehaving, unruly children deserving of harsh punishment. This way of thinking, born from an exceptionalist mindset, justified limitless atrocious warfare in the archipelago. On June 19, 1899, Secretary of State John Hay wrote to Jacob Gould Schurman that it was "heart breaking to see how much punishment those misguided Filipinos insist on, but it must go on until they learn the things that belong to their peace. Then will come the time for you to put forth the bases of an orderly and beneficent government for them."

While concepts of American Exceptionalism circulated widely among imperialists, they were not the only ones to draw on them to justify their cause. America's anti-imperialists, who formed the Anti-Imperialist League in 1898, did so as well. Denying the very righteousness of U.S. imperialism, they argued that U.S. domination of overseas territory and formal colonial rule invalidated all claims to exceptionality. In their view, the U.S. was acting like any other European great power driven by the lust for power, conquest, rule, and exploitation of foreign peoples. Andrew Carnegie, steel magnate and one of the leading anti-imperialist voices in the U.S., was so irritated about the U.S. in the Philippines acting so much like the British imperialists that he even offered to buy the islands for $20 million to restore them to independence.

Other anti-imperialists saw colonial rule as a burden that was expensive, involved a lot of responsibility, and was likely to draw the U.S. into wars overseas. They argued that the U.S. would have to maintain a costly army and navy to enforce its rule in other world regions; also, administering colonies would cost a lot of money—money that could be better used for domestic purposes. Another strand in the anti-imperialist argument, from a conviction of cultural superiority, claimed that the U.S. would dump large sums of money into uncivilized countries that would never assimilate to American standards. Informal domination of overseas territory, therefore, appeared to be the cheaper and more beneficial alternative to direct colonial rule.

Most importantly, however, anti-imperialists also exploited the race question insofar as they argued that the U.S. would lose its white, Anglo-Saxon purity when integrating mixed-race populations or nonwhite populations into its order. Democratic senator John W. Daniel of Virginia thus warned that if the Philippines were taken, the conquering nation would no longer be known as the United States of America but would descend to the depths of "The United States of America and Asia," as Americans and Filipinos would become "one flesh." Whiteness, therefore, seemed to be the bulwark of American Exceptionalism.

THE BIRTH OF WILSONIANISM FROM THE SPIRIT OF WORLD WAR I

From a U.S. perspective, the history of World War I had two phases, the period of neutrality lasting from August 1914 to the spring of 1917, and the period of involvement beginning with the U.S. declaration of war on

Germany on April 6, 1917, and ending with the refusal of the U.S. Senate to ratify the Versailles peace treaty on November 19, 1919. In both phases, American Exceptionalism played an important role in justifying U.S. foreign policy.

When war broke out in Europe, President Woodrow Wilson asked his countrymen on August 19, 1914, to stay neutral "in thought, as well as action," and this was a plausible thing to do. The U.S. had little or nothing directly to do with the coming of the war, which originated from a complex set of intra-European conflicts. The Wilson administration and many U.S. citizens saw the war as a European war that was symptomatic of all the bad things that Europe stood for in American eyes: coercive government, irrationality, barbarism, feudalism, backwardness, decadence, and corruption. World War I literally appeared as a war of the Old World waged for conquest, territorial aggrandizement, and national glory. In such a war, the U.S., as a youthful country, seemingly had nothing to gain but everything to lose, most importantly its own moral superiority. Neutrality was what the vast majority of Americans wanted in the summer of 1914 and beyond, and in November 1916, they reelected Wilson under the campaign slogan "He Kept Us Out of War."

Only half a year later, Wilson was confronted with the task of persuading the country to enter the war. The reasons for the U.S. entry were highly complex. Economically speaking, the U.S. had become a war party by 1917, as its neutrality policy did not preclude private businesses from trading with European powers. As a result, U.S. industries provided an increasingly large share of weapons, ammunition, and other military supplies needed on the European battlefields. However, it was not this growing U.S. economic involvement that eventually led to the U.S. entering the war. This was, rather, provoked by a combination of Germany's unrestricted submarine warfare and President Wilson's rigorously dogmatic stance on neutral rights.

Under the auspices of unrestricted submarine warfare, German submarines would attack every enemy merchant ship in the North Sea without prior warning and preceding search. Wilson, feeling that this was a massive violation of international law, radically expanded the meaning of neutral rights. On February 10, 1915, six days after the German government had declared the North Sea a war zone, he announced that the U.S. government would hold Germany to "strict accountability" for any loss of U.S. ships, trading goods, or lives on the high sea. In Wilson's understanding, neutral rights not only meant that U.S. vessels should be protected by international law no matter where they went, even in wartime, but also that neutral rights protected U.S. goods and citizens even on enemy ships. When, on May 7, 1915, a German submarine attack on the British passenger vessel *Lusitania* caused the death of 128 U.S. citizens, Wilson responded with three increasingly sharp diplomatic notes of protest, in which he not only demanded compensation for the material losses but also an immediate halt to all German attacks on passenger vessels, declaring that "nothing less high and sacred" was at stake "than the rights of humanity." German submarine warfare had become a matter of principle.

Faced with growing U.S. diplomatic pressure, Germany gave in and announced on September 18, 1915, that it would end its campaign of unrestricted submarine warfare. However, this pledge lasted less than two years. On February 1, 1917, Germany resumed its indiscriminate attacks on ships in the North Sea. Wilson broke off all diplomatic relations with Germany on February 3, 1917, but he did not move to have war declared on Germany at once, despite the fact that an enraged public opinion was calling increasingly loudly for war.

Then, on February 24, 1917, the British government made known the contents of the Zimmermann Telegram, which it had intercepted and deciphered. In it, the German foreign minister, Arthur Zimmermann, authorized the German ambassador in Mexico City to talk the Mexican government into entering the war as Germany's ally. In this capacity, Mexico was to invade the U.S. with German help, and as a reward, it would get back the territory it had lost in the Treaty of Guadalupe Hidalgo. The news was in all leading American newspapers on March 1, 1917, and on April 2, 1917, President Wilson addressed a joint session of Congress, asking the legislators to declare war on Germany.

In this session, he delivered his famous War Message, which is the basic programmatic text defining liberal internationalism as the U.S. foreign policy agenda in the globalized, entangled, and interdependent world of the twentieth century. The term *liberal internationalism*, sometimes also called *Wilsonianism*, describes a political course that sees it as the U.S. duty and interest to export democracy and free-market capitalism overseas to create a world of widely shared prosperity and everlasting peace.

The philosophical premises for this policy agenda were laid down by the eminent philosopher of the Enlightenment, Immanuel Kant, who formulated the idea of a republican peace at the end of the eighteenth century. He suggested that democracies were inherently peaceful political orders that did not go to war against each other because it was impossible to organize popular support for a war in a system based on free elections and majority rule. War in this reading was inherent to monarchies and other autocratic systems because decision makers did not have to ask anyone when they wanted war. Under the premises of this thinking, a world of democracies would be a world without war.

The War Message is one of Wilson's best speeches ever. Utilizing the full range of rhetoric techniques, Wilson, in simple but powerful words, strove to define war aims worth sacrificing American lives for, and he saw the protection and spreading of democracy as the only worthy ones. Clad in a rhetoric of selflessness, the War Message framed the conflict as a matter of universal concern, suggesting that Germany's submarine war was "a warfare against mankind [. . .] a war against all nations" because it violated all norms of international law. In light of this assessment, Wilson argued that "the vindication of right, of human right, of which we are only a single champion" was the only goal that the U.S. could possibly pursue in a war.

Interpreting the war as a conflict of political systems, Wilson saw the U.S. as fighting for the "the principles of peace and justice in the life of the world [. . .] against selfish and autocratic power." The ideological divide of World War I thus ran between democracy and autocracy—of which Prussia was but a manifestation. For Wilson, autocracies posed a structural threat to the "the peace of the world [. . .] and the freedom of its peoples." In an autocratic government like the Prussian one, not only could the U.S. "never have a friend," Wilson stated, but also, as long as autocratic governments existed, there could be "no assured security for the democratic Governments of the world" because autocracies were the "natural foe to liberty." Having laid out this diagnosis, Wilson then promised that the U.S. would "spend the whole force of the nation" to destroy autocracy and make the world "safe for democracy."

In going to war, therefore, Wilson wanted to shape the peace of the postwar world, which in his understanding, could only be "planted upon the tested foundations of political liberty." When asking Congress to declare war on Germany, Wilson thus argued for a new world order from which the causes of war, bloodshed, and human misery would be eradicated once and for all. He saw it as the U.S. mission to bring about this new world order because the very success of the exceptional experiment in liberty and democracy that had begun with the American Revolution at the end of the eighteenth century suggested exporting the American model into the world. In April 1917, Wilson declared, the day had come "when America is privileged to spend her blood and her might for the principles that gave her birth and happiness and the peace which she has treasured."

This eloquent use of an exceptionalist rhetoric and agenda had an effect: On April 4, the U.S. Senate voted 82 to 6 that a state of war existed with Germany, and early in the morning of April 6 the U.S. House of Representatives joined in by a vote of 373 to 50. For the first time in its history the U.S. entered a war on the European continent.

In his War Message, President Wilson defined the basic coordinates of liberal internationalism. In his State of the Union address of January 8, 1918, he staked out the details of the new world order in his famous Fourteen Points. Demanding that "the world be made fit and safe to live in," especially for free and open societies organized on the basis of individual freedom and self-determination, Wilson claimed that all nations of the world were "in effect partners in this interest." Therefore, they should work together in international organizations to guarantee the rule of international law and to solve international conflicts by way of negotiations on the basis of commonly shared liberal values.

The most important principles upon which Wilson based the U.S. "programme of the world's peace," which he, with all the moral rigor he was capable of, declared to be "the only possible programme," were free trade based on the freedom of the seas, the reduction of armaments, and the "absolutely impartial adjustment of all colonial claims" taking into consideration both the "equitable claims" of the colonial powers and the right of all nations to self-determination. The keystone of Wilson's vision of a new liberal world order was the League of Nations, which he conceived of as a "general association of nations" that worked to afford "mutual guarantees of political independence and territorial integrity to great and small states alike," and served as the guarantor of the liberal world order.

In the conceptual history of American Exceptionalism, Wilson's agenda of liberal internationalism was a major turning point insofar as it ideologized democracy and reformulated the well-known exceptionalist ideas, themes, and concepts in a global frame. Under the pressure of having to define a war aim justifying all the sacrifices to be expected from an industrial war like World War I, Wilson abandoned the long tradition of U.S. continentalism and announced a new course of internationalism that saw the U.S. embarked on a mission to create an international environment that was safe for democracies. Deeply convinced of America's exceptionality, Wilson saw the U.S. as morally legitimated and obligated to claim leadership in making the world safe for democracy. An active interventionist foreign policy to support market democracies all over the world and expand the sphere of democracy, liberty, and free-market capitalism became a matter of U.S. identity politics: Liberal internationalism would serve to perpetuate and even rejuvenate American Exceptionalism. In making the world safe for democracy, the U.S. would continue its mission of building an ideal world that was started with John Winthrop's "city upon a hill" and continued with the experiment in liberty of the American Revolution, which was then translated into the Manifest Destiny of creating an "Empire of liberty" on the North American continent.

Everything, however, depended on whether Americans would be ready, willing, and able to fight and sacrifice for liberty and democracy abroad. Written into Wilson's foreign policy agenda of liberal internationalism was the by now familiar pattern linking a sense of American chosenness and mission to a rhetoric of responsibility, service, and the possibility of failure. This put the U.S. under pressure to make the right political decisions in the here and now if it wanted to realize the full potential of its own claims to exceptionalism and uniqueness.

Measured against these high-flying ideals of a new world order, the Versailles Peace Treaty of 1919 could appear as a bitter disappointment. Although Wilson, as the first U.S. president ever to go abroad, personally headed the U.S. delegation to the Paris peace conference and negotiated directly with the statesmen of the world, the Versailles Treaty was not the "peace without victory" he had envisioned and promised in an address to the U.S. Senate on January 22, 1917. Rather, it was a harsh peace that put all the blame on Germany and aimed to punish it for having begun the war. That, however, was not why the U.S. Senate refused to ratify the treaty on November 19, 1919, although many Americans including Wilson were convinced that Germany deserved punishment for having provoked the unspeakable carnage of the past four years.

The most contentious issue of the Versailles Treaty in the U.S. was the League of Nations. Its founding charter was part of the Versailles Treaty package, and ratifying the treaty would have meant U.S. membership in the international organization that was to guarantee the new world order envisioned by Wilson. The political controversy in the U.S., therefore, revolved around the question of whether the U.S. should join the League. This debate was not primarily between isolationists and internationalists. To be sure, there was a small minority of roughly twelve to fifteen "Irreconcilables"—U.S. senators who, like William Borah, Robert La Follette, and Hiram Johnson, were adamantly opposed to any form of U.S. internationalism because they felt that this was a major break with all U.S. foreign policy traditions. The real conflict, however, was one between competing versions of internationalism. More specifically, it was a struggle between those who advocated a multilateral internationalism that wanted the U.S. to work with and through international organizations to pursue its goals, and those who wanted to pursue a unilateral form of internationalism that gave the U.S. a free hand in its dealings with other powers. The unilateralists did not want to join the League of Nations because they feared that this would limit U.S. policy options and would hinder the country in pursuing its national interests in the international system.

All factions in the political debate drew on American Exceptionalism to justify their cause. The isolationists argued that only retreat from the world would keep America exceptional, and they could look back to George Washington in stating their cause. The multilateralists embraced Wilson's position and his interpretation of American Exceptionalism, and while the unilateralists were also convinced that it was America's destiny to make the world over, they wanted the U.S. to do it alone. For the unilateralists, America's economic dominance and the powerful allure of its way of life were tools for the single-handed creation of a new world of widely shared prosperity and peace. Like the multilateral internationalists, the unilateralists were convinced that, being an exceptional country, the U.S. had the right and the moral responsibility to realize this utopian vision of a world free of wars and want.

THE UNILATERALIST INTERNATIONALISM OF THE 1920S
AND THE TRADITIONS OF AMERICAN EXCEPTIONALISM

U.S. foreign policy of the 1920s has often been described as isolationist, but that is a misconception. While there indeed was a strong isolationist undercurrent in significant parts of the American population during the 1920s, especially in the rural areas of the heartland, this should not blind us to the continuing power of internationalism in a rapidly globalizing America. Although the U.S. did not join the League of Nations, it did not retreat from the world during the 1920s. Rather, it pursued a unilateral internationalism that led to a massive economic and cultural expansion of the U.S. abroad.

The U.S. economy emerged unscathed and on full steam from World War I, while Europe lay in shambles. The U.S. had developed from the debtor nation to the creditor nation of the Old World; New York's Wall Street replaced the City of London as the center of the world's financial system. The international economic system ran on U.S. capital, and U.S. businesses began to penetrate Europe, investing money, setting up factories, and selling their products all over the continent. During the 1920s, Coca-Cola, Ford automobiles, refrigerators, vacuum cleaners, washing machines, and other American consumer goods were widely available in Europe. This economic penetration went hand in hand with the spreading of American material and popular culture. Jazz, tap dancing, and Hollywood movies were wildly popular in Europe during the 1920s–1930s. The new and massive presence of U.S. businesses, products, and culture led many European contemporaries to speak of the "Americanization of Europe"; it was altogether unclear whether they liked it or not.

The economic and cultural expansion of the U.S. during the 1920s was a mix of private enterprise and state action that relied on economic and financial power to pursue policy goals. This approach has been called "dollar diplomacy." It was an altogether new way of conducting international politics, which broke with the mechanisms of traditional European power politics. Dollar diplomacy refrained from employing military force, and it relied on economic expansion as a way to forge friendly ties between nations that, for trading with each other, would not go to war against each other. Economic power and business orientation thus became foreign policy tools. Theologian Reinhold Niebuhr, in *Harper's* magazine in June 1932, even suggested that the representatives of the emerging American market empire were "not admirals or proconsuls, but bankers."

THE RETURN OF LIBERAL INTERNATIONALISM IN WORLD WAR II

The 1930s not only experienced the Great Depression but also witnessed the return of liberal internationalism. While the Great Depression severely raised questions about all notions of American Exceptionalism built around liberal democracy, free-market capitalism, and affluence, the agenda of liberal internationalism reaffirmed them.

The rise of communist- or fascist-style totalitarianism during the 1930s defined a fundamental challenge to the liberal world order in general and the American way of life in particular because totalitarian regimes were anti-democracies, insofar as their entire legitimacy rested on the denial of liberal principles. Despite all of their substantial ideological differences, fascism and communism had several things in common. They both favored a strong, centralized state and authoritarian forms of rule; they rejected individualism, liberal democracy, societal pluralism, as well as the liberal world order of collective security, peaceful negotiations of conflicts, and free trade advocated by the makers of U.S. foreign policy.

Faced with the rise of totalitarian regimes during the 1930s, the U.S. largely watched from the sidelines; a series of four Neutrality Acts passed by Congress between 1935 and 1939 cemented the isolationist position. These acts declared the U.S. absolutely neutral in all military conflicts around the globe. They outlawed U.S. arms sales and loans to nations at war, even to those engaged in civil wars, and they strictly barred Americans from traveling on the ships of belligerent powers. The isolationist sentiment written into these Neutrality Acts was widely shared by the American public.

This was the context in which a growing number of political, intellectual, and business elites used American Exceptionalism to advocate the return to an active and interventionist foreign policy. Convinced that the U.S. could not afford to not care about the world, President Franklin D. Roosevelt and his political friends began to forge a new geopolitical mindedness, suggesting that the U.S. should actively counter the totalitarian threat. To justify America's international involvement, define its goals, and mobilize support for it, Roosevelt drew heavily on Wilson's ideas of a liberal world order.

Already, in his State of the Union address of January 4, 1939, Roosevelt stressed that forces of aggression were growing stronger and that there should be serious cooperative efforts to resist them. The U.S., he said, should use all means "short of war" to deter aggression, and in his Fireside Chat of December 29, 1940, he argued that it should work to secure economic support for overseas democracies fighting the right-wing totalitarian threat. In this context, he created the powerful image of the U.S. as an "arsenal of democracy" that was supplying free and democratic peoples all over the world with all the war supplies and money they needed to win the fight against totalitarian aggressors.

Opening his radio address, Roosevelt declared that this was "not a fireside chat on war" but rather "a talk on national security" given in "the presence of a world crisis" that threatened the peace, security, and prosperity of the U.S. "Never before since Jamestown and Plymouth Rock has our American civilization been in such danger as now," he said, and went on to conjure up the image of a world engaged in a Manichean battle between freedom-loving peoples and the right-wing totalitarian regimes of Germany, Italy, and Japan. In the interconnected world of industrial modernity, the U.S. was no longer protected by mighty oceans, Roosevelt said, and Americans could not "escape danger, or the fear of danger, by crawling into bed and pulling the covers over our heads." As long as there were totalitarian anti-democracies in the world, there could never be peace for the U.S. Roosevelt saw Great Britain and its allies as waging war against "this unholy alliance," which is why America's "own future security" greatly depended "on the outcome of that fight." The U.S., therefore, should support the British war effort by serving as the "arsenal of democracy" that supplied Great Britain and its allies with the much needed "implements of war, the planes, the tanks, the guns, the freighters which will enable them to fight for their liberty and for our security."

In his Fireside Chat of December 29, Roosevelt already envisioned the possibility of the "building of a better civilization in the future." In his State of the Union address of January 6, 1941, known as the "Four Freedoms" speech, Roosevelt developed this vision further. Calling for a determined U.S. effort to meet the challenge and seize the opportunity to create a new world order, Roosevelt defined four freedoms that the U.S. was fighting for in this war. Like President Wilson during World War I, President Roosevelt interpreted the U.S. involvement in the then-current war as the chance to shape the postwar world by casting it into the American mold. "In the future days, which we seek to make secure," Roosevelt said, "we look forward to a world founded upon four essential human freedoms." These four freedoms were the "freedom of speech and expression," the "freedom of every person to worship God in his own way," the "freedom from want" that would "secure to every nation a healthy peacetime life for its inhabitants," and finally, the "freedom from fear," which for Roosevelt meant the "world-wide reduction of armaments to such a point and in such a thorough fashion that no nation will be in a position to commit an act of physical aggression against any neighbor." In defining these four freedoms, Roosevelt was keen on insisting that they should count "everywhere in the world." With this, Roosevelt globalized the American way of life, and he envisioned a new liberal world order based on the "cooperation of free countries, working together in a friendly, civilized society" to ensure the rule of international law, guarantee human rights, and fend off authoritarian aggressions of all sorts.

Roosevelt's Four Freedoms speech inspired Henry Luce to write his famous editorial "The American Century" for *LIFE* magazine on February 17, 1941; the piece argued that the U.S. had the potential and the opportunity to turn the twentieth century into an American century, a century fundamentally shaped by the benevolent hegemony of the U.S., which would use its political, economic, and moral power to make the world like America. However, this vision of an Americanized globe could only be realized, Luce claimed, if the U.S. accepted the responsibilities of leadership resulting from its status as the world power that it actually already was. Diagnosing a deep "moral and intellectual confusion" about the U.S. place and role in international affairs, Luce urged his readers to end the period of self-deception and "accommodate themselves spiritually and practically" to the fact that the U.S. had developed into the "most powerful and most vital nation" of the twentieth century.

No country in the world would be able to win the war without American help, Luce declared, which is why every country of the free world, even Great Britain, would accept American leadership. The "complete opportunity of leadership is OURS," Luce stated, demanding that the U.S. seize this "creative" opportunity or bear "the responsibility of refusal." He argued that continued isolationism would be "moral and practical bankruptcy." Calling for a "truly AMERICAN internationalism," Luce suggested that the U.S. should work to export the American way of life all over world as the only avenue to universal peace, affluence, safety, and human happiness. To realize this utopian vision of an American Century, the U.S. should create a global market integrated by free trade, work to end poverty and famine in the world, and export both its "technical and artistic skills" as well as its political and social values around the globe. "We must undertake now to be the Good Samaritan of the entire world," Luce wrote. "It is the manifest duty of this country to undertake to feed all the people of the world who as a result of this worldwide collapse of civilization are hungry and destitute." The much larger goal, however, was to include "a passionate devotion to great American ideals" in "our vision of America as a world power." Driven by a deep sense of exceptionalism, Luce's vision of an American Century not only anticipated an American victory over the totalitarian anti-democracies in Europe and Asia at a time when the country actually was not yet at war but also provided the moral authority to call for a systematic Americanization of the postwar world.

LIBERAL INTERNATIONALISM AND THE COLD WAR

The term *Cold War* refers to the Soviet-American conflict that spanned the four and a half decades from 1947 to 1991. It was an irreconcilable conflict between two mutually incompatible ways of organizing politics, society, the economy, and culture. In political terms, the Cold War was a conflict between liberal democracy and totalitarian communist-style dictatorship. In economic terms, it was the rivalry between free-market capitalism and a planned economy. In social and cultural terms, it was the antagonism between an open and pluralistic civil society based on individualism, liberty, and self-determination, and a socialist society that saw the collective as superior to the individual, that did not allow for plurality, and that defined the working class as the leading social group.

The Cold War had a powerful influence on both U.S. foreign and domestic policies, and it marked a major break with the American tradition of limited government. In the pursuit of its Cold War agenda, the U.S. ended its long tradition of refraining from entangling alliances and built a system of permanent alliances that aimed at encircling the Soviet Union. The founding of NATO on April 4, 1949, is the most prominent case in point. In addition, the U.S. systematically expanded and modernized its armed forces and created a military apparatus that was as huge as it was permanent. This military buildup served to deter the Soviet Union from attacking the U.S. and its allies, but it was also done to force it into an arms race that it could not possibly win technologically and economically. Thus, the Cold War constellation created what one could call a *Cold War complex* in the U.S., that is, a vast agglomeration of government institutions, armed forces, private companies, universities, and research institutions all working together to prepare for an anticipated war against the Soviet Union and its allies.

The Cold War created big government in the U.S., which, in organizing the multidimensional global campaign against communism with an increasingly large apparatus of state agencies, intervened deeply in American society, economy, and culture. The U.S. military buildup was huge, its defense budgets were astronomically high, and the Pentagon became the biggest client of American industry. In addition, the U.S. Cold War governments deeply interfered with the private lives of their citizens by sending them to fight wars in Korea and Vietnam, or by persecuting real and imagined communist enemies within, for example during the McCarthy era. Time and again, the Cold War governments suspended their own rules and laws to wage the global fight against communism, for example when Hollywood actors, directors, scriptwriters, and other entertainment professionals were blacklisted in the 1940s and 1950s on the suspicion that their work was communist inspired, or when the Reagan administration illegally channeled money from arms sales to Iran to support anticommunist Contra rebels in Nicaragua and El Salvador during the 1980s.

Throughout the Cold War, American Exceptionalism was an important cultural resource used to justify policies and make citizens accept the administrative state. It was especially functional in constructing the Soviet Union as an ideological enemy working to destroy the American way of life. What Prussian autocracy had been during World War I and fascism during World War II, communism now became, that is, an ideological antagonist posing an existential threat to the values that the U.S. was built on. The only way to counter this threat, so the U.S. perspective on the Cold War suggested, was to put all political, military, economic, and cultural resources to the service of a global battle to contain and eventually destroy communism. This policy was framed in a series of programmatic documents that described the Cold War constellation, assessed threats, defined policy options, and anticipated solutions to the crisis. All of these documents were written between 1946 and 1950.

George F. Kennan, career diplomat and the leading expert on the Soviet Union at the time, was the first to describe the unbridgeable ideological and political antagonism of the systems. His eight-thousand-word Long Telegram of February 22, 1946, defined America's Cold War outlook and articulated the dominant frame of reference within which Soviet actions would be perceived by U.S. officials to the very end of the conflict. It was triggered by Josef Stalin's remarks in a speech of February 9, 1946, in which the Soviet leader saw the Soviet Union dangerously encircled by a group of capitalist countries determined to end the Soviet experiment in socialism. He went on to say that a peaceful coexistence between the Soviet Union and the capitalist world was impossible and that this irrepressible conflict would be decided by war sooner or later.

After Stalin's speech, the Department of State asked Kennan, who then was an attaché at the U.S. embassy in Moscow, to analyze Stalin's speech. Kennan's answer was the Long Telegram. In it, he painted the picture of a Soviet Union that was relentlessly working to destroy the Free World defined by liberal democracy and free-market capitalism integrated under U.S. leadership. Soviet policy moved on two planes, Kennan stated, an official plane and a "subterranean plane of actions undertaken by agencies for which Soviet Government does not admit responsibility." On the official plane, Moscow would commit all its energies to increasing the strength and prestige of Soviet power through systematic industrialization, a massive military buildup, and aggressively expansionist policies all over the globe, especially in Third World countries. Furthermore, the Soviet Union would officially participate in the United Nations (UN) and other international organizations but not because it was devoted to the liberal world order and systems of collective security but, rather, because it offered an opportunity to extend

Soviet power. On the unofficial plane, the Soviet Union would engage in a widespread and multifaceted policy of subversion in the Free World, carried out by local Communist Parties and a wide variety of national nonparty organizations like labor unions, youth leagues, women's organizations, racial societies, and media corporations. The aim of this systematic infiltration was to undermine the political and strategic potential of the Free World, and to encourage "all forms of disunity" in it. "In summary," Kennan concluded, "we have here a political force committed fanatically to the belief that with US there can be no permanent modus vivendi that it is desirable and necessary that the internal harmony of our society be disrupted, our traditional way of life be destroyed, the international authority of our state be broken, if Soviet power is to be secure."

The only adequate U.S. response to the Soviet challenge, in Kennan's eyes, was a determined policy of containment that sought to prevent the further spread of communism in the world. This policy was to rely on the systematic export of liberal democracy, free-market prosperity, and the American way of life. Kennan argued that the inner unity of a "Western World" integrated on the basis of American ways and values was the best protection against Soviet communism. Arguing that much depended on the "health and vigor of our own society," Kennan suggested that the Americans should have "courage and self-confidence to cling to our own methods and conceptions of human society" and should systematically work to spread their way of life around the world to contain and eventually destroy the Soviet Union. Although Kennan argued for a determined policy of strength to deter Moscow from any aggressions, he did not advise militarizing the conflict. Rather, Kennan was convinced that the Cold War problem was in America's power to solve "without recourse to any general military conflict" by solely relying on the strength and attractiveness of the American way of life.

Kennan's Long Telegram framed the conflict and made internal policy suggestions. President Harry S. Truman translated it into a foreign policy agenda that committed the U.S. to a determined global fight against communism. His Truman Doctrine, which is considered by many to be the American declaration of the Cold War, was triggered by events in Greece and Turkey and the British abdication as hegemon guaranteeing the economic and military stability of that world region in February 1947.

After Great Britain had informed Washington that it could no longer afford to maintain a military presence in Greece and Turkey—two countries destabilized by communist uprisings—the Truman administration seized the moment to officially declare it the U.S. duty to step in. Asking a reluctant Congress for $400 million in military and economic aid for Turkey and Greece on March 12, 1947, Truman made the global containment of communism the general line of U.S. foreign policy. Truman suggested that, should Greece fall into the hands of the communists, other countries in that region would also fall; "totalitarian regimes imposed on free peoples, by direct or indirect aggression, undermine the foundations of international peace and hence the security of the United States." Therefore, "it must be the policy of the United States to support free peoples who are resisting attempted subjugation by armed minorities or by outside pressures." To protect its own way of life at home, Truman argued, the U.S. had to fight communism abroad by supporting and spreading liberal market democracies.

The economic substantiation of the Truman Doctrine was the Marshall Plan. Based on the European Recovery Program passed by Congress on April 3, 1948, after months of heated and controversial debates, the Marshall Plan was a huge economic aid program that pumped billions of dollars across the Atlantic to reconstruct the economies of sixteen Western European countries and Turkey. It aimed at rebuilding Western Europe as a zone of free-market capitalism that would produce the kind of prosperity needed to stabilize liberal democracy and fend off the communist challenge. The Truman administration was convinced that Europe would be unable to recover from the damages the war had wrought all by itself, and the resulting hardship and poverty would favor the rise of a political radicalism that would give the Soviet Union an easy path to expanding its control over Europe. The rationale of containment here merged with the economic necessity of rebuilding Europe as a market for American goods. After all, Washington's financial aid to Europe was also to ensure that the U.S. had the strong trading partners it needed for its own booming economy. The U.S., having emerged unscathed from the destruction of World War II, was producing much more than could possibly be consumed at home.

The plan to build strong market democracies in Europe through U.S. financial aid and make them immune to communism was first developed by George C. Marshall in a commencement address delivered at Harvard University on June 5, 1947. In it, Marshall stated that Europe's need for food and other essential products exceeded its financial capacities by far, so that it must either have "substantial additional help" provided by the U.S., "or face economic, social, and political deterioration of a very grave character." Should the U.S. leave Europe all to itself, this would have a "demoralizing effect on the world at large," which would most likely trigger "disturbances arising as a result of the desperation of the people concerned." Therefore, it was only logical that the U.S. should assist Europe "in the return of normal economic health in the world, without which there can be no political stability and no assured peace." The purpose of U.S. financial aid to Europe "should be the revival of a working economy in the world" that would "permit the emergence of political and social conditions in which free institutions can exist."

Before 1950, therefore, the major instruments of containment policy were economic and moral in nature. Both Kennan and Marshall relied on economic measures to stop the advance of communism, and they wanted the U.S. to lead through the example of its exceptional way of life, which appeared to be what other nations were striving for. In the formative period of the U.S. containment policy, there was only very little talk about armaments, military build-up, and deterrence.

This changed in 1950. By then, the division of Germany was complete, Soviet control over Eastern Europe was firmly in place, and communists under the leadership of Mao Zedong had founded the People's Republic of China. In January 1950, therefore, the Free World seemed under pressure worldwide and even on the retreat. Containment seemed to have proven a failure—the export of democracy and prosperity alone could obviously not stop the advance of communism.

In this situation, the Truman administration ordered the chief of the State Department's policy planning staff, Paul Nitze, successor to Kennan, to critically assess U.S. containment policy, and to produce a strategy paper that would define the future course of America's foreign policy. The result of this internal discussion and planning effort was the "National Security Council Memorandum No 68" (NSC-68) that ushered in the far-reaching militarization of America's Cold War strategy. This document repeated the assessment that the U.S. and the Soviet Union were the two superpowers in a bipolar world without precedent in history. It reiterated Kennan's original claim that the Soviet Union, "animated by a new fanatic faith, anti-thetical to our own," was striving for the absolute domination of the world. NSC-68 restated the containment of communism as U.S. grand strategy and urged the government to continue to pursue a policy "designed to foster a world environment in which the American system can survive and flourish." To achieve these goals, the paper advocated a policy that continued to rely on U.S. economic and cultural power, but it added a strong military component to the fray. NSC-68 called for a systematic alliance policy aimed at encircling the Soviet Union, and it demanded a massive military buildup that included nuclear and conventional armaments for powerful and standing armed forces "to deter, if possible, Soviet expansion, and to defeat, if necessary, aggressive Soviet or Soviet-directed actions of a limited or total character."

Overall, therefore, the U.S. Cold War ideology was firmly in place by 1950. Drawing on American Exceptionalism as an identity narrative that assessed the world situation, formulated threats, staked out policy options, and structured policy agendas, the documents discussed above defined the overall framework within which U.S. Cold War policies (despite the repeated and well-known changes and transformations during the long forty-year period of the East-West conflict) moved. It adapted the premises and strategies of liberal internationalism to the bipolar world of the Cold War.

FROM CONTAINMENT TO ENLARGEMENT: U.S. FOREIGN POLICY IN THE 1990S

The Cold War ended with the fall of the Berlin Wall in November 1989 and the collapse of the Soviet Union in 1991. The U.S. stood triumphant, and the outcome of the forty-year conflict seemed to be the ultimate proof that the American way of life indeed was superior to all other forms of social organization. The very allure of the American model, many argued, had eventually decided the Cold War in favor of the U.S. and the Free World.

The outcome of the Cold War reinforced notions of American Exceptionalism, and the clearest and most enthusiastic celebration of this were the writings of Francis Fukuyama, for whom the end of the Cold War was not just the end of a historical epoch to be followed by another historical epoch but, rather, "the end of history." Before his widely received book came out under that title in 1992, he had already developed his thoughts in a 1989 essay for *The National Interest*. With the Berlin Wall not yet having fallen, Fukuyama declared: "What we may be witnessing is not just the end of the Cold War, or the passing of a particular period of post-war history, but the end of history as such: that is, the end point of mankind's ideological evolution and the universalization of Western liberal democracy as the final form of human government." For Fukuyama, history thus was a process driven and structured by ideological antagonisms and attempts to create ideal worlds based on ideological premises. The Cold War was the last of these ideological battles, and with the Cold War being won by the U.S., Fukuyama suggested that from now on liberal democracy and free-market capitalism would be the only games in town.

In the final days of the Cold War, President George H. W. Bush constantly spoke of a "New World Order" under the auspices of a Pax Americana. Bush, therefore, wanted the U.S. to continue its deep involvement in international affairs to finally create the best of all possible worlds. However, President Bill Clinton, who was convinced that nobody in the U.S. actually cared about world affairs, won the presidential election of 1992 with a domestic agenda, running on the slogan "It's the economy, stupid."

The end of the Cold War thus left the U.S. both triumphant about its victory in the battle of the systems and uncertain about its future role in the world. While some conservatives and liberals favored a reduction of U.S. foreign policy activities to all but the most vital national security areas, others—neoconservatives as well as idealistic liberals—pressured for the continuation of an activist foreign policy that would secure American global hegemony and advance human rights all over the world. In this situation, the Clinton administration embraced the rhetoric and agenda of liberal internationalism, adapting it to the post–Cold War world.

The crucial programmatic foreign policy statement of the Clinton administration was the speech "From Containment to Enlargement" that National Security advisor Anthony Lake delivered on September 21, 1993, at Johns Hopkins University in Washington, DC. In it, Lake argued that the successor to a policy of containment should be one of enlargement, that is, the active spreading of liberal democracy and free-market capitalism to countries where they did not yet exist. Lake built his argument on the observation that with the end of the Cold War, "America's core concepts—democracy and market economics," were "more broadly accepted than ever." Still, there were vast regions in the world still waiting to be opened up to democracy, Lake argued, and he was convinced that the U.S. should use this historical moment to enlarge the sphere of "market democracies." Lake saw the U.S as the dominant power of the new era ushered in by the end of the Cold War. In this unipolar world, the U.S. had a responsibility to lead. It could not and should not retreat from the world, especially since there were still threats to U.S. security, Lake argued, and he mentioned terrorism, proliferating weapons of mass destruction, ethnic conflicts, and environmental destruction. The best way to counter these security threats was the "enlargement of the world's free community of market democracies."

Despite this clear programmatic basis, U.S. foreign policy of the 1990s lacked inner coherence and force. There was, of course, the U.S. intervention in the Balkan wars, and there was a bit of an intervention on behalf of democracy in Haiti—but all of this was haphazard. Vis-à-vis Russia and China, the Clinton administration pursued a pragmatic course that was more interested in enlarging business opportunities than democracy there. This lack of an inner orientation had a lot to do with a missing ideological antagonist threatening the very essence of the American way of life. This changed substantially with the 9/11 attacks on the World Trade Center and the Pentagon in 2001.

9/11 AND THE WAR ON TERROR

The attacks of September 11, 2001, created a new enemy image in the U.S.: Middle Eastern terrorists. This enemy was an ideological enemy just as the enemies of the twentieth century had been, an antagonistic force systematically working to destroy the American way of life at its foundation. Nine days after 9/11, President George W. Bush, in an address to a joint session of Congress, already declared the terrorists of Al Qaeda to be "enemies of freedom" who had "committed an act of war against our country" that put "freedom itself [. . .] under attack." Al Qaeda's goal, Bush said, was to remake the world and impose its "radical beliefs on people everywhere." The network of radical Islamic terrorists masterminded by Osama bin Laden was out there to "disrupt and end a way of life" because they rejected liberal democracy, free-market capitalism, pluralism, religious tolerance, diversity, and Judeo-Christian culture. "They hate," Bush said, addressing both houses of Congress, "what we see right here in this chamber—a democratically elected government. Their leaders are self-appointed. They hate our freedoms—our freedom of religion, our freedom of speech, our freedom to vote and assemble and disagree with each other." He went on to put Al Qaeda terrorists in line with the totalitarian threats to U.S. democracy. "We have seen their kind before," he said. "They are the heirs of all the murderous ideologies of the 20th century. By sacrificing human life to serve their radical visions—by abandoning every value except the will to power—they follow in the path of fascism, and Nazism, and totalitarianism."

To fight terrorism, the George W. Bush administration took liberal internationalism and all of its exceptionalist baggage into the twenty-first century. Believing that the U.S. should use its power to democratize the Middle East as the best and only way to solve the many conflicts in that region, Bush embraced the idea of "regime change," which was to turn dictatorial countries like Iraq, Iran, and North Korea into liberal democracies and free-market economies. While he thus shared Wilson's determination to use U.S. power to promote American values and interests by spreading democracy around the world, the president did not subscribe to Wilson's multilateral internationalism, which worked through international institutions to accomplish U.S. goals. On the contrary, Bush was an assertive nationalist whose internationalism was decidedly unilateral. Working to shed restraints on the use of U.S. power, President Bush wanted the U.S. to do it alone. Zeroing in on Iraq as a "rogue state" supposedly in possession of weapons of mass destruction, Bush, in his State of the Union address of January 2002, redirected the focus of the U.S "War on Terror" from Afghanistan to Iraq. The president stressed that Saddam Hussein's brutal dictatorial regime had to be changed, if necessary, through the use of force, and he left no doubt that the U.S. was willing to proceed in that manner.

This determined U.S. unilateralism met with a lot of criticism in Europe, where especially France and Germany were absolutely against a military confrontation in the Middle East, advocating international inspections operated through the UN to verify the existence of weapons of mass destruction in Iraq. Among the Bush administration and its political friends, this European opposition reinforced notions of American Exceptionalism. Secretary of Defense Donald Rumsfeld dismissed America's longtime allies as "old Europe," which had lost its willingness and ability to fight. Robert Kagan, neoconservative historian and foreign policy commentator, went so far as to suggest that Americans and Europeans were living on different planets. In his widely read treatise *Of Paradise and Power*, published in 2003, he belittled Europeans for living on Venus—named after the ancient Roman goddess of peace—while Americans were from Mars, the planet of the Roman god of war.

After President Bush had begun talking about "rogue states" and "regime changes" rather haphazardly shortly after the 9/11 attacks, the U.S. National Security Strategy of September 2002 officially redefined the country's foreign policy agenda. With this strategy paper, the Bush administration framed the international situation it saw itself acting in after 9/11, defined the threats emerging from it, and suggested solutions to the problem in the form of a coherent strategy that was to guide U.S. foreign policy in the years to come. In doing so, it transcended the 9/11 moment, putting the events into a bigger picture, and reflecting U.S. reactions to it in the context of U.S. foreign policy traditions.

The preamble stated that "the great struggles of the twentieth century between liberty and totalitarianism" had "ended with a decisive victory for the forces of freedom." Individual liberty, liberal democracy, and free enterprise had emerged from these struggles as the "single sustainable model for national success" for the twenty-first century. Insisting on the universal applicability of U.S. values, the National Security Strategy claimed that people everywhere wanted to be

> able to speak freely; choose who will govern them; worship as they please; educate their children—male and female; own property; and enjoy the benefits of their labor. These values of freedom are right and true for every person, in every society—and the duty of protecting these values against their enemies is the common calling of freedom-loving people across the globe and across the ages.

Stating that the U.S. was the only remaining superpower in a unipolar world enjoying "a position of unparalleled military strength and great economic and political influence," the National Security Strategy stated that the U.S. was seeking "to create a balance of power that favors human freedom." To achieve this goal, the U.S. would "defend the peace by fighting terrorists and tyrants" while at the same time "encouraging free and open societies on every continent." It defined terrorists as a new kind of enemy that changed the government's task of defending the U.S. dramatically:

> Enemies in the past needed great armies and great industrial capabilities to endanger America. Now, shadowy networks of individuals can bring great chaos and suffering to our shores for less than it costs to purchase a single tank. Terrorists are organized to penetrate open societies and to turn the power of modern technologies against us.

While terrorism thus proved to be a new kind of enemy, the threat it posed to the U.S. was the same as before. Interestingly, and this is also in keeping with the traditions of exceptionalist mindsets in U.S. culture, the National Security Strategy saw the threats posed by terrorism as a historical moment of opportunity in which the foundations for a new world order could be laid and the democratization of the world could be completed under American leadership. The text stated that "the United States will use this moment of opportunity to extend the benefits of freedom across the globe. We will actively work to bring the hope of democracy, development, free markets, and free trade to every corner of the world."

Most of the foreign policy measures that the National Security Strategy suggested to execute the new foreign policy agenda were largely based on the traditions of liberal internationalism. New, however, was the idea of a preemptive strike, that is, a proactive policy seeking to destroy perceived threats before they could actually harm the U.S. Faced with weapons of mass destruction in the hands of terrorists and states supporting them, the National Security Strategy called it "a matter of common sense and self-defense" if the U.S. acted against "emerging threats before they are fully formed." The U.S. would, therefore, defend its "interests at home and abroad by identifying and destroying the threat before it reaches our borders." In the pursuit of this policy, the U.S. would "constantly strive to enlist the support of the international community," but it would "not hesitate to act alone, if necessary, to exercise our right of self-defense by acting preemptively against such terrorists, to prevent them from doing harm against our people and our country."

This doctrine of the preemptive strike was a deep break with the traditions of liberal internationalism, but it was not a break with the exceptionalist mindset that carried them. The neoconservative reformulation of Wilson's internationalist agenda turned the U.S. into a crusader state that would no longer confine itself to containing threats and solving international conflicts peacefully by way of negotiations. Rather, it would proactively and preemptively work to destroy threats to U.S. security and spread American values with the use of force. In contrast to Wilson, the Bush administration contemplated using unilateral military force preemptively to make the world safe for democracy. This policy continued to rest on the moral certainty that the U.S., by being an exceptional nation, had the right, even the duty, to cast the world into its own mold.

President Barack Obama continued the liberal internationalist agenda in the fight against terrorism. While he was convinced that the war in Iraq was a disastrous mistake, he did not question the legitimacy of the "War on Terror" as such. Although he emphatically insisted that the U.S. was not at war against Islam, stressing the partnership with the Muslim world that was critical to U.S. security and other interests, he left no doubt that the extremist perpetrators of the 9/11 attacks needed to be fought and destroyed. The real battleground of the "War on Terror" for him was Afghanistan, which is why under Obama's presidency, U.S. military efforts were redirected from Iraq to south-central Asia. This went hand in hand with a much more pragmatic approach that abandoned the idea of far-reaching regime changes in favor of stability. Still, the Obama administration, convinced of America's exceptionality, continued to work for the liberal world order the U.S. had been building under the auspices of liberal internationalism since 1917.

It is too early to answer the question of how the "America First" nationalism of the Trump administration fit into the traditions of U.S. foreign policy and how it tapped into the cultural resource of American Exceptionalism. If the Trump administration pursued something like a grand strategy at all, it looked like a return to the unilateral internationalism and the "dollar diplomacy" of the 1920s. Although it was altogether incoherent, haphazard, and erratic, President Trump's foreign policy did mark a break with the liberal internationalism pursued by U.S. administrations since 1945. Some Americans loved it, others stood in dumbfounded bewilderment, while many of the U.S.'s closest longtime allies were thoroughly alienated by it. Whether the Trump administration's foreign policy agenda was but an episode, or whether it had a lasting transformational effect remains to the seen. While the first hundred days of Joe Biden's presidency pointed in the direction of a return to a pre-Trump normalcy in the field of U.S. foreign relations, it is still too early to call which future course U.S. foreign policy will take. Judging by President Biden's inaugural address, however, it seems certain that the spirit of exceptionalism will continue to inform U.S. foreign policy—as it has done since 1789 in one way or another.

This chapter has shown that American Exceptionalism has served as a powerful cultural resource to motivate, guide, and justify U.S. foreign policy agendas throughout U.S. history. Driven by the question of what kind of foreign policy was befitting a self-declared exceptional nation, U.S. foreign policy was never only about national security and the pursuit of political and economic interests. It was just as much a matter of identity; here, the identity narratives building on concepts of American Exceptionalism translated into the most different foreign policy programs. This chapter has shown how exceptionalist persuasions were used to justify expansionist and anti-expansionist, internationalist and isolationist, as well as multilateral and unilateral agendas. At the heart of the multifaceted debate was a sense of mission to make the world over, which, however, was inseparably tied to a vibrant nervousness about the permanence of the American republic and its experiment in liberty. The question of what kind of foreign policy would stabilize and perpetuate American democracy and the way of life it was built on triggered intense debates about the direction of U.S. foreign policy; the answers given have been subjects of an ongoing debate that has not yet ended.

Furthermore, this chapter has revealed the complex racist dynamics of U.S. foreign policies built on exceptionalist persuasions. Strongly intertwined with notions of whiteness and Anglo-Saxonism, American Exceptionalism as a cultural resource informed foreign policy agendas that, as different and contradictory as they may have been, all pursued the interests of white Euro-American power elites.

6

Promissory Notes

Exceptionalism and African American Self-Empowerment

WHEN SWEDISH NOBEL-LAUREATE ECONOMIST Gunnar Myrdal investigated the situation of African Americans in the U.S. during the 1940s, he detected an "American Dilemma." Painstakingly detailing the many obstacles to full participation in U.S. politics, society, economy, and culture that African Americans faced in a country waging war to defend freedom and democracy abroad, Myrdal felt that the U.S. was living in a fundamental paradox: Founded on the promise of individual liberty and self-determined pursuits of happiness, it discriminated against African Americans for racist reasons, undermining the very universalism of its founding credo, according to which *all* men had been created equal. In 1944, when he published his magisterial tome *An American Dilemma: The Negro Problem and Modern Democracy*, Myrdal was convinced that the then-current war for freedom and against Nazi racism, in which young Americans, including blacks, were dying in large numbers for the cause of democracy, only deepened the ideological contradictions of the American way of life.

The racist marginalization of African Americans that Myrdal identified as a "dilemma" was not just some systemic error that had somehow happened. Rather, the exclusion of African Americans from full participation in America's democracy was the result of decisions, and these decisions were justified *with* the liberal creed of the American Revolution. The basic pattern went like this: The U.S. founding documents declared all human beings to have been created free and equal, which is why they had inalienable rights that could not be taken away from them and must not be infringed upon. At the same time, this natural-rights egalitarianism was inseparably tied to the question of who was to be classified as a human being—because, in this way of thinking, only full human beings were entitled to natural rights and citizenship in America's democracy. Accordingly, whites justified the exclusion of African Americans based on their supposed deficient humanity. Under the premises of racist thinking, blacks were widely held to be intellectually and mentally unfit for self-determination and self-government. White racists represented African Americans as either brutal savages or docile children, but in any case, as racially inferior to European American humanity, and incapable of ever reaching that superior state of development that European Americans had supposedly reached. The universal founding credo of natural-rights liberalism—and notions American Exceptionalism based on it—was, therefore, initially used to justify the hegemony of white, Euro-American, mostly Protestant men.

Yet America's liberal founding ideology developed a subversive, counter-hegemonic dynamic, insofar as it offered African Americans the chance to use it in order to formulate their own claims to emancipation, citizenship, and participation in America's democracy. This counter-hegemonic potential of American Exceptionalism resulted from the very universalism of America's revolutionary ideology, as the very discrepancy between the egalitarian ideals and the racist realities in America produced a tension fueling the struggle for black emancipation throughout U.S. history. African Americans could always argue that America's exceptionality still lay ahead, was yet to come, or was a potentiality but not a reality as long as they were not given equal rights and opportunities. However, American Exceptionalism developed its counter-hegemonic potential only in connection with integrationist visions of America's future, that is, visions that saw blacks and whites living together in one and the same society integrated on the basis of a shared natural-rights consensus.

THE AMERICAN REVOLUTION AND THE BIRTH OF THE AMERICAN DILEMMA

The American revolutionaries did not want to be treated like slaves. When he wrote his pamphlet *A Dissertation on the Canon and Feudal Law* at the height of the Stamp Act crisis in 1765, John Adams saw the North

American colonies as being on their way to becoming slaves to Great Britain, and he argued that this must never be accepted by the colonists, since "consenting to slavery" was "a sacrilegious breach of trust" and an offense to God Almighty who had "promulgated from heaven, liberty, peace, and good-will to man!" On October 14, 1765, Adams, writing under his penname Humphry Ploughjogger in the *Boston Gazette*, snarled at Great Britain: "[W]e won't be their negroes." Providence had never intended the American colonists "for negroes [. . .] and therefore never intended us for slaves." The American colonists in Adams's eyes were white Englishmen, and therefore free.

By 1774, this way of looking at the colonial protest as resistance against enslavement attempted by the mother country had become commonplace in the pamphlet literature of the day, and it caused slavery at home to become a problem, too. Richard Wells, who identified himself as a "citizen of Philadelphia" in his *A Few Political Reflections Submitted to the Consideration of the British Colonies*, argued in 1774 that the "exercise of slavery" was impossible to reconcile "with our professions of freedom." What Gunnar Myrdal in 1944 called the "American Dilemma" had thus already been diagnosed by the contemporaries of the American Revolution.

Yet on the eve of July 4, 1776, slavery existed in all thirteen colonies of the future United States. While the Southern states held on to slavery, in the North, the revolutionary ideology triggered political movements for its abolition. This revolutionary abolitionism to a very large extent was fueled by the ideological contradictions between the universal claims to liberty formulated in the Declaration of Independence and the reality of slavery, to the effect that by 1804 all states north of Maryland had passed laws providing for the gradual abolition of slavery. Around 1820, the institution had vanished from New England and most of the Mid-Atlantic states.

The abolition of slavery in the North and its continuation in the South only deepened the ideological contradictions in the U.S., undermining all claims to exceptionality. On July 11, 1787, James Wilson, a Pennsylvania delegate to the Constitutional Convention in Philadelphia, asked whether the slaves should be considered "property" or "citizens." If they were property, they would have no rights at all. If they were citizens, they could not be slaves. The delegates of the Constitutional Convention thus were faced with "the dilemma of doing injustice to the Southern States or to human nature," as his colleague in the Pennsylvania delegation, Gouverneur Morris, summarized.

Whites, however, were not the only ones to see this contradiction. African Americans did so, too, and it is interesting to see how the revolutionary ideals of liberty were used by blacks, free and non-free, to already question slavery during the American Revolution. Boston slave Quock Walker thus had the Massachusetts Supreme Judicial Court decide the question of why he was considered the private property of Nathaniel Jennison in 1781. One year later, in the "Petition of an African slave to the Legislature of Massachusetts," a slave named Belinda asked to be compensated for forty years of labor for her master, drawing on the revolutionary rhetoric of freedom and rights. Finally, an explicit reference to the Declaration of Independence is found in Benjamin Banneker's letter to Thomas Jefferson of August 19, 1791. Banneker, the eldest child of a free black couple owning a tobacco farm in Maryland, asked Jefferson to recall "that time in which the Arms and tyranny of the British Crown were exerted with every powerful effort in order to reduce you to a State of Servitude." This, Banneker went on to elaborate, "was a time in which you clearly saw into the injustice of a State of Slavery." Under the impression of the "horrors" of slavery and full of "abhorrence thereof," Jefferson had, as Banneker reminded him, written the Declaration of Independence stating the self-evident truth that all men were created equal. "Here Sir," Banneker wrote, "was a time in which your tender feelings for your selves had engaged you thus to declare, you were then impressed with proper ideas of the great valuation of liberty, and the free possession of those blessings to which you were entitled by nature." How could he, Jefferson, therefore, detain "by fraud and violence so numerous a part of my brethren under groaning captivity and cruel oppression, that you should at the Same time be found guilty of that most criminal act, which you professedly detested in others, with respect to yourselves."

Reference to the ideological contradictions of American Exceptionalism was not solely confined to written statements in a rational debate. It could also be the fuel for acts of violent resistance against slavery. Gabriel Prosser's planned slave uprising of 1800 emerged from it, with one of the uprising's slaves, possibly Prosser himself, declaring after having been captured: "I have nothing more to offer than what General Washington would have had to offer, had he been taken by the British and put on trial by them. I have adventured my life in endeavoring to obtain the liberty of my countrymen, and am willing sacrifice to their cause." African Americans thus began to use the revolutionary language of rights and liberty to expose the ideological dilemma undermining all American claims to exceptionalism and to fight for their inclusion in the liberal founding consensus of America's democracy in many different shapes, styles, and forms.

A NEW BIRTH OF FREEDOM? AMERICAN EXCEPTIONALISM AND THE ABOLITION OF SLAVERY

A black abolitionist movement emerged in the first half of the nineteenth century, which after 1830, entered into a rather uneasy alliance with white abolitionists who found their strongman in William Lloyd Garrison. It was, therefore, a colorful group of white northern liberals; evangelical Christians, many of them women; and a significant number of free blacks who carried the abolitionist movement in antebellum America. Within this lot of activists, the group of black abolitionists was diverse in and of itself. Some, like Martin Delany, advocated a race-conscious separation of blacks from white society as the only possible condition for black liberation. Cultivating the idea of blacks as "a nation within a nation," Delany and his political friends in antebellum America feared the total absorption and disappearance of the black race through integration and assimilation to the standards of white society. Therefore, they suggested, among other measures, colonizing parts of Africa as a homeland for American blacks as a way to achieve self-determination.

Others in the black abolitionist movement pursued an integrationist agenda that claimed civil and voting rights for blacks to enable their participation in America's democracy. The premise for their political struggle was an understanding of the Declaration of Independence as an antislavery document whose universal language included blacks when it declared that all men had inalienable rights to life, liberty, and the pursuit of happiness. A black convention held in New York thus passed *Resolutions of the People of Color, at a Meeting Held on the 25th of January, 1831*, in which they claimed the U.S., and not Africa, as "THE PLACE OF OUR BIRTH." Considering the U.S. to be their homeland, they suggested that the "time must come when the declaration of independence will be felt in the heart as well as uttered from the mouth, and when the rights of all shall be properly acknowledged and appreciated." Rejecting all colonization projects in Africa and elsewhere, they anticipated that the liberal promise of the Declaration of Independence would one day also include them.

One of the most famous examples of how antebellum African American activists used the language of American Exceptionalism to fundamentally criticize slavery and to justify the abolitionist cause was a speech by Frederick Douglass now known as "What to the Slave Is the Fourth of July?" Douglass, a former slave, author of a widely read slave narrative, and one of the leading representatives of the abolitionist movement, had been asked to give an Independence Day address to the Ladies' Anti-Slavery Society in Rochester, New York. On July 5, 1852, he delivered his speech to an audience of five hundred to six hundred people.

In his address, he depicted the American Revolution as the heroic act of founding a new nation based on fundamental, universal, and even "eternal" principles. These "saving principles" were laid down in the Declaration of Independence; they were true "on all occasions." He spoke of the signers of the Declaration of Independence as "brave" and "great men" that gave "fame to a great age," and he also identified the U.S. Constitution as a "GLORIOUS LIBERTY DOCUMENT." He congratulated his audience on the birthday of *their* nation, only to sharply distinguish between white Americans and black Americans, who had nothing to celebrate on the Fourth of July. The "blessings" resulting from America's independence were not extended to them. "Fellow-citizens, pardon me"; Douglass asked, "[W]hy am I called upon to speak here to-day? What have I, or those I represent, to do with your national independence? [. . .] I am not included within the pale of this glorious anniversary!"

Douglass went on to say that his subject was not American freedom but American slavery, which he identified as "the great sin and shame of America!" Contrasting the festive jubilation of white America on Independence Day with the situation of African American slaves, Douglass stressed that the Fourth of July revealed to them "more than all other days in the year, the gross injustice and cruelty" to which they were constant victims. To them, the Fourth of July only revealed the full extent of American hypocrisy. From the slaves' perspectives, Douglass told his white audience, "[Y]our celebration is a sham; your boasted liberty, an unholy license; your national greatness, swelling vanity; your sounds of rejoicing are empty and heartless; your denunciations of tyrants, brass fronted impudence; your shouts of liberty and equality, hollow mockery." In this reading, all narratives of American Exceptionalism are but "a thin veil to cover up crimes which would disgrace a nation of savages." In this context, Douglass identified a negative American Exceptionalism insofar as there was "not a nation on the earth guilty of practices, more shocking and bloody, than are the people of these United States, at this very hour." Regarding "revolting barbarity and shameless hypocrisy," Douglass cried, "America reigns without a rival."

Douglass's eloquent diagnosis of the American dilemma had two sides. On the one hand, he criticized the U.S. for not living up to its own ideals and saw the very fact of slavery as destroying all claims to exceptionality. On the other hand, he celebrated the revolutionary founding documents as statements of universal truths defining the basis for an ideal society. As long as slavery existed, this exceptional society was only a potentiality, not yet a reality, but one could hope that it would become a reality one day.

The end of slavery in the U.S. came with Abraham Lincoln's Emancipation Proclamation of January 1, 1863, and the Thirteenth Amendment to the U.S. Constitution, ratified in 1865. These two documents were informed by an understanding of the meaning of the Civil War as laid down in Lincoln's Gettysburg Address. Lincoln delivered this speech, one of the most memorable in the history of U.S. oratory, on November 19, 1863, at the dedication of a war cemetery for Union soldiers who had fallen at the Battle of Gettysburg, in Pennsylvania. The legendary battle, which ended with a decisive victory for the North, left fifty-one thousand Confederate and Union soldiers wounded, missing, or dead. The battle was not only the turning point of the war that paved the path to Northern victory, it also triggered meaning-making efforts that reinterpreted the war. With the Gettysburg Address, President Lincoln, as interpreter in chief of U.S. history, no longer saw the war primarily as a war to save the union but as a war to finally realize America's exceptionalist potential. In that address, Lincoln repeated the arguments that abolitionists like Frederick Douglass had been making all along.

The first sentence of the speech (the speech consisted of only 272 words) established an immediate connection between the *now* of the Civil War, and the *then* of the American Revolution. The iconic formulation "[f]our score and seven years ago" linked the year of 1863 directly to the year of 1776 and the Declaration of Independence, which was explicitly referenced by Lincoln. Eighty-seven years ago, Lincoln said, "[O]ur fathers brought forth, upon this continent, a new nation, conceived in liberty, and dedicated to the proposition that 'all men are created equal.'" With this first sentence, as elegant and short as it is, Lincoln defined the Declaration of Independence as America's founding document, and the radical egalitarianism formulated by it as the essence of the American way of life.

From there, Lincoln moved on to reflect on the place and significance of the Civil War in the course of American history when he said: "Now we are engaged in a great civil war, testing whether that nation, or any nation so conceived, and so dedicated, can long endure." The sense of instability and the possibility of failure, both of them crucial to the mindset of American Exceptionalism, surfaced in these words that interpreted the crisis of the Civil War as a test deciding the future fate of liberty and democracy.

Having identified the historical significance of the moment, Lincoln, in the third and final paragraph of his speech, talked about the tasks lying ahead for all Americans. In his view, the enormous number of war dead—and here he was referring to all fallen soldiers, Union and Confederate soldiers alike—would have a meaning only if the American nation had "a new birth of freedom" by ending slavery, and if it demonstrated to the world that "government of the people by the people for the people" would "not perish from the earth."

With these words, the Gettysburg Address demanded a transformation of America's democracy because it suggested that the American promise was not yet fully fulfilled and that it needed an expansion of freedom to finally realize it. Like Frederick Douglass in "What to the Slave Is the Fourth of July?" Lincoln in his Gettysburg Address treated American Exceptionalism as something that still lay ahead, something that still needed to be fulfilled.

It was not fulfilled in the aftermath of the Civil War, as already discussed in chapter 2. The system of slavery gave way to legal discrimination against blacks under the auspices of Jim Crow. It went hand in hand with multiple forms of de facto economic discrimination against African Americans in the North and South that thrust the vast majority into a vicious cycle of poverty and debt. Blacks continued to be marginalized in a democratic order that had fought a civil war to end slavery and that had constitutionally guaranteed equal rights to African Americans.

LIBERAL INTERNATIONALISM AND THE DEEPENING OF THE AMERICAN DILEMMA

In 1903, W. E. B. Du Bois wrote in his famous *The Souls of Black Folk*, "The problem of the Twentieth Century is the problem of the color line," and right he was. The decades after 1900 witnessed the rise of a powerful African American civil rights movement, which was probably the single most important social movement of the twentieth century, not only because it eventually ended the long history of legal discrimination against blacks, but also because it implanted a rights consciousness into U.S. political culture that led to other hitherto marginalized groups claiming their right to participation and self-determination in the wake of the African American freedom struggle.

The African American civil rights movement did not begin in the 1950s. Rather, it emerged gradually over the course of the twentieth century, and it largely fed on the ideological contradictions of a supposedly exceptional American way of life. These contradictions became even more pronounced during the two world wars, in which the U.S. fought for democracy abroad and against totalitarian regimes worldwide. The U.S. foreign policy agenda of liberal internationalism ideologized liberty and democracy, and it expected African Americans to defend the liberty and democracy abroad that were withheld from them at home.

African Americans fought and died for the revolutionary founding ideas of America's democracy in large numbers and with patriotic dedication in both world wars. During World War I, more than 350,000 African Americans were drafted for the American Expeditionary Force (AEF); roughly 50,000 of them were sent to fight on the French and Belgian fronts in the summer of 1918. World War II saw an even greater mobilization of African Americans for the cause of freedom and democracy. More than a million black soldiers served in the U.S. armed forces, and, unlike during World War I, when most of them had worked behind the front lines as stevedores, servants, and construction workers, an increasing number of them now fought in combat units. Given the severe destruction of World War II and its enormous causalities, the U.S. armed forces could no longer afford to uphold their established practices of racist discrimination, such as segregated units, the refusal to promote blacks to officer's ranks, or not using blacks in combat units. In both world wars, African Americans not only contributed their share to the American war effort as soldiers but also as workers in war industries.

The African American contributions to and sacrifices in both world wars not only deepened the American dilemma, but they also boosted the determination among African Americans to fight the system of legal segregation and racist discrimination at home. To push their cause and mobilize support, civil rights activists exploited the subversive potential of American Exceptionalism.

A first powerful articulation of this new determination was W. E. B. Du Bois's piece "Returning Soldiers," published in *The Crisis* in May 1919. Stating that tens of thousands of black men had "fought gladly and to the last drop of blood" against "German race arrogance" and "for America and her highest ideals," he contrasted this with the reality of race relations in the U.S. In defending democracy abroad, Du Bois pointed out, black soldiers had also helped defend a "dominant southern oligarchy entrenched in Washington" and the America *it* stood for, an America "that represents and gloats in lynching, disfranchisement, caste, brutality and devilish insult." Identifying the African American GIs as "Soldiers of Democracy," Du Bois said that they would be "cowards and jackasses," if they, now that the war was over, did not "marshal every ounce" of their "brain and brawn to fight a sterner, longer, more unbending battle against the forces of hell in our own land." He concluded: "We return. We return from fighting. We return fighting. Make way for Democracy! We saved it in France, and by the Great Jehovah, we will save it in the United States of America, or know the reason why."

World War II made African Americans even more determined to end racist discrimination at home. This war, which was not only a war against right-wing totalitarianism but also, explicitly, against Nazi racism, questioned the ideology of white supremacy and the racist premises on which it rested even more than World War I had done. From early on in the war, black leaders and black media were calling for a "Double Victory" that should encompass both the victory over the Axis powers abroad as well as over Jim Crow at home. The slogan was coined by the African American newspaper *The Pittsburgh Courier* on February 7, 1942, in response to the letter, "Should I Sacrifice to Live 'Half American?'" written by twenty-six-year-old reader James G. Thompson. Calls for legal equality for African Americans at home became increasingly louder in the course of World War II, and they became even more assertive after 1945, when the postwar situation gave way to the Cold War constellation that witnessed the U.S. as protector of the "Free World" involved in a global struggle against another enemy challenging American Exceptionalism and its ideological premises: communism.

The Cold War, explained in greater detail in chapter 5, was a global rivalry between liberal democracy and Soviet-style communism. It turned Jim Crow segregation into a global problem for the U.S. No longer just a matter of home rule, the continuing legal discrimination against African Americans created a multitude of negative images of the U.S. abroad, and it seriously undermined America's position and credibility as world leader. How could a country that was working hard to export freedom, democracy, and free-market capitalism all over the world to contain communism possibly afford a system of racist discrimination at home without destroying the moral authority behind its leadership claim? In the Cold War context, the American dilemma took on a global dimension.

Internationally, the U.S. was faced with increasingly massive criticism. The Soviet Union used every opportunity it could find to exploit the ideological contradictions of the supposedly superior American way of life for its own propagandistic purposes. Diplomats from Third World countries like Pakistan, India, and Burma repeatedly rubbed salt into the open wound of America's body politic, but America's Western allies also charged the U.S. with hypocrisy. Segregation, Walter Lippmann wrote in an article titled "Today and Tomorrow: The Grace of Humility" for the *Washington Post* on September 24, 1957, "mocks us and haunts us whenever we become eloquent and indignant in the United Nations." Referring to Jim Crow legislation, Lippmann continued: "The caste system in this country [. . .] is an enormous, indeed an almost insuperable, obstacle to our leadership in the cause of freedom and human equality." The Cold War thus magnified the problem of segregation, and it questioned all claims to exceptionalism that motivated and justified the U.S. global struggle for freedom and against Soviet totalitarianism.

AMERICAN EXCEPTIONALISM AND THE CIVIL RIGHTS MOVEMENT OF THE 1950S AND 1960S

The experience of two world wars, the ideological energy of the Cold War, and the fact that the vast majority of blacks continued to live in dire poverty in a society that, due to the lasting economic boom of the 1950s and 1960s, was becoming more and more affluent fueled the transformation of the African American civil rights movement in the postwar era. Prior to 1945, the civil rights movement had not been a mass movement generating much public attention. The National Association for the Advancement of Colored People (NAACP) was an alliance of educated elites, and its activities primarily unfolded as consciousness-raising efforts among the black community and a tedious march through the courts. This changed substantially in the 1950s, when millions of blacks took to the streets, putting their bodies on the line to claim their freedom, willing to suffer beatings and other violent acts of white racists, and tacitly accepting jail for their conscious violation of the Jim Crow laws. The new appeal of the movement went hand in hand with new forms of protest that required mass action like sit-ins, boycotts, protest marches, or Freedom Rides. Many of these direct-action campaigns reached a nationwide audience through the new technology of television, which was spreading like wildfire in the 1950s. Television, for the first time in U.S. history, created a national audience where there had only been highly fragmented local and regional ones before. It allowed the whole nation to witness directly the structural violence of Jim Crow segregation and the hate potential of racism.

The transformation of the civil rights movement after 1945 was also driven by a new type of leader. The NAACP had recruited its members from intellectual circles and did not really have a prominent position in the everyday lives of the vast majority of African Americans. The NAACP's language of protest was mostly academic, legalistic, dry, and uninspiring, and most of the leading NAACP activists were past their prime in the 1950s and 1960s. In contrast, the most prominent leaders of the postwar civil rights movement were young and charismatic, many of them serving as ministers in black congregations. Being part of the rich and powerful tradition of religious oratory, these leaders created a new language of protest interspersed with biblical vocabulary, images, and metaphors.

This is the context of the March on Washington of August 28, 1963, which, to this day, is the largest protest action in U.S. history. On this occasion, Martin Luther King Jr. gave his seminal "I Have a Dream" speech. By 1963, King had become the face and the voice of the civil rights movement, and he was introduced by A. Philip Randolph as the "moral leader of our nation," when he mounted the rostrum at the Lincoln Memorial at the end of a long day of protest to deliver what is clearly a masterpiece of American oratory. In it, King exploited the subversive potential of American Exceptionalism to its fullest extent, demanding the immediate end of Jim Crow segregation, and outlining a powerful vision of an integrated society in which blacks and whites interacted on the basis of equal rights and opportunities.

Already with his first sentence, King established a connection between August 1963 and the Declaration of Independence that defined the exceptionalist promise of America. "Five score years ago, a great American, in whose symbolic shadow we stand today, signed the Emancipation Proclamation," King said, and with this, he was referring to Abraham Lincoln and his deed of 1863. Using the opening words "five score years ago," King also played with Lincoln's iconic "four score and seven years ago" of the Gettysburg Address that had established a direct link between 1863 and 1776. The formulation "five score years ago" thus reaches from 1963 all the way back to July 4, 1776.

Moving on with his speech, King elaborated on the stark contrasts between the promise of freedom and self-determination laid down in both the Declaration of Independence and the Emancipation Proclamation, on the one hand, and the ongoing marginalization of African Americans, on the other. America's blacks, King said, were "sadly crippled by the manacles of segregation and the chains of discrimination," were living "on a lonely island of poverty in the midst of a vast ocean of material prosperity," and found themselves exiles in their own land.

The reality of racial discrimination thus destroyed all of America's exceptionalist potential. As long as the U.S. did not live up to the universal ideals of its founding credo, exceptionalism remained something that still lay ahead. However, King showed himself convinced that the U.S. indeed could live up to its own idealistic claims; the way to do it was to take the universalism of their founding ideas seriously, end racist discrimination, and include African Americans in the civil rights consensus.

That is why he identified the Declaration of Independence and the U.S. Constitution as "promissory note[s]" written by "the architects of our republic" stating "that all men, yes, black men as well as white men, would be guaranteed the 'unalienable Rights' of 'Life, Liberty and the pursuit of Happiness.'" As the U.S. had "defaulted on this promissory note" as far as African Americans were concerned, they had now come to Washington, DC, "to cash this check" that was to redeem the promise of a life led in liberty and self-determination and "to make justice a reality for all of God's children."

Suggesting that 1963 was "not an end, but a beginning," King went on to say that a growing number of whites had "come to realize that their destiny is tied up with our destiny. And they have come to realize that their freedom is inextricably bound to our freedom." America's exceptionalism would thus materialize only in a racially integrated society in which all members enjoyed the same natural rights that formed the core of America's founding credo. "I have a dream," King exclaimed, "that one day this nation will rise up and live out the true meaning of its creed: 'We hold these truths to be self-evident, that all men are created equal.'" He thus was right in arguing that his dream was "deeply rooted in the American dream."

The realization of that dream would deeply transform American society as it then existed insofar as "the sons of former slaves and the sons of former slave owners" would be able "to sit down together at the table of brotherhood." It would turn the state of Mississippi, then a state "sweltering with the heat of injustice, sweltering with the heat of oppression," into "an oasis of freedom and justice," and it would create a society whose members would "not be judged by the color of their skin but by the content of their character." To realize its exceptionalist potential, so King argued, America had to turn his dream into a reality. "And if America is to be a great nation," he said, "this must become true."

The March on Washington was the culmination of a decade of direct-action protests, and was a powerful demonstration of the civil rights movement's broad popular support that helped clear the path to the Civil Rights Act of 1964 and the Voting Rights Act of 1965. This legislation ended de jure discrimination against African Americans and secured them equality of opportunity. Both acts changed the lives of many African Americans in several important respects. One of the most important changes occurred in the field of education. In the fifty years since the passing of both laws, financial aid available to blacks grew, predominantly white universities were increasingly willing to admit black students, and a host of affirmative action programs in the field of education worked to right some of the wrongs of the past. As a result, there was significant growth in the number of black children completing high school; also, the percentage of African Americans graduating from college has risen exponentially since the 1960s.

As improved educational credentials for blacks and a greater willingness of employers to treat blacks equitably led to better-paying jobs, the material situation of African Americans improved. With more and more African Americans working as physicians, lawyers, professors, or officers in the armed forces, incomes rose and standards of living improved. This went hand in hand with a new presence and visibility of African Americans in top-ranking positions. A rising number of blacks Americans elected to public offices, and in 2009, Barack Obama became the first black person to be inaugurated to the office of U.S. president. Even more remarkable is the fact that he was reelected in 2012. Looking back at the civil rights movement from this angle, it appears to be a successful struggle for equal opportunities that has the potential of reaffirming notions of American Exceptionalism.

Not surprisingly, it was Obama himself who frequently used the fact of his being elected to speak of America as an exceptional country. Actually, he was the first president since Ronald Reagan to publicly use the term American Exceptionalism. Time and again, as Donald Pease writes in his book *The New American Exceptionalism*, Obama represented his own biography as the manifestation of three core ideas: "the immigrant's dream of escape from economic poverty and political persecution, the minoritized American's endlessly deferred dream of 'one day' being included within the American dream, and the white middle-class Americans' dream of future prosperity."

When he announced his candidacy for the presidency on February 10, 2007, Obama, standing at the Old State Capitol in Springfield, Illinois, where Abraham Lincoln had begun his political career, had already skillfully run the gamut of American Exceptionalism. Wanting to "play a small part in building a better America," Obama found the "genius of our Founders" in the fact that "they designed a system of government that can be changed." He went on to recall the major transformational crises of U.S. history and how they all contributed to America's exceptionality. "In the face of tyranny, a band of patriots brought an empire to its knees. In the face of secession, we unified a nation and set the captives free. In the face of Depression, we put people back to work and lifted millions out of poverty," Obama said; he continued: "We welcomed immigrants to our shores. We opened railroads to the west. We landed a man on the moon. And we heard a King's call to 'let justice roll down like water, and righteousness like a mighty stream.'"

The story of American Exceptionalism that Obama told on the steps of the Old State Capitol in Springfield was one of slavery, discrimination, racism, and brutal violence, but it was also a story of a continued "march for freedom" that overcame all of these problems to unify the nation and help build America's greatness. Abraham Lincoln had his doubts, defeats, and setbacks, Obama said, but "through his will and his words, he moved a nation and helped free a people," which is why Americans were "no longer divided, North and South, slave and free." Framing his candidacy as an "improbable quest," he asked his followers whether they, like himself, felt "destiny calling," and saw "a future of endless possibility stretching before us." Should this be the case, Obama said that he was "ready to take up the cause, and march with you, and work with you" to "finish the work that needs to be done, and usher in a new birth of freedom on this Earth."

Once elected president, Obama continued to work as interpreter-in-chief of American Exceptionalism. Seven years into his presidency, he gave one of his best speeches in Selma, Alabama, on March 7, 2015. His "Remarks at the 50th Anniversary of the Selma to Montgomery Marches" commemorated a pivotal event of the civil rights movement when six hundred peaceful protesters, trying to cross Edmund Pettus Bridge on their fifty-mile march to Montgomery for voting rights, were brutally attacked by police officers with billy clubs and tear gas. Looking back on March 7, 1965, Obama identified Selma as a place where America's destiny had been decided. "In one afternoon 50 years ago, so much of our turbulent history—the stain of slavery and anguish of civil war; the yoke of segregation and tyranny of Jim Crow; the death of four little girls in Birmingham; and the dream of a Baptist preacher—all that history met on this bridge."

In Obama's view, the struggle for African American civil rights was "a contest to determine the true meaning of America," and this true meaning for Obama, like for the civil rights activists of the 1960s, was "the idea of a just America and a fair America, an inclusive America, and a generous America." That idea, in Obama's view of U.S. history, had "ultimately triumphed." The civil rights activists had had "enormous faith" in God and America when they embarked on their freedom struggle, Obama said. "They marched as Americans who had endured hundreds of years of brutal violence, countless daily indignities—but they didn't seek special treatment, just the equal treatment promised to them almost a century before."

Obama went on to argue that what happened at Selma fifty years ago was very American, in that it was a great "expression of faith in the American experiment" demonstrating "the belief that America is not yet finished, that we are strong enough to be self-critical, that each successive generation can look upon our imperfections and decide that it is in our power to remake this nation to more closely align with our highest ideals." The Selma protests were "not some outlier in the American experience" but rather the "manifestation of a creed written into our founding documents: 'We the People . . . in order to form a more perfect union.' 'We hold these truths to be self-evident, that all men are created equal.'" Taking his own political biography as evidence substantiating his views, Obama portrayed the civil rights struggle as a success story born from the American love of liberty that effected an unprecedented presence of African Americans in boardrooms, on the bench, and in "elected office from small towns to big cities; from the Congressional Black Caucus all the way to the Oval Office."

However, Obama also confronted the persistence of racism in the U.S. Giving his speech just days after the Justice Department, investigating the police shootings at Ferguson, Missouri, that killed an unarmed black teenager, had excoriated the town's police department as a hotbed of racist oppression, Obama addressed the issue of police brutality, and "rejected the notion that nothing's changed. What happened in Ferguson may not be unique, but it's no longer endemic. It's no longer sanctioned by law or by custom. And before the Civil Rights Movement, it most surely was."

Speaking about a "long journey toward freedom" structured by occasional disruptions, Obama characterized America as "a constant work in progress" leading to the gradual but steady expansion of the "boundaries of freedom." Obama argued that everybody who risked everything to realize America's promise showed "what it means to love America. That's what it means to believe in America. That's what it means when we say America is exceptional." Although he acknowledged that America's "march is not yet finished," Obama still argued that Americans were nearing its end. "Two hundred and thirty-nine years after this nation's founding," he said, "our union is not yet perfect, but we are getting closer." This, in Obama's view, defined the very exceptionality of America—the fact that it was getting there, that it was ceaselessly working to realize its promise.

Black critics of Obama like Columbia University professor Frederick Harris, Georgetown University's Michael Eric Dyson, or black feminist Brittney Cooper, and other liberal intellectuals, black and white, have criticized Obama for his paradoxical version of American Exceptionalism and charged him with abandoning his focus on racial inequality and blinding the nation to the multiple patterns and structures of continuing racist discrimination against African Americans. These patterns become manifest in their higher poverty rates and lower median incomes, their significant underrepresentation in well-paying jobs, and their grotesque overrepresentation in America's prison population, or in the de facto segregation of the housing market that keeps African Americans trapped either in isolated rural areas or in urban ghettos with their vicious cycles of poverty, welfare dependency, crime, drug addiction, and AIDS. Seen against the backdrop of the continuing racial inequalities in contemporary U.S. society, liberal critics have argued that Obama's reaffirmation of American Exceptionalism encouraged post-racial illusions among white Americans who felt that by voting for Obama, they cleared themselves and the nation of the racist charge and wiped out America's original sins of slavery and racism once and for all. Ironically, Obama himself was acceptable to many whites because they perceived him as an exceptional member of his race, as an exceptional black man to whom racist stereotypes about African Americans did not apply. This brings us to the limits of American Exceptionalism's subversive power.

BLACK NATIONALISM AND THE LIMITS OF AMERICAN EXCEPTIONALISM'S SUBVERSIVE POWER

American Exceptionalism develops its subversive power only in connection with integrationist visions of black emancipation. Integrationism understands integration as the replacement of prejudice and discrimination with colorblind reason, neutrality, and a universally applied natural-rights consensus as the ultimate definition of racial justice. Integrationism denies that race as a category of social distinction matters at all, and it delegitimizes all forms of race consciousness, including black race consciousness, suggesting that all members of a society could and should interact as individuals and members of a common humanity.

The alternative to such a view, which can be encountered in U.S. history since the antebellum period, is black nationalism because it radically questions whether blacks will ever be able to achieve self-determination as long as they live together with whites in one and the same society. Black nationalism doubts whether blacks will ever be fully accepted as equals by whites, and it sees integration as black assimilation to white standards, which in the end forces blacks to give up their racial identity anchored in blackness. Pursuing a race-conscious approach to black liberation, black nationalism seeks to transcend individualist notions of society and sees a widely shared and consciously practiced black group identity as liberating. Along with this goes an analysis of racial injustice that locates racial domination and inequality in the economic base of the historically specific power relations between whites and blacks in America. The social bonds of a race-conscious identity, recognition, and solidarity, therefore, are seen as the very condition of possibility of black emancipation and self-determination. Black nationalism has existed in different shapes and forms in U.S. history since the antebellum period. We have already encountered Martin Delany above. In the urban-industrial world of the twentieth and twenty-first centuries, some form of black nationalism was pursued by activists like Marcus Garvey, W. E. B. Du Bois, the Black Muslims, Malcolm X, Stokely Carmichael, Amiri Baraka, and the Black Panthers, to name a few.

From a black nationalist perspective, American Exceptionalism has nothing to offer for the struggle of black emancipation. This is best demonstrated by Malcolm X, who in his speech "The Ballot or the Bullet," delivered on April 3, 1964, at Cory Methodist Church in Cleveland, Ohio, eloquently rejected all attempts at utilizing ideas, themes, and strands of American Exceptionalism for the African American cause. Identifying himself as "one of the 22 million black people who are the victims of Americanism," he argued that U.S. democracy was "nothing but disguised hypocrisy." Blacks had not seen "any American dream," all they had experienced was "an American nightmare." Along with this, Malcolm X rejected the narrative of American history and the civil rights movement's place in it, as described by Martin Luther King Jr. or Barack Obama. "To those of us whose philosophy is black nationalism," Malcolm X argued, "the only way you can get involved in the civil-rights struggle is give it a new interpretation. That old interpretation excluded us. It kept us out."

From a black nationalist perspective, an exceptionalist reading of the civil rights movement not only kept out African Americans, it was also actually a way to perpetuate white racial dominance and to destroy the black race through forced assimilation to the liberal founding credo of the U.S. Black nationalism's language of protest, therefore, did not even try to appropriate American Exceptionalism to tap its counter-hegemonic power. Rather, it used an altogether different language of protest and pursued an altogether different idea of black emancipation.

In summary, this chapter has shown that by using ideas, concepts, and themes of American Exceptionalism for themselves, activists of the African American civil rights movement embraced the principles of American individualism, the liberal theory of state, and the credo of limited government. From this identification with the core values of the American way of life resulted the enormous transformational power of the civil rights movement, and it was also why it was able to generate support among whites and majorities in the U.S. Congress, where it was, after all, white legislators who passed the Civil Rights Acts. At the same time, this civil rights agenda set very narrow limits on all demands for equitable compensation for past wrongs, group rights, the preferential treatment of hitherto marginalized groups, the redistribution of property, and an active state acting as agent of racial justice. While American

Exceptionalism was a powerful cultural resource for African American activists pursuing integrationist visions of black emancipation, it held nothing in store for race-conscious black nationalists, who suggested that the only path to true black self-determination was a complete separation from white society.

7

Perfectible Union

American Exceptionalism and Reform

THE IDEA OF A PERFECTIBLE UNION is a core theme of American Exceptionalism. Accordingly, America was an ongoing experiment in liberty and self-government that never was quite finished, a promise still awaiting fulfillment. Inseparably connected to it was the conviction that free men and women were capable of shaping their own destiny, and because they were, they *had* to do it and perfect the yet imperfect Union. This mindset triggered, motivated, and structured reform movements of different size, shape, and impact throughout U.S. history. The host of reform initiatives in Jacksonian America, ranging from Sunday school reform and the temperance movement to abolitionism and the emerging women's movement, is what comes to mind immediately, as does the Progressive Era, with its multiple and contradictory quests for social and moral reform to fight the many problems, inequities, and hardships of America's now fully developed industrial society. Finally, the more recent conservative grassroots movement of the New Right, spearheaded by populist activists like Phyllis Schlafly, Jeremy Falwell, Beverly LaHaye, Stephen Bannon, or Donald Trump for that matter, could also be mentioned in this context. Reform movements inspired, driven, and structured by the persuasions of American Exceptionalism can be found in all parts of America's political spectrum. They are not progressive per se, which only shows once more how malleable and politically elusive the idea of American Exceptionalism is.

The reform movements structuring U.S. history are way too different in terms of agendas, membership, character, and form to be discussed in all their details here. That is why this chapter will discuss three exemplary cases highlighting the complex and ambivalent relationship between American Exceptionalism and reform in U.S. history: the early women's movement, the New Deal, and the labor movement.

REMEMBER THE LADIES: AMERICAN EXCEPTIONALISM AND THE QUEST FOR WOMEN'S EMANCIPATION

The American Revolution witnessed the birth of an American feminism that worked to include women in the egalitarian natural-rights ideology proclaimed by the Declaration of Independence, from which they were originally left out. This feminist agenda demanded citizenship for women and their full participation in America's democracy, and it was born from the same spirit of natural-rights liberalism that also informed colonial resistance against England in the last third of the eighteenth century. The revolutionary rhetoric of the defense of freedom and the fight against monarchic despotism led to a general questioning of power relationships, hierarchies, and government in the broadest sense.

This debate also affected gender relationships. None other than Abigail Adams, the wife of the leading revolutionary and second U.S. president-to-be, John Adams, called for a reordering of gender relations under the auspices of America's liberal founding ideology, even before the Declaration of Independence was drafted. In a letter to her husband, who was away from the New England family farm serving as the Massachusetts delegate to the Second Continental Congress, Abigail Adams wrote on March 31, 1776, that she longed for independence to be declared. Writing about the revolutionary rhetoric of freedom, despotism, and tyranny, she famously asked her husband and his co-revolutionaries to "Remember the Ladies, and be more generous and favorable to them than your ancestors. Do not put such unlimited power into the hands of the Husbands. Remember all Men would be tyrants if they could." Should particular "care and attention" not be paid to the women, she continued, they were "determined to foment a Rebel[l]ion" and would not hold themselves "bound by any Laws in which we have no voice, or Representation." In this context, she especially asked for education, as this would enable women to participate in the civic culture of the new republic. Envisioning the future of the U.S. as an exceptional state built on liberty, Abigail Adams wrote to her husband, John, on August 14, 1776: "If we mean to have heroes, statesmen and philosophers, we should have learned women."

This call for female education as the basis for their emancipation and participation in America's democracy was even stronger in Judith Sargent Murray's essay "On the Equality of the Sexes," written in 1790. In it she argued that patriarchy and gender stereotypes portraying women as intellectually inferior to men and incapable of higher learning kept women from developing their full intellectual capabilities. Deconstructing these gender ideas as myths, Murray suggested that women had the same intellectual capabilities as men, which is why they should also be allowed to get education as the basis of a life led in self-determination and self-reliance. Unfolding to a large extent as an educational movement, early American feminism demanded the expansion of women's education not only for their own benefit but also as a means to perpetuate the new republic, because only learned women would be effective "Republican mothers" educating their children to be good, liberty-loving and liberty-defending citizens and future civic leaders. Women's education was thus both a path to female self-determination and a contribution to the ongoing perfection of America's exceptional experiment in liberty.

The feminism of the Early Republic did not confine itself for long to the question of education and informal participation in America's civic culture under the auspices of Republican Motherhood. More and more women began demanding equality before the law, asserted the right to pursue careers outside the home and enter the professions, and asked for participation in public affairs. In the 1830s and 1840s, the feminist energies circulating in America since the Declaration of Independence translated into an institutionalized first women's movement that emerged at the confluence of several reform movements fighting for things like free public schools, improved treatment for the mentally ill, prison reform, the restriction of alcohol consumption, and the abolition of slavery. All of these movements mobilized women for politics in Jacksonian America, and they participated widely in many of them. Especially strong was the interconnection of the abolitionist movement with the emerging fight for women's rights. Lucretia Mott and Elizabeth Cady Stanton were both active in the fight against slavery, only to discover that they were not accepted as equals and were treated as second-class activists by male reformers. Frustrated by being subordinated to male domination and chauvinism, they began thinking about women's rights as an emancipatory cause all its own that would help bring the U.S. closer to its own ideals.

In 1848, Mott and Stanton organized the first ever women's rights convention, meeting on July 19–20 in Seneca Falls, New York. This meeting passed the Declaration of Sentiments drafted by Stanton, who rewrote the Declaration of Independence to include the words "and women," where the founding fathers had only spoken of men. The Declaration of Sentiments thus stated: "We hold these truths to be self-evident: that all men and women are created equal; that they are endowed by their Creator with certain inalienable rights; that among these are life, liberty, and the pursuit of happiness." The Declaration of Sentiments went on to imitate the wording and the line of argumentation of the Declaration of Independence, giving it a feminist twist insofar as men were now charged with working to establish "an absolute tyranny over" women. The facts "submitted to a candid world" to prove this point were, among others, the disenfranchisement of women, the withdrawal from them of the right to property, the law of coverture that denied married women the status of legal personhood, and divorce laws anchored in "the false supposition of the supremacy of man, and giving all power into his hands." Having diagnosed the "entire disfranchisement of one-half the people of this country," and having described the "social and religious degradation" of women to the fullest extent, the signers of the Declaration of Sentiments insisted that women "have immediate admission to all the rights and privileges which belong to them as citizens of these United States."

The Seneca Falls convention also passed a series of resolutions set up by Stanton. The resolutions stated that "woman is man's equal," and declared that all laws that kept women in an inferior state and prevented them from self-determinedly pursuing their notions of a good and happy life had "no force or authority." Speaking of the "equality of human rights," and suggesting that it was time for women to "move in the enlarged sphere" outside the narrow confines of the home, the Seneca Falls convention also resolved that it was the "duty of the women of this country to secure to themselves their sacred right to the elective franchise." The right to vote appeared so outlandish at that time that even a significant minority of the women present at the Seneca Falls convention rejected it. In the end, it was Frederick Douglass, the former slave and famous abolitionist, who persuaded a narrow majority to accept the call for woman suffrage. Still, many Americans of Jacksonian America, men and women alike, were shocked by the Seneca Falls convention, classifying it as a female insurrection, and fearfully anticipating a "Reign of Petticoats."

This did not stop the emerging women's movement in its fight for women's rights. Together with Lucretia Mott and later Susan B. Anthony, Elizabeth Cady Stanton continued to sponsor conventions, write articles, deliver lectures, and appear before legislative bodies to work for better educational opportunities, equal wages, property rights for women, marriage reform, and easier divorce laws. Suffrage, however, was becoming an increasingly important issue, which the more formalized first women's movement began to organize around. The 1850s witnessed a series of eleven National Women's Rights Conventions that embraced women's suffrage with increasing determination, and after the Civil War, two organizations emerged that pursued the single issue of women's suffrage: the National Woman Suffrage Association, formed on May 15, 1869, by Susan B. Anthony and Elizabeth Cady Stanton in New York City, and the American Woman Suffrage Association founded in Boston in November of that year and headed by Lucy Stone as president. On February 18, 1890, the organizations merged to become the National American Woman Suffrage Association (NAWSA), led by Susan B. Anthony until she retired in 1900. Carrie Chapman Catt succeeded her in the office of president of NAWSA.

In their struggle for the vote, America's suffragists exploited the ideas, themes, and language of American Exceptionalism to present women's suffrage as a way to finally perfect a still imperfect union. Their political argumentation unfolded as a feminist reinterpretation of the Declaration of Independence and the U.S. Constitution that aimed to show that the founding credo of natural rights, self-determination, and popular sovereignty had included women all along.

"First let me speak of the constitution of the United States," Isabella Beecher Hooker began her speech, titled "The Constitutional Rights of the Women of the United States," "and assert that there is not a line in it, nor a word, forbidding women to vote; but properly interpreted, that is, interpreted by the Declaration of Independence, and by the assertions of the Fathers, it actually guarantees to women the right to vote in all elections, both state and national." In this address delivered to the founding session of the International Council of Women in March 1888, Hooker reminded her audience that the U.S. Constitution "plainly embraced women in all its provisions."

Hooker appropriated the universalism of the founding documents to expose America's hypocrisy, which undermined its very claim to exceptionality. One could not, Hooker said, proclaim "over the whole earth that governments derive their just powers from the consent of the governed and that taxation without representation is tyranny" and then deprive one-half of the people of representation. With these remarks, Hooker, on the one hand, affirmed the emancipatory promise of the American Revolution, and on the other, questioned the very notion of American Exceptionalism, which would never materialize as long as women continued to be discriminated against.

Carrie Chapman Catt, in her essay "Will of the People," published in *The Forum* magazine in June 1910, gave this argument an even more radical twist when she suggested that for not having enfranchised women so far, the U.S. was actually a backward, barbaric country. Taking women's suffrage as a marker of progress, Catt saw Australia as being far ahead of the U.S. for having already given women the vote. Compared to Australians, Americans, who had enfranchised African Americans, American Indians, and "immigrants from all quarters of the globe" while withholding the vote to women, were "mere democratic masquerade[rs]." While Americans would not hesitate to criticize the "brutal barbarism" of countries like China and Turkey for denying "personal liberty to woman," they obviously had no problem with withholding the vote and full citizenship from their own women.

In all, therefore, suffragists saw themselves as spearheading a movement that would make the U.S. live up to its revolutionary ideals and thereby realize its exceptionalist claims. They linked the sense of mission connected to both the Puritan "city upon a hill" image and Thomas Paine's revolutionary enthusiasm for making the world over to a now-or-never rhetoric that calculated the equal treatment of women as the test that the country had to pass to live up to its own ideals. Already in the "Address to Congress" adopted on May 10, 1866, the Eleventh National Women's Rights Convention held in New York City reminded Americans: "The nations of the earth stand watching and waiting to see if our

Revolutionary idea, 'all men are created equal,' can be realized in government. Crush not, we pray you, the million hopes that hang on our success."

Forty-five years later, Max Eastman, a founding member of the Men's League for Woman Suffrage, established in 1909, made the same argument. In his essay "Is Woman Suffrage Important?" published in the *North American Review* in January 1911, he depicted the U.S. as the "laboratory" for an experiment in freedom that Americans were conducting, and he felt that it was the Americans' "business is to try out the experiment until the last breath of hope is gone out of us." He identified the present situation in 1911 as a serious threat to the successful completion of this experiment. Continuing "to discriminate against an approximate half of the Citizens" was "to betray our hypothesis and destroy our experiment at its crucial point," he wrote.

When Eastman made this claim, the suffrage movement was pushing hard for a constitutional amendment. Before 1900, suffragists had pursued the plan to acquire women's voting rights state by state. In 1890, Wyoming was the first state to grant full participation in all elections, and by 1914, eleven of the forty-eight states of the Union had granted universal suffrage to women. On the eve of World War I, the battle for universal women's suffrage throughout the country was in full swing—but it took the war to generate majorities for an amendment.

President Wilson's agenda of liberal internationalism, which interpreted the war as an ideological fight between liberty and autocracy and expected Americans to fight a war to make the world safe for democracy, significantly deepened America's ideological paradox that women's rights activists had been talking about all along. This was especially true because President Wilson, who ideologized democracy and expected women to do their share for the war effort, continued to oppose women's suffrage. This drew massive criticism from women activists, who picketed the White House carrying banners that compared President Wilson to America's archenemy Kaiser Wilhelm II of Germany. The Poster Record Group 165 of the War Department's Records (General and Special Staff) holds a photo showing an unnamed female suffragist presenting a banner that read: "Kaiser Wilson. Have you forgotten your sympathy with the poor Germans because they were not self-governed? 20.000.000 American Women are not self-governed. Take the beam out of your own eye."

With Germany's defeat and in light of the enormous sacrifices for democracy made by both men and women on the battlefield as well as on the home front, the continued discrimination against women defined a dilemma that could no longer be borne. In 1919, Congress submitted the Nineteenth Amendment, which gave women the vote. It had originally been introduced in Congress in 1878 by Senator Aaron A. Sargent and given to the states for ratification. It was adopted on August 18, 1920, and it read: "The right of citizens of the United States to vote shall not be denied or abridged by the United States or by any State on account of sex." Women's rights activists celebrated it as the completion of America's democracy and the fulfillment of all of its exceptionalist claims.

AMERICAN EXCEPTIONALISM AND SOCIAL REFORM IN AN INDUSTRIAL WORLD

America's democracy was founded in an agrarian world, and the themes, concepts, and narratives of American Exceptionalism were anchored in the experiences of an agrarian republic that was rapidly expanding westward. The tumultuous industrial transformation of the U.S. and the corporate reconstruction of American capitalism that created an economic order dominated by gigantic business enterprises undermined the very foundations of American Exceptionalism. In a business world of brutal cutthroat competition driven by vicious cycles of boom and bust, in an economy in which huge trusts like U.S. Steel, Standard Oil, and the Ford Motor Company monopolized whole segments of the market, and in an industrial society in which business tycoons like Andrew Carnegie, John D. Rockefeller, and Henry Ford amassed enormous fortunes while the vast majority of industrial workers lived in dire poverty with only a small prospect of social improvement—in such a world, the ideas of rugged individualism, self-reliance, equality of opportunity, limited government, and democratic self-determination had seemingly run their course.

Furthermore, the rampant materialism, brutal business practices of unfettered corporate capitalism, and blatant culture of greed that we have come to identify with the Gilded Age gave little reason to posit America's moral superiority vis-à-vis Europe. In *Democratic Vistas*, published in 1871, Walt Whitman presented a sobering diagnosis of the situation in the U.S. The eminent poet, who before the Civil War had sung the most exuberant praises of America's democratic virtues, moral strength, and artistic creativity in *Leaves of Grass*, now spoke of the "depravity of the business classes of our country," whose one sole aim was "pecuniary gain." He saw government in America "saturated in corruption, bribery, falsehood, maladministration," and he felt that America's "best class" was "but a mob of fashionably dress'd speculators and vulgarians."

While writers and other intellectuals criticized and satirized greed and political corruption and characterized it as undermining all claims to exceptionality, the captains of industry cultivated an altogether different perspective on the changes and transformations going on in the U.S. in the last third of the nineteenth century. In his essay "The Gospel of Wealth," written in 1889, none other than Andrew Carnegie, who had pulled himself up on a shoestring to become the master and face of the American steel industry, praised the highly competitive order of corporate America as an indicator and factor of mankind's progress. In his eyes, the industrial order of the U.S. represented the latest and most advanced stage of human development. Adopting ideas of Social Darwinism, Carnegie suggested that the progress of mankind was driven by brutal competition in a relentless struggle for existence that was survived only by the fittest. In his view, business leaders like him were the fittest because they had created huge trusts that had emerged as the last man standing from the competitive struggle for economic survival on the free market.

The evolution of industrial capitalism, therefore, necessarily produced inequalities in terms of wealth, political influence, and social status. Carnegie elaborated on the rigid caste system that sharply distinguished between employers and employees, capital and labor, rich and poor. He clearly saw that the substantial political and social equality of the preindustrial age had in his own time given way to an unequal distribution of wealth and power. This, he felt, was not to be deplored but to be welcomed as the necessary and inevitable result of the "law of competition" promoting human progress. While the struggle for survival driven by the law of competition was, as Carnegie willingly admitted, "hard for the individual, it is best for the race, because it insures the survival of the fittest in every department." In Carnegie's analysis, therefore, business concentration was the inevitable outcome of free-market competition; it put the economic and political power into the hands of a few, which was, he felt, "not only beneficial but essential for the future progress of the race." Industrial capitalism, therefore, produced social inequality, created petrified class societies featuring a class of permanently poor workers who had nothing but their labor to offer, and limited upward social mobility.

In accepting social inequality as a given, Carnegie's views, which were widely circulating among America's middle classes at the turn of the twentieth century, invalidated most of the premises, ideas, and values upon which American Exceptionalism rested. Interestingly enough, the serious threat that the corporate transformation of American capitalism posed to American Exceptionalism was best diagnosed by none other than Herbert Hoover in his book-length essay *American Individualism*, published in 1922. Hoover, a champion of a conservative Republican agenda (and as of 1929, the thirty-first president of the U.S.) would never be suspected of leaning left, yet he felt that the emergence of big business threatened the very foundations of the American way of life anchored in individual liberty, self-determination, and equality of opportunity.

Hoover wrote his piece under the impression of the Great October Revolution in Russia that led to the foundation of the Soviet Union. This new order marked the great alternative to everything the U.S. stood for, and in light of the communist challenge, Hoover confessed that his faith "in the essential truth, strength, and vitality of the developing creed by which we have hitherto lived in this country" was still unbroken. This creed was centered in an individualism that was decidedly American, insofar as it balanced individualism's selfish potential with equality of opportunity, free competition, and service to the community. Behind this assessment was an awareness that an individualism unchecked was prone to produce a destructive egotism that undermined solidarity and dissolved all social cohesion. Key to America's uniqueness was that, while American society was built "UPON THE ATTAINMENT OF THE INDIVIDUAL," it was also safeguarding "TO EVERY INDIVIDUAL AN EQUALITY OF OPPORTUNITY TO TAKE THAT POSITION IN THE COMMUNITY TO WHICH HIS INTELLIGENCE, CHARACTER, ABILITY, AND AMBITION ENTITLE HIM."

It was exactly this value system that was seriously questioned by the corporate reconstruction of American capitalism and the formation of an industrial society in the U.S., as Hoover was willing to admit. Looking back on American history prior to the Civil War, he wrote: "When we were almost wholly an agricultural people our form of organization and administration, both in the governmental and economic fields, could be simple." However, the "enormous shift in growth to industry and commerce" had produced gigantic business enterprises that many denounced as "Frankensteins," Hoover wrote. This concentration of economic power threatened equality of opportunity so that everything depended on whether the corporations could be controlled.

Although Hoover was convinced that big business could be controlled and put to the service of the common good, and although he wholeheartedly embraced the idea and practice of limited government as the American way, Hoover admitted that the future of America's exceptionality depended on whether the government was able to assure equality of opportunity in the industrial world. Government, Hoover wrote, had actually become the "most potent force for maintenance or destruction of our American individualism." He clearly saw the challenge resulting from it: Curbing "the forces in business which would destroy equality of opportunity" and maintaining "the initiative and creative faculties" of the American people were the "twin objects" that needed to be attained through government activity, he suggested. While even a conservative Republican like Herbert Hoover was willing to let government play a greater role in regulating the economy, he remained convinced that it "must keep out of production and distribution of commodities and services." He thus supported the idea of a laissez-faire state that largely refrained from intervening in economic and social processes and that was willing to let the market forces have their way as long as business practices were fair, just, and legal.

It was exactly this agenda that was discredited by the Great Depression of the 1930s. At the time the longest and deepest economic crisis in U.S. history, it was one of the great transformational crises in U.S. history insofar as it led to the foundation of an American-style welfare state under the auspices of the New Deal. This largest social-reform initiative in U.S. history put the idea of government as such on a new footing. The New Deal state, founded under the presidency of Franklin D. Roosevelt, and then gradually expanded under Presidents Harry S. Truman, Dwight D. Eisenhower, John F. Kennedy, and Lyndon B. Johnson, functioned as an agent of economic and social justice that worked to protect wage earners and consumers against the uncertainties and hazards of unregulated free-market capitalism. The New Deal state provided for unemployment insurance and old-age pensions, laid the foundations for a health insurance system, aimed at stabilizing the purchasing power of U.S. citizens, redistributed wealth from the top to the bottom on behalf of social justice, worked to improve the overall living conditions of the wage-earning classes, and aimed at ensuring a minimum standard of living for the poor. In addition, it accepted the right of workers to unionize and bargain collectively, regulated the market to stabilize the economy, defined standards for workplace security and the quality of goods, pushed the rights of consumers, and was active in the field of environmental protection. In short, the New Deal state defined the social-democratic moment of American history, which lasted from 1933 roughly to the end of the 1960s. It was supported by a broad New Deal consensus in the U.S. that let even Republicans like President Eisenhower accept the basic legitimacy and necessity of the welfare state to reform free-market capitalism.

This new thinking about the role of government was a major departure from the traditions of limited government in America; Franklin D. Roosevelt himself privately acknowledged that his agenda was "taking an enormous step away from the philosophy of equalitarianism and laissezfaire." Had that philosophy not been bankrupted by the Great Depression, he went on, Herbert Hoover would still be sitting in the White House.

While the New Deal state may have been a major departure from the traditions of limited government, it was most certainly not a break with the ideas of American Exceptionalism. Quite the contrary, the creation of a welfare state was seen by its proponents as an attempt to secure the foundations and ideological core of the American way of life against those threats emerging from corporate capitalism that even a conservative like Hoover had identified as lethal. The New Deal, therefore, sought to adapt American government to the realities and necessities of an industrial economy in order to keep the American promise of lives led in liberty, self-determination, and the pursuit of happiness.

In his first inaugural address, delivered on March 4, 1933, Franklin D. Roosevelt utilized many exceptionalist ideas and themes to justify his demand for "broad Executive power to wage a war" against the miseries and hardships of the Great Depression. He spoke of the U.S. as a great nation, he mentioned the "perils which our forefathers conquered," and he referenced "the American spirit of the pioneer" as the "way to recovery." Famously, he pointed out that the only thing Americans had to fear was "fear itself." Spreading his contagious optimism, Roosevelt showed himself convinced that the American nation would "revive" and "prosper" through the reform project he was about to initiate.

The Great Depression, in his view, did not come from "failure of substance" and was not a problem inherent to America's political, social, economic, and cultural order. Rather, it was the result of the greed and incompetence of big business elites and the "[p]ractices of the unscrupulous money changers" who had recklessly pursued selfish interests at the expense of the public good. It was now time for a substantial change in business ethics to restore the "ancient truths" of American civilization; this restoration of America to its people should happen through the government.

Roosevelt called for public programs that would put people back to work; stimulate the economy; supervise the sectors of transportation, communications, and public utilities; and regulate the banking sector. In calling for this deep change in government, Roosevelt felt he was covered by the U.S. Constitution, which, in his view, was so "simple and practical" that it could "meet extraordinary needs by changes in emphasis and arrangement without loss of essential form." One could, therefore, redefine the role of government in the existing constitutional frame, and this was what he intended to do. Thus, the U.S. Constitution itself became a manifestation of American Exceptionalism because it was, as Roosevelt said, the "most superbly enduring political mechanism the modern world has produced." These words show that the New Deal was not meant to be a revolution; rather, it aimed at protecting the liberal foundations of the American way of life through welfare-state activity. It developed into, as Jill Quadagno has convincingly argued in her book *The Color of Welfare*, an "Equal Opportunity Welfare State" that worked to guarantee equal chances to all members of an industrial society but that largely refrained from universal social programs and direct payments to the poor.

During the Cold War, the New Deal was taken to new dimensions with the Fair Deal under President Harry S. Truman. In his State of the Union address of January 5, 1949, the thirty-third president proposed his ambitious program of wide-ranging social legislation that included national health insurance, public housing, civil rights legislation, and federal aid for education. While the New Deal was started to fight the economic hardships of the Great Depression, Truman's Fair Deal was not primarily about overcoming scarcity. Rather, it aimed at having as many Americans as possible participate in America's wealth. Truman thus envisioned an affluent society integrated by a widely shared prosperity produced by a continuous economic growth stimulated by the welfare state.

Looking back on the reform agenda of the past sixteen years, Truman stated in his address that Americans had "been creating a society which offers new opportunities for every man to enjoy his share of the good things of life." Under the auspices of the New Deal reforms, Americans had "abandoned the 'trickledown' concept of national prosperity. Instead, we believe that our economic system should rest on a democratic foundation and that wealth should be created for the benefit of all." Through the welfare measures of the Fair Deal, Truman sought to further improve this new society created by the New Deal. Poverty, he said, was just as wasteful and just as unnecessary as "preventable disease." America's common resources should be used "to help one another in the hazards and struggles of individual life," and a U.S. citizen should not be barred "from an education, or from good health, or from a job that he is capable of performing" for whatever reason. The creation of such a society, Truman concluded, demanded "the best efforts of every citizen in every walk of life," but it also imposed "increasing responsibilities on the Government."

With this, Truman embraced the New Deal legacy and radicalized its idea of a strong government that was acting on behalf of social, economic, and also racial justice. However, Truman was very keen to point out that this new understanding of the role of government was no radical break with American values but, rather, that it served to protect them. "In this society," Truman said, "we are conservative about the values and principles which we cherish; but we are forward-looking in protecting those values and principles and in extending their benefits." He thus wanted the government to closely cooperate with industry, labor, and farmers to keep the U.S. economy "running at full speed." At the same time, the government had to see "that every American has a chance to obtain his fair share of our increasing abundance. These responsibilities go hand in hand." America could not maintain prosperity without a "fair distribution of opportunity" and "a widespread consumption of the products of our factories and farms." Social reform under the auspices of the Fair Deal not only aimed at protecting wage-earners and consumers against the hazards and unpredictabilities of industrial capitalism, it also served to hold the consumers in the market by stabilizing their purchasing power even in times of unemployment and economic downturn.

The social reform impulse reached its climax with U.S. president Lyndon B. Johnson's vision of a "Great Society" and his fight against poverty in the U.S. In his State of the Union address of January 8, 1964, Johnson declared his administration's "unconditional war on poverty," and he asked Congress to legislate the most far-reaching package of social legislation in U.S. history. Federal spending for education, health, retraining of the unemployed, and help for the economically and the physically handicapped, for Johnson, was a way to help people realize the American Dream. Poverty prevented people from doing just that, Johnson argued, which is why his legislative program would serve to

> help each and every American citizen fulfill his basic hopes—his hopes for a fair chance to make good; his hopes for fair play from the law; his hopes for a full-time job on full-time pay; his hopes for a decent home for his family in a decent community; his hopes for a good school for his children with good teachers; and his hopes for security when faced with sickness or unemployment or old age.

When he developed his plan for a "war on poverty," Johnson was driven by the utopian vision of a "nation that is free from want and a world that is free from hate—a world of peace and justice, and freedom and abundance, for our time and for all time to come." While this may appear to be just another iteration of the utopian longing characteristic of American Exceptionalism, the Cold War context in which Johnson uttered it gave it a new twist. In light of the global antagonism between liberal market democracies and communism, Johnson identified the year 1964 as offering "a unique opportunity and obligation—to prove the success of our system; to disprove those cynics and critics at home and abroad who question our purpose and our competence." The success of the American system, therefore, was defined insofar as it managed to eradicate poverty and spread prosperity to all strata of society.

The welfare programs that he advocated, in Johnson's view, offered a chance to realize the utopian world of a Great Society integrated on the basis of liberty, peace, and prosperity for all. However, since the year 1964 offered this "unique opportunity," Americans also had the obligation to seize it. Should they fail, should Americans "fritter and fumble away our opportunity in needless, senseless quarrels between Democrats and Republicans, or between the House and the Senate, or between the South and North, or between the Congress and the administration, then history will rightfully judge us harshly." This combination of a sense of mission with the possibility of failure is a conceptual link written into American Exceptionalism encountered time and again in this book. It can be traced all the way back to John Winthrop.

In all, therefore, the New Deal impulse for social reform rested on the conviction that it required an active and interventionist government working to regulate free-market capitalism on behalf of stability, justice, and equal chances to preserve and expand the American promise in the world of corporate capitalism. While the New Dealers thus tapped American Exceptionalism as a cultural resource to justify the welfare state, the reformist potential emerging from exceptionalist mindsets reached its limits at the point where reforms moved beyond the pursuit of equal opportunity into the fields of racial injustice and civil rights, universal social welfare programs, direct services and payments to the poor, and the redistribution of wealth from top to bottom.

Some of the major questions discussed in connection with American Exceptionalism relate to the welfare state. Why was it never fully developed in the U.S. as it was in Europe? Why were most welfare programs underfunded? Why did the New Deal fail to consolidate wide-ranging universal welfare programs? Why was the welfare state contested in U.S. political culture from the start, and remained so throughout the Cold War, until Ronald Reagan and the New Right began dismantling it? The answers to these questions are manifold and far too complex to be sufficiently discussed here. In the context of this book, however, two things should be highlighted.

First, the liberal reformulation of American Exceptionalism justifying the welfare state, born from the economic catastrophe of the Great Depression and nurtured by the Cold War conflict between liberal market democracies and communism, never took the same deep roots in

America's political culture as the version presented by Herbert Hoover in *American Individualism* did. A conservative opposition against the New Deal emerged already in the 1930s. In 1935–1936, the U.S. Supreme Court declared key legislation of the New Deal, the National Recovery Act and the Agricultural Adjustment Act, unconstitutional. In 1942, Representative Charles Gifford, a Republican from Massachusetts, called on Congress to "win the war from the New Deal." In 1964, Barry Goldwater, a Republican senator from Arizona, ran for president on an anti-government agenda that brought out two figureheads of the emerging New Right, Ronald Reagan and Phyllis Schlafly, in support for him. Eventually, it was Reagan, who in his first inaugural address of January 20, 1981, spoke of America as an "exemplar of freedom" and a "beacon of hope," only to argue that government was not the solution to the problem, but rather that it was the problem.

Second, the coalition carrying out the New Deal for three decades was a paradoxical mix of Southern Democrats, industrial wage workers from the North, farmers, small businessmen, African Americans, and other minorities. It thus united racial conservatives from the Jim Crow South with the Northern industrial working class, which (due to the Great Migration of African Americans from the rural South to the industrial centers of the North) included a growing number of blacks. In this constellation, Southern Democrats from the still "Solid South" defined the limits of the welfare legislation and were a bastion of resistance against fighting racial injustice through the federal government pushing for equal opportunities for African Americans. This shaped the evolution of the American welfare state to a great extent. While the New Deal thus worked to protect the industrial working class and improve its standard of living, at the same time, it reinforced and even deepened racial segregation because of how the federal welfare programs, labor policies, and housing policies were set up, administered, and executed. Jill Quadagno has explained this in great detail in her widely received study *The Color of Welfare: How Racism Undermined the War on Poverty*.

What is important for us to note is that the welfare state largely remained accepted as long as it did not challenge America's racial order anchored in white supremacy. When the welfare state started to become an agent of racial justice—and this happened with President Johnson's War on Poverty—the New Deal coalition splintered, and support for reform legislation waned. The antipoverty programs became linked to the question of civil rights in that being poor and being black were frequently the same thing in the 1960s. In fighting poverty, the Johnson administration aimed at providing economic security to African Americans so that they could compete without impediment on the basis of equal opportunities and fairness. In all, therefore, President Johnson's ambitious welfare agenda sought to end the racial bias of the New Deal state, and in doing so, it alienated large numbers of southern Democrats who went on to become key players in the emerging New Right. This new conservative movement was born at the confluence of a fiscal and social conservatism that opposed government interventions of all forms with a racial conservatism that remained publicly committed to racial equality while opposing a forceful implementation of civil rights legislation.

If one looks at the political struggle over the welfare state through the lens of American Exceptionalism, it becomes clear once more that it was fueled, validated, and legitimated by two mutually exclusive interpretations of the concept. The liberal camp interpreted the welfare state as the means to perfect an imperfect union and to finally fulfill America's promise of self-determination and prosperity in an inclusive society organized around human dignity. In contrast, the new conservatism born from the spirit of fundamental opposition to the New Deal state championed a version of American Exceptionalism that embraced the principles of individual liberty, equality of opportunity, private property, and anti-statism to reject the very premises of social reform and the welfare state as an aberration from the true American way of life. Although the conservative interpretation of American Exceptionalism comes across as universal and colorblind, it is inseparably connected to an unwritten subtext of white, Anglo-Saxon, and Protestant hegemony, and it can easily collude with notions of white supremacy.

WHY IS THERE NO SOCIALISM IN THE U.S.? AMERICAN EXCEPTIONALISM AND THE LABOR MOVEMENT

Werner Sombart had a problem. Conceiving of the U.S. as "capitalism's land of promise," where everything was working to let capitalism reach "the most advanced state," Sombart was puzzled by the lack of a strong socialist labor movement in America. Why was this a problem for the colorful German professor of sociology, who never set foot on North American soil? Well, the history of industrialization in Europe and the teachings of Karl Marx both suggested that the purer the capitalism developed in a country, the stronger the class-conscious, socialist labor movement would be. Under the premises of this thinking, the U.S., being "more suited than any other country to provide capitalism with the means for conquering the world," should also have the strongest socialist labor movement in the world. Yet wherever Sombart looked in the U.S., he found neither strong industrial unions nor a powerful socialist party supported by a class-conscious industrial working class. The Marxist "doctrine of the inevitable Socialist future" was, as Sombart had to admit, "refuted by the facts" of American life.

This let Sombart raise the question of *Why is there no Socialism in the United States?* in a book published in 1906, and this question leads to the core of this section's problem: American labor exceptionalism, which Kim Voss, in her 1993 study *The Making of American Exceptionalism*, identified as the "unexpected combination of weak working-class institutions and unions' political conservatism." While labor movements in Europe created strong unions organizing all industrial workers and supported political parties pushing for the reform of capitalism, the nationalization of key industries, and the redistribution of wealth from top to bottom, the labor movement in the U.S. generally was not a very powerful agent of progressive social reform effectively promoting collective solidarity and a class-conscious opposition to the capitalist system.

The trade unions operating under the umbrella of the American Federation of Labor (AFL) organized only skilled workers, who were always a minority in an industrial workforce dominated by unskilled and semiskilled workers. The AFL unions were preoccupied with bread-and-butter issues. They worked to get higher wages and maximum fringe benefits for their members. They fought to reduce working hours, improve working conditions, and raise safety standards in the workplace—but AFL unions did not see capitalism as the root of all workers' misery. They basically accepted the capitalist system and strove to better the living and working conditions of their members *within* the system. The AFL unions generally embraced the philosophy of a trade unionism that tried to balance the employers' monopoly of production with a union monopoly of labor. In a letter written to federal judge Peter Grosscup in September 1894, Samuel Gompers, founder and longtime president of the AFL, argued that trade unions were of "service to the laboring man" within the industrial order, and "not a menace to the lawful institutions" of the U.S. The industrial transformation of the country had "utilized and monopolized" the vast natural and social resources of the U.S. "for the benefit of the comparative few." In light of this economic concentration, workers had to learn "that only by the power of organization, and common concert of action, can either their manhood be maintained, their rights to life (work to sustain it) be recognized, and liberty and rights secured." The formation of huge business conglomerations and trusts had weakened the individual, depriving him of all influence "in deciding what the wages, hours of toil and conditions of employment shall be." How could the "old siren song that the workingman should depend entirely upon his own 'individual effort'" possibly still be sung, Gompers wanted to know. Denying that labor had any "quarrel with capital, as such," Gompers saw the role of trade unions in the industrial world as necessary and useful institutions standing for "right, for justice, for liberty," and working to have this recognized for the workers, too. With this political language and agenda, Gompers and the trade unions basically accepted the liberal core values that America's democracy was built on. They did not want to change the system but only secure the worker's right and opportunity to participate in it. In the long run, AFL unions indeed managed to better conditions for their members, but they left the vast majority of workers out, and in the pursuit of their goals, they embraced both xenophobic and racist practices. The AFL was all for immigration restriction, and it refused to accept blacks into its ranks. This, the AFL did both to exclude from the labor market potential competitors willing to work for less.

While American labor history did witness the emergence of radical unions like the Knights of Labor or the Industrial Workers of the World (IWW) that were dedicated to the idea of organizing *all* workers of an industry, they were transient phenomena on the radical fringe of the American working class. The IWW never had more than five thousand to ten thousand members at any given time, and membership was fluid. Furthermore, there was a Socialist Party of America. It was formed by a merger of several socialist groups in 1901, and was quite active and visible in the years prior to World War I. The party embraced a rhetoric and practice of class struggle, and wanted to overthrow the system of wage labor and end private ownership of the means of production. Its strongman Eugene V. Debs, one of the founding members of the IWW, identified capitalism as an oppressive system, and he felt that the labor movement should do more than work to increase wages, shorten working hours, and improve the living conditions of blue-collar workers. Rather, it should destroy capitalism to liberate the working class. With this agenda, the Socialist Party generated some limited success. In the years before the onset of World War I, the Socialist Party had more than a thousand elected officeholders in more than three hundred municipalities throughout the U.S.; Debs ran for president altogether five times. In 1912, he received more than nine hundred thousand votes, which to this day is the best performance of a Socialist candidate in a national election. However, it was not more than 6 percent of the popular vote. Unlike Socialist parties in Europe, the Socialist Party of America did not have a mass base; party membership reached its peak in 1912 at roughly 113,000 members.

Only during the Great Depression did industrial unionism, as institutionalized in the Congress of Industrial Organizations (CIO) led by John L. Lewis, take root in the U.S. This was the result of both the heavy strike activities of the 1930s triggered by the desperate economic situation and the New Deal legislation. The seminal National Labor Relations Act of 1935 (Wagner Act) guaranteed workers the right to freely unionize, engage in collective bargaining, and take collective strike actions to realize their goals. The New Deal finally accepted the unions as representatives of the working class and made them partners in a cooperative partnership between capital, labor, and the government that served to stabilize the free-market economy, promote growth, and spread prosperity as widely as possible within American society. In the 1930s, the AFL and CIO labor unions, which in 1955 united as the AFL-CIO, thus became integral parts of the New Deal state that dished out social benefits to the wage earners, to the effect that a reformed free-market capitalism was restored in a time when the capitalist system as such was shaken to its very foundations. In the 1930s, the labor unions became thoroughly intertwined with the American welfare state and the New Deal consensus on which it rested, and they shared its fate. The conservative backlash against the New Deal, which we discussed in the preceding section, unfolded to a large extent as the eventually successful attempt to reduce union influence and push back the gains regarding industrial democracy. In all, therefore, the militancy of the American working class, as became manifest in a long and continuous series of walkouts and violent strikes, never translated into strong labor unions and Socialist parties in the U.S. that could have carried a sustained effort of progressive social reform.

In 1906, Sombart was the first to diagnose this exceptional trajectory of American labor history, and his question *Why is there no Socialism in the United States?* has structured the evolution of American labor history as an academic discipline to a very large extent. Labor history has given profound, complex, but also contradictory, answers to why the labor movement in the U.S. developed the way it did, and to what extent it indeed was exceptional compared to labor movements in Europe. Labor historians have identified the split between skilled and unskilled workers as well as the ethnic and linguistic diversity of the labor force as the most important factors hampering the formation of an overarching working-class solidarity. They have also pointed to the determination of American businesses to keep the unions out of their shops. Compared to employers in Europe, American employers were much better organized, fought more bitterly against the unions, and brought more resources to the battle against them. In addition, the formal neutrality of U.S. governments in labor disputes effectively helped the employers' side. Before the New Deal, state authorities never took action to neutralize intransigent employers nor to mediate in labor conflicts, let alone to intervene on behalf of workers' interests. At the same time, American courts generally leaned toward the employers' side, helping them break strikes through court injunctions.

Overall, therefore, it appears that American capital countered the labor movement with effective organization of its own to keep unions out, and in their struggle against the unions, American employers could count on labor politics and an institutional environment of a state that, prior to the New Deal, was generally more favorable to the interests of capital than to those of labor. American labor exceptionalism, therefore, was not foreordained. Rather, it was made, and made from the contexts of U.S. history.

This chapter, however, is not primarily interested in the structures, institutional patterns, economic constellations, and other historical factors explaining the distinctive trajectory of American labor history. Rather, it deals with how American Exceptionalism, as a mindset and cognitive map, as an identity narrative, and as a form of nationalism, impacted the history of the labor movement in the U.S. In this context, the chapter argues that many of the American workers and most of the labor organizations accepted the premises of the concept. They thus tended to embrace a meritocratic work ethic that understood material wealth as a proof of achievement, merit, and superior talent, while to be poor was a sign of personal failure. Hardship, misfortune, and poverty were thus not blamed on the economic system but on individual shortcomings and deficiencies. At the same time, many American workers shared a strong nationalist pride in the U.S. as an exceptional nation they considered themselves to be part of.

Aspects of this were already presented by Sombart himself, who portrayed the U.S. as a country of widespread materialism, where everybody was striving to get rich, and where success was measured solely in terms of monetary value. Sombart found that neither the great majority among America's wage laborers nor the most important of their leaders in the national unions embraced the spirit of socialism. One felt, he wrote, that the American workers generally were "not on the whole dissatisfied with the present conditions of things." Rather, they had a "most rosy and optimistic conception of the world." Among them was none of the "envy, embitterment, and hatred against all those who have more and who live extravagantly" that was the source of class-conscious opposition to industrial capitalism in Europe. In Sombart's view, American workers had internalized the American way of life's "restless striving after profit." They had subscribed to America's "commercial drive and the passion for business," trying to earn as much through their work as possible, while, at the same time, striving to "be as unrestrained as possible."

This defined, according to Sombart, the "fundamentally capitalist disposition" of the American working class that did not stand in fundamental opposition to the basic values of the American order but, rather, worked within the system to better their economic situation, increase their political weight, and participate in America's democracy. Sombart also found that American workers were generally better off than industrial workers in Europe, and that the fluidity of American society allowed for an upward mobility, nurturing the optimistic view among workers that they were not stuck in their class but indeed could rise up the social ladder. Workers thus subscribed to the ideal of individual self-advancement that precluded the formation of a class-consciousness. A second major reason the American workers identified with "the present American State," in Sombart's view, was their patriotism and nationalist pride. American workers shared, Sombart pointed out, a "belief in the mission and greatness" of their country, which, of course, means that they embraced exceptionalism as an identity narrative.

What Sombart diagnosed from afar through the window of his German ivory tower can be traced in ever so many autobiographical self-descriptions of American workers. When, for example, Harriet H. Robinson and Lucy Larcom, in autobiographies written at the end of the nineteenth century, looked back on their youth as workers in the textile mills of Lowell, Massachusetts, during the 1830s and 1840s, they created their own narratives of American Exceptionalism. Larcom, in *A New England Girlhood* (1889), and Robinson, in *Loom and Spindle* (1898), presented themselves as self-made women and their lives as success stories. According to their autobiographies, both had risen to affluence and repute from humble beginnings as mill girls in the emerging textile industry. Both celebrated U.S. political values as giving them the chance to rise in the world and liberate themselves. They felt that even as mill girls in Massachusetts, they had been in a much better social position, enjoying much better living conditions, than European mill workers. In their autobiographies, both the working conditions and the standard of living of the American workers appeared as exceptional in comparison to those of Europe.

Their descriptions of factory life are carried along by a work ethic that saw work as an end in itself and as a way to rise in the world. Work for Larcom and Robinson was defined as a thing of honor and as a source of pride, and they both reflected on work in terms of accomplishment and merit. Larcom and Robinson both saw the wages they earned not as a manifestation of capitalist exploitation but as the basis for their own economic independence, and as a first step toward their full empowerment.

Neither Larcom nor Robinson defined their individual identity through class, and they refused to see their fellow workers as members of a collective. "When I look back into the factory life of fifty or sixty years ago," Robinson wrote, "I do not see what is called 'a class' of young men and women going to and from their daily work." Rather, she saw them "as individuals, with personalities of their own." Her reflections culminated in the statement that all the women she worked with in Lowell were "self-made in the truest sense." Against this backdrop, Robinson considered herself a "woman who has risen to have once been a factory-girl"—and she was proud of it. With their autobiographies, both Larcom and Robinson thus actively contributed to constructing an ideology of American Exceptionalism from a working-class perspective.

Both of these New England mill girls experienced an early phase of industrialization in the U.S. When the industrialization of the U.S. entered a new phase after the Civil War, turning the U.S. into the number-one industrial country in the world, the much-needed supply of workers was largely drawn from the vast pool of immigrants from southern and eastern Europe. While this wave of mass immigration brought some radicals to the U.S., most of the newly immigrated people worked in the factories to get ahead and realize their personal American Dream: a life led in prosperity, freedom, and recognition. In her autobiography *The Promised Land*, published in 1912, Mary Antin, a Russian Jew from Polotsk who came to the U.S. in 1894, looked back on her days in Boston's Dover Street slums as being "pregnant with possibilities." She praised America as an "open workshop" that had allowed a "child of the slums" to rise to affluence and repute.

The 1930s was a decade of intense strike activity, and the mood among the millions of unemployed was rebellious. Historians have identified the 1930s as a "Red Decade," when communist agitation was strong in the U.S., and when there was a quite radical mood among the lower classes of U.S. society. However, even during these hard times, most Americans concentrated on making do, not on overthrowing capitalism; Studs Terkel's famous oral history of the Great Depression, *Hard Times*, gives ample evidence of this. In it, you can find the report of Larry Van Dusen, a labor organizer in the early thirties, who blamed the poverty he lived in on his father's failure. Van Dusen thus regretted that his father, a carpenter, somehow never had done better, "that he hadn't gotten the breaks." His father had felt a sense of shame in having to accept government aid in times of economic hardship. Men like his father, Van Dusen said, "suffered indignity" working at government projects "they considered alien to the American concept of productive labor."

At the same time, most working people continued to respect the property rights of companies and businessmen. A very telling example is provided by Howard Zinn in his *A People's History of the United States: 1492–Present*, which actually highlights moments of radicalism in America's past. He reports about an Aunt Molly Jackson, who in the 1930s, walked into a local store with a pistol to get a sack of sugar to feed her seven children. At gunpoint, she told the shopkeeper that she would shoot him if he did not give it to her for free but that she would be back in ninety days to pay for it. This mindset went hand in hand with the refusal to perceive American society in terms of class. Hank Oettinger, a linotype operator, told Studs Terkel that his father, even during the Great Depression, would not "accept the idea that there were different classes in America." For his father, who was violently anticommunist, it was "still the Great America," and therefore, he did not see "any benefits in social legislation." Against this backdrop, it fits in nicely that many Communist agitators of the thirties deplored the lack of class-consciousness, even among the protesting and militant workers.

The economic boom of World War II and the widely shared war nationalism of the decade pacified workers even more, and after the war, one of the longest and most dynamic economic growth periods of a reformed and regulated capitalism improved workers' living and working conditions well beyond anything that could reasonably have been anticipated from the perspective of the 1930s. Joe Morrison, a coal miner from Indiana, who was interviewed by Terkel in the 1960s, thus looked back on the Great Depression as a time of unrest, radicalism, and the political mobilization of working men and women, only to contrast this with the post-1945 era, when there was no longer "much political talk any more among workingmen. You go to a tavern now, it's around ball games, something like that. Seldom ever politics or war." Morrison identified "an apathy" among the working class where everybody was "so busy trying to keep their bills paid" that they did not care very much about politics, socialism, or even communism anymore.

Morrison's generational perspective is supported by Gregory, born in 1946, who told Terkel that he did not know anything about the labor struggles of the 1930s, as neither his grandfather nor his uncle, both autoworkers for life, had ever talked to him about them. In that same vein, Howard, born in 1947, also told Terkel that his grandfather had never mentioned any strikes to him. He had actually been strongly anti-union, Howard reminisced about his grandfather, and he concluded, "He didn't want Negroes to come into the plant. That's why he wanted it unionized, to keep his job and keep them out. On the other hand, he was against unions."

This chapter has examined three exemplary case studies to reflect American Exceptionalism as a factor triggering, structuring, and defining the goals of reform movements in U.S. history. We have seen how the concept was used to justify the most diverse reform issues, and had we looked at more reform movements, we would have found even more issues; as different as the reform movements were, their basic theme was the discrepancy between the ideal and the real, between the claims to exceptionality and the realities in American life. While it thus functioned as an important cultural resource providing a political language to motivate reform, American Exceptionalism was so malleable a concept that it could be used to drive outright contradictory reform agendas. It could be used to justify the enfranchisement or disenfranchisement of women, the creation or dismantling of the welfare state, the legalization or criminalization of unions.

The latter is important insofar as U.S. labor history is one of the major fields triggering and shaping the debate about American Exceptionalism. The lack of socialism in a developed capitalist country like the U.S. is just as important a theme in the conceptual history of American Exceptionalism as that of the city-upon-a-hill imagery or the frontier thesis. While the answer to why there is no socialism in the U.S. is very complex and involves many aspects and dimensions, this chapter has made the point that American Exceptionalism as an identity narrative was widely shared by America's working classes, to the effect that exceptionalist mindsets took a lot of the radical wind out of the labor movement's sails. American Exceptionalism, therefore, has both enabled and hampered reform movements in U.S. history, and in some cases, it prevented them altogether.

8

People of Plenty

American Exceptionalism and Affluence

IN HER 1963 BOOK *ON REVOLUTION*, Hannah Arendt famously observed that America's prosperity, and not the new form of government created by the American Revolution, had "revolutionized the spirit of men, first in Europe and then all over the world." America, as the new continent, had become a "refuge, an 'asylum' and a meeting ground of the poor," who, thanks to the rich abundance of the American land, the liberty they enjoyed, and the system of government they lived under, had every chance to become affluent and advance in the world. As a result, American society had largely eradicated poverty from its midst, and this was, Arendt suggested, America's real claim to exceptionality.

When Arendt made her point, she stood in the shadow of a large archive of texts, images, and material artifacts that all thematized abundance and a widely shared prosperity as an outstanding feature of American life. They all contributed to highlighting both the experience and expectation of abundance and material wealth as major elements of the American Dream, which is the central idea and metaphor in the conceptual toolbox of American Exceptionalism. The American Dream suggests that individual initiative can lead to material prosperity and that everybody can acquire property and social standing, if only they work hard enough, live a frugal and law-abiding life, and rely on themselves for their own advancement.

American Dreams centering on abundance and material wealth originated in colonial America, and they underwent repeated reformulations in the changing contexts of an economic history that witnessed the U.S. developing from an agrarian republic to the leading industrial power dominating the world economy well into the 1970s. In light of the deep economic and social transformations that the U.S. went through since roughly the mid-1970s, it is currently not at all clear whether claims to America's exceptionality can still draw on the widely shared experience of prosperity, a constantly growing standard of living, and an optimistic outlook into the future connected to it.

AMERICAN DREAMS IN THE AGRARIAN REPUBLIC

From the beginning of European settlement on the North American continent in the seventeenth century, the experience and expectation of material wealth was the most important element in the exceptionalist imagination. Prior to the industrial transformation of the U.S. in the nineteenth century, the images of America as a place of great and widely shared prosperity were anchored in agriculture. Notions of wealth and a good life revolved around land ownership, fertile soils, and abundant natural resources available for everybody to exploit. The ability of the American land, its flora, and fauna to provide not only sustenance but also affluence to a hard-working agrarian people, was, as explained in chapter 1, an important theme of American Exceptionalism from the seventeenth century onward.

In the eighteenth century, these ideas and experiences were condensed into first versions of the American Dream, an intellectual formation centering on the concepts of individual prosperity, success, and upward social mobility achieved under conditions of equal opportunity and solely through one's own abilities, talent, and skills, regardless of social class or circumstances of birth. In this context, there is no getting around John Hector St. John de Crèvecœur and Benjamin Franklin as two early prophets of the American Dream.

In the third of his *Letters from an American Farmer*, published in 1782, John Hector St. John de Crèvecoeur depicted revolutionary America as an "asylum" for the "poor of Europe," who by working hard and leading frugal, honest lives, could become respectable farmers on their own land, enjoying all the freedom and status resulting from land ownership. In Crèvecœur's letter, the Mid-Atlantic region appeared as the site of a widely shared prosperity inhabited by a well-fed society that generally had a much higher standard of living than any European society. "The meanest of our log houses is a dry and comfortable habitation," Crèvecœur wrote, contrasting them with the "clay-built hut[s]" and "miserable cabin[s]" in which Europe's poor dwelled in "meanness, smoke, and indigence."

The reasons for the general prosperity in North America were multiple. Crèvecœur mentioned the abundance of natural resources, the easy availability of exceptionally fertile land, and a political and legal system that, lacking feudal structures, set individuals free, encouraged their initiative, and let them fully enjoy the fruits of their labor. This constellation of factors formed a society of freeholders owning medium-sized property. American society of the Mid-Atlantic region thus did not feature excessively large fortunes, but it also lacked extreme poverty. Instead of polarized wealth, American society offered homogeneity on a middle ground, a "pleasing uniformity" that led to the rich and the poor not being "so far removed from each other" as they were in Europe. In contrast to Europe "with all its pomp," Crèvecœur suggested that North America was a "continent for men of middle stations and labourers."

By migrating to North America, poor Europeans thus could rise from poverty, dependence, and servitude to affluence, independence, and freedom. Under North American skies, Europeans, Crèvecœur suggested, could thus metamorphose into Americans, and this transformation basically ensued "[f]rom nothing to start into being; from a servant to the rank of a master; from being a slave of some despotic prince, to become a free man, invested with lands to which every municipal blessing is annexed."

With this, Crèvecœur presented nothing less than an agrarian version of the American Dream. The rise from rags to riches that he described in several shapes and forms in his *Letters from an American Farmer* was anchored in land ownership. It did not, however, exhaust itself in material wealth, insofar as notions of freedom, self-determination, civic responsibility, and participation in the broadest sense were inseparably tied to the possession of landed property. The agrarian-style American Dream that Crèvecœur constructed in his writing was enveloped by a discourse on morality and virtue. He made it unmistakably clear that only honest, industrious, sober, and frugal individuals would be successful in revolutionary North America.

This connection between affluence and repute resulting from a virtuous life is even more explicit in Benjamin Franklin's autobiography (discussed in chapter 4), which eminent Franklin scholar J. A. Leo Lemay has called the "definitive formulation of the American Dream." In his autobiography, Franklin described his life as a self-made rise from "the Poverty and Obscurity in which I was born and bred, to a State of Affluence and some Degree of Reputation in the World." Arguing that his life was "fit to be imitated" and capable of serving as a model to others, Franklin suggested that everybody in America could do as he did. Thus his memoir was an autobiographical manual to success.

Franklin's life writing unfolded as a report about self-education, self-improvement, and self-creation. It depicted him as an avid reader who used every spare minute for study and exercise to improve his language, knowledge, intellectual capabilities, and skills as a printer. This relentless, self-directed activity fueled a personal rise that had two sides: the economic success that made him one of the richest men in colonial North America and a growing reputation as a member of Philadelphia's civil society. This success story, as the autobiography suggested, was enabled and driven by Franklin's own industry, frugality, honesty, reliability, and superior skills as a printer. In great detail, Franklin described how he started out working for the Philadelphia printer Samuel Keimer, quickly developed into the best of Keimer's workmen, teamed up with his friend Hugh Meredith to set up his own print shop, was the better and more reliable printer of the two, finally bought Meredith out to become the sole proprietor of the business, and bested all of his competitors due to his skill, industry, reliability, honesty, and business talent.

This business success went hand in hand with a deepening involvement in public-improvement projects and colonial politics. Franklin began to get involved in public-improvement projects around the time he set up his own business in the late 1720s. In 1727, he was a founding member of the Junto, a voluntary association of mostly young Philadelphians from different occupational backgrounds who committed themselves to civic improvements and debating the urgent political, social, and economic questions of the day. Under Franklin's hidden leadership, the Junto initiated, among other things, the Library Company of Philadelphia (1731), the American Philosophical Society (1743), the Academy of Philadelphia (1749), the Pennsylvania Hospital (1751), and the College and Academy of Philadelphia (1755). All of these initiatives contributed to enhancing Franklin's reputation and social standing, which in turn was good for his business relationships, too.

The American Dream that Franklin created in his autobiography thus had self-made prosperity as the basic theme, but it did not exhaust itself in economic success. Material wealth did not appear as an end in itself but, rather, only as the basis for a life lived in civic responsibility and dedicated to public improvement and public service. It constructed the normative ideal of a way of life centering on a rationally planned moral self-improvement as the condition of possibility for a self-engineered rise in the world, and it celebrated America as the only place in the world where this was possible. His account let America appear as a land of opportunity, where—in contrast to Europe—individuals had choices and could shape their lives into any form they chose. Striving for material wealth thus appeared as a natural thing to do—and America was the place where one could pursue one's notions of material and nonmaterial happiness unfettered by European traditions, institutions, and hierarchies.

Franklin died in 1790, and numerous unauthorized, cheap, and popular editions of his autobiography were quickly published. They usually contained only the first of the four parts of the manuscript, which detailed Franklin's economic success story and did not reflect very much on morality and civic responsibility. This is symptomatic of what happened to Franklin's broad and multifaceted American Dream that found its fulfillment in a reputation resulting from moral conduct just as much as from affluence—it was narrowed down to the rags-to-riches theme and reduced to its economic aspect, to the effect that, starting with Jacksonian America, a rather blunt materialism moved to the center of exceptionalist notions about the U.S.

In his seminal *Democracy in America*, the French aristocrat and analyst of American society Alexis de Tocqueville described the U.S. as an exceptionally affluent country, in which the "passion for material prosperity" was widely shared and "felt by all." Every American in his depiction was freely following the "natural and instinctive taste for comfort," so that the "love of comfort" had become "the dominant taste of the

[American] nation." This for him was the result of the general equality of conditions in the U.S., where "distinctions of class" were "blurred and privileges abolished," and social structures were so fluid that every hardworking and honest person could actually become prosperous and climb the social ladder through work. In such a society, fortunes were made and lost within a lifetime or over generations, which is why the equality of opportunity and individual freedom in Tocqueville's analysis created restlessness among Americans. The "poor man's imagination," Tocqueville wrote, desired to obtain material wealth and the comfort that came from it, while "the rich man's mind" was "overtaken by the fear of losing it." As a result of this relentless quest for prosperity, "a lot of modest fortunes" were created in the U.S., with their owners having "enough physical comforts to have a liking for them but not enough to be content."

From this resulted restlessness in the midst of prosperity, which Tocqueville identified as a major feature of American society in Jacksonian America. The "passion for material prosperity," Tocqueville explained, let every American think about the "shortest route" to wealth, which is why they were constantly buying and selling things. "In the United States," Tocqueville wrote,

> a man will carefully construct a home in which to spend his old age and sell it before the roof is on; he will plant a garden and will rent it out just as he was about to enjoy its fruit; he will clear a field and leave others to reap the harvest. He will take up a profession and then give it up. He will settle in one place only to go off elsewhere shortly afterwards with a new set of desires.

The U.S. thus appeared as a country in which the taste for material wealth and physical comfort ran freely because neither laws nor custom held anyone in their place. In the U.S., Tocqueville explained, all "privileges of birth and wealth" had been destroyed, all professions had been opened to all, and everybody could climb to the top on their own merits. Equality of opportunity thus allowed "each citizen to imagine unlimited hopes." His account is but one of many describing the U.S. as a farmers' heaven, a land for hardworking white people to make a good living and widely share in the affluence of the first half of the nineteenth century.

AMERICAN DREAMS IN THE INDUSTRIAL WORLD

Within just fifty years of the end of the Civil War in 1865, the U.S. developed from an economically backward and still largely agrarian nation into the number-one industrial country of the world, producing more than the next two countries on the list, England and Germany, combined. This tumultuous and disruptive process produced a few private fortunes of a size the world had hardly seen before. Business tycoons like Andrew Carnegie, John D. Rockefeller, and John Pierpont Morgan became iconic personifications of self-made wealth. While the industrial transformation of the U.S. produced great wealth and comfort at the top, it produced even greater poverty and hardship at the bottom, where the industrial workers, especially the unskilled ones, led precarious lives in the inner-city slums with little chance to rise in the world. The muckraking journalist and social photographer Jacob Riis documented the plight of the industrial working class in his seminal *How the Other Half Lives*, published in 1890. Sixteen years later, Upton Sinclair, in his novel *The Jungle*, gave a gripping and shocking description of workers' lives in Chicago's meatpacking industry.

The polarization of wealth, inequality of living conditions, and increasingly petrified social structures of the emerging industrial class society transformed Franklin's American Dream and gave it a new meaning. It was largely deprived of its complex civic ethos of service and reduced to purely material success. Horatio Alger became the prophet of the rags-to-riches success story, suggesting that even in industrial America everybody could rise from dishwasher to millionaire. Writing in the last third of the nineteenth century, Alger, a schoolteacher and Unitarian minister in Brewster, Massachusetts, who was forced to leave the pulpit after allegations of sexual activities with local boys in 1866, was the author of more than one hundred young-adult dime novels that sold more than twenty million copies. His astonishing writing career was founded on the sensational success of *Ragged Dick; or, Street Life in New York with the Bootblacks*. Published in 1867–1868, it told the story of a poor but honest, hardworking and humble shoeshine boy who rose to wealth. It developed the from-rags-to-riches formula that Alger clung to in all of his subsequent novels. His educational stories featured characters like Ragged Dick, John Oakley, or Tattered Tom, and they made "Alger hero" a household term in the U.S.

In Horatio Alger's world, America's exceptionality was defined by the fact that it was a country whose political institutions, social order, and cultural values allowed for spectacular stories of individual material success. In setting individuals free, forcing them to rely on themselves, allowing them to pursue their notions of a good life, and letting them enjoy the fruits of their labor, the U.S. created an environment that systematically produced affluence, comfort, and a standard of living that let even the American poor live much better lives than the poor in any other region of the world, past and present. The narratives of affluence suggested that the sole source of economic growth and general affluence was the individual who, in pursuing their private material dreams, was also contributing to the general welfare of the country.

While this may appear as but a continuation of the pre–Civil War narratives celebrating the U.S. as a land of affluence, it is important to note that Alger's American Dream stories had a different meaning and function in the context of American corporate capitalism. This economic order actually hindered if not precluded individual rises from rags to riches because it accepted social inequality, petrified class structures, and the polarization of wealth as givens. Preaching the "Gospel of Wealth" in 1900, steel magnate Andrew Carnegie (see chapter 7), who more or less *was* America's steel industry at that time, reflected on the enormous fortunes created in the course of America's industrial transformation and diagnosed the great inequality of opportunity in corporate America. Arguing that industrialization had revolutionized "the conditions of human life," he pointed to the great polarization of wealth that came with it. While in former days there had been "little difference in the dwelling, dress, food, and environment" of master and servant, employer and employee, entrepreneur and laborer, social conditions in industrial societies were now a lot more diverse, differentiated, and polarized. "The contrast between the palace of the millionaire and the cottage of the laborer" was great and was a visible manifestation of the social transformations that had come with industrialization. "This change," Carnegie wrote, "is not to be deplored, but welcomed as highly beneficial," insofar as in contemporary societies, even the poor were much better off than in former times. Social inequality, in Carnegie's view, was the necessary result of industrial capitalism, and therefore to be accepted.

Seen against this backdrop, Horatio Alger's success stories served to justify American corporate capitalism, suggesting that individual rises from rags to riches were still possible. Alger heroes demonstrated that America had not given up on its promise of equal opportunities that defined its claim to exceptionality to a very large extent. Ironically, this illusion produced a characteristic friction that is visible in every Alger tale; because in the end, it always takes a lucky break in the form of unanticipated support by a benevolent patron for the hardworking, honest, and thrifty Ragged Dicks and Tattered Toms to really strike it rich.

Be that as it may, Horatio Alger's rags-to-riches stories did their share in reducing the American Dream to the quest for material wealth, and not everyone in the U.S. liked it. Starting in the Gilded Age and the Progressive Era and stretching to the twenty-first century, a long list of U.S. writers, playwrights, artists, photographers, filmmakers, publicists, and other intellectuals criticized the shallow materialism of American consumer capitalism, diagnosed the loss of morality in the quest for wealth, and seriously questioned whether the American Dream still worked.

A case in point is William Dean Howells's novel *The Rise of Silas Lapham*, published in 1885. It told the story of the barefooted son of poor farmers who makes a fortune in the paint business but lacks the etiquette, status, and standing of the old-money families in Boston. Lapham puts all his capital and effort into building a pompous house in Boston's fashionable Back Bay neighborhood without ever being acknowledged by Boston's elite as one of their own. Lapham loses much of his fortune when he refuses to strike an unethical business deal that would have saved him from financial ruin, his new house on Beacon Street burns down, and he is forced to return to his ancestral home in the countryside.

Fifteen years later, Theodore Dreiser's novel *Sister Carrie* painted an even more hopeless portrait of a society dedicated to limitless materialism. His book was about the young, beautiful, and naïve Carrie Meeber, who leaves her rural home in Wisconsin for Chicago to become famous and get ahead in this world. In a scene at the Marshall Fields department store, she is blinded by all the nice consumer goods on display there, falling prey to the temptations of materialism, and losing all her sense of morality. Her insatiable appetite for luxury goods and fame destroys the middle-aged George Hurstwood, who, captivated by Carrie's beauty and vitality, gives up his respectable middle-class life to be with her. Hurstwood pursues highly unethical business practices to be able to afford Carrie's highflying lifestyle. After he loses all his money, Carrie, who is on her way to becoming a famous actress, drops him from one day to the next. While her rise to affluence and fame continues, an impoverished Hurstwood commits suicide in the end.

In an even more drastic way than Howells, Dreiser highlighted the destructive effects of the hunt for wealth and repute at all costs, showing how it was all built on fraud and sand. In that same vein, F. Scott Fitzgerald wrote his iconic 1925 novel *The Great Gatsby*, in which Jay Gatsby, a self-made man in New York, regularly throws extremely extravagant parties at his lavish country residence in West Egg, Long Island. His miraculous fortune is of uncertain origin, but it most certainly was not the result of hard work, industry, and frugality, but of criminal activities. It becomes clear that all Gatsby wants is to win back his old love Daisy, who is married to Tom Buchanan. Gatsby puts all his wealth on display to literally buy her back, but Daisy is far too spoiled, hollow, and mindless to be able to love anyone. In the end, Gatsby is murdered, his life and dreams destroyed, without anybody caring much about the death of their party host. In his novel, Fitzgerald makes explicit references to Franklin's autobiography, especially its famous chart of virtues that guided Franklin's project of moral self-improvement. Accordingly, the young Gatsby tried to live by the principles and rules staked out in Franklin's autobiography, only to discover that they no longer applied to life in the industrial age. His attempt to follow Franklin's advice and pull himself up by his bootstraps ends in complete disaster. The American Dream and the premises it was built on had seemingly become defunct. Yet even this intellectual critique of American materialism moved within exceptionalist mindsets, insofar as it criticized the situation in the U.S. from the vantage point of a supposedly higher morality that was key to the notion of American Exceptionalism from the start. The novelistic diagnoses of life in industrial America presented by Howells, Dreiser, Fitzgerald, and many others suggested that the shallow materialism dominating American life undermined and destroyed the American potential for a superior morality.

However, the literary critique of American materialism and consumerism was only one side of the coin. It should not blind us to the fact that, starting around 1900, many contemporaries celebrated America's corporate capitalism as the quintessence of American Exceptionalism. Anchored in individual freedom, free labor, the ethics of the marketplace, the imaginative use of technology, and a pervasive entrepreneurial spirit, U.S. business culture was celebrated for its unparalleled efficiency in the production of goods and services. The years from 1890 to 1930 were the formative period of a specifically American consumer capitalism anchored in the mass consumption of mass-produced consumer goods ranging from shoes, clothing, furniture, and interior decorations to the newly invented vacuum cleaners, refrigerators, washing machines, and automobiles. Innovations like department stores, mail-order catalogues, chain stores, magazines, movies, and advertising were institutions of an emerging consumer culture that provided consumer goods of different quality and price for all strata of society. The turn of the twentieth century witnessed the formation of an anonymous but highly differentiated mass market that gave individuals the opportunity to define themselves and their social rank through consumer goods. In this emerging consumer society, you were what you owned and could afford.

In *The Theory of the Leisure Class*, published in 1899, the Norwegian American economist and sociologist Thorstein Veblen described the structures and mechanisms of the modern consumer society unfolding before his eyes. He argued that in modern industrial societies, the only remaining markers of social rank and status were "conspicuous leisure" and "conspicuous consumption." The ostentatious display of consumer goods for everybody to see and the visible performance of leisure activities demonstrating to everyone that one could afford *not* to work thus defined the status and standing of an individual. The utility of conspicuous leisure and consumption "for the purposes of reputability lies in the element of waste that is common to both," Veblen wrote. "In the one case it is a waste of time and effort, in the other it is a waste of goods." The mechanisms of the newly forming consumer society allowed members of the middle and working classes to emulate the lifestyle of the upper classes through consumption and leisure activities that demonstrated their financial prowess and their material wealth. The standard of living measured in consumer goods and degrees of comfort thus became indicators of social status.

This standard of living was enabled by an unprecedentedly efficient industrial economy that produced standardized consumer goods in large quantities for sale on an anonymous mass market. Industrial mass production of consumer goods for mass consumption—that is the formula of American consumer capitalism, which came to full fruition in the 1920s and reached unprecedented heights in the 1950s and 1960s, making the U.S. the country with the highest standard of living in the world. This was the result of a business culture that was built on the principles of Fordism and Taylorism. *Fordism* refers to the mechanized assembly-line production of standardized consumer goods made from prefabricated interchangeable parts in combination with a policy of high wages that enabled the workers to buy the products they produced. *Taylorism* refers to scientific management, that is, the application of scientific methods to improve the efficiency of the production process.

In his autobiography *My Life and Work*, published in 1922, Henry Ford gave the most systematic account of his business philosophy. He operated on the premise that the function of business was "to produce for consumption and not for money or speculation." He wanted to make high-quality products for sale at low consumer prices so that many could afford the goods. The consumer products should first and foremost serve the people, "and not merely the producer." Key to Fordism was the idea of lowering the production costs of an article through the most efficient time- and labor-saving means of production. The reduced cost of production would then be used to lower consumer prices even further. The lowering of production costs, therefore, was not to be translated into higher profit margins for the producer but into lower prices for the consumer. "My financial policy is the result of my sales policy," he wrote; he continued, "I hold that it is better to sell a large number of articles at a small profit than to sell a few at a large profit."

Ford's business philosophy was thus driven by the vision of a consumer society in which everybody was a producer and a consumer, a buyer and a seller, at the same time. This required, however, that the producers of cars, the assembly-line workers, were affluent enough to afford all the nice things that American industry was producing. Convinced that it was "bad financial policy to reduce wages because it also reduces buying power," Ford paid high wages to his workers: five dollars for an eight-hour workday. While Ford's high-wage policy was also meant to keep labor unions out of the motor company's shops, it was primarily aimed at increasing the buying power of the population, allowing the majority of society to participate in consumption according to their financial means.

Akin to Fordism were Frederick Winslow Taylor's ideas about "national efficiency" as laid down in his 1911 treatise *The Principles of Scientific Management*. His primary concern was to combat the widespread "waste of human effort" through the most efficient and effective use of human labor. Criticizing the omnipresent "inefficiency in almost all of our daily acts," Taylor advocated "systematic management," rather than the search "for some unusual or extraordinary man" as the best remedy for what he saw as the national problem of inefficiency. He sought to prove "that the best management is a true science, resting upon clearly defined laws, rules, and principles, as a foundation." As such, the "fundamental principles of scientific management" were "applicable to all kinds of human activities, from our simplest individual acts to the work of our great corporations, which call for the most elaborate cooperation."

Like Ford, Taylor believed that it was more profitable to sell a large number of products at a low price than to sell a few at high ones. Therefore, he showed himself convinced that the "maximum prosperity for the employer" was inseparably "coupled with the maximum prosperity for each employee." Maximum prosperity, for him, was not only related to pecuniary factors (i.e., large dividends for the companies and high wages for the workers) but also involved the "development of every branch of the business to its highest state of excellence" and the "development of each man to his state of maximum efficiency, so that he may be able to do, generally speaking, the highest grade of work for which his natural abilities fit him." To achieve these two goals was the overall aim of scientific management, and Taylor argued that only such a wide-ranging ethos of efficiency would make prosperity permanent in the industrial world.

The core elements of scientific management were the time-and-motion studies that Taylor and his large teams of scientists conducted in factories. They thoroughly analyzed the individual tasks involved in the assembly-line production of a car or a refrigerator, measuring the time it took to perform each task and charting the body motions involved. From this analysis, they would then suggest new ways of organizing the process that were more efficient because "unnecessary motions" were eliminated, and slow and inefficient motions were substituted for fast and more efficient ones. Through time-and-motion studies, scientific managers sought to increase output by showing how each task in the production process could be done in the quickest time and with the most efficient use of the human body. This greater output should then translate into lower consumer prices to supply the demand of the mass market.

Together, the values, principles, and practices of Fordism and Taylorism created a specifically U.S. form of consumer capitalism that between 1890 and 1930 produced a standard of living in the U.S. that became the envy of the world. Things like electricity, automobiles, telephones, and washing machines, which gained a significant presence in Europe only after World War I, had become commonplace in America by 1914. This reinforced perceptions of U.S. uniqueness. In 1901–1902, Max Goldberger, a German economist who traveled in the U.S. for eight months, was thus overwhelmed by the "gigantic economic strength of the nation" (*gigantische Stärke der Nation*). In his 1903 book *Das Land der unbegrenzten Möglichkeiten: Beobachtungen über das Wirtschaftsleben der Vereinigten Staaten von Amerika* (*The Land of Unlimited Possibilities: Observations on the Economic Life of the United States of America*), Goldberger spoke of the U.S. economy as a "mighty motor" (*das mächtige Getriebe*) fueled by a "fantastic" (*wunderbar*) supply of raw materials, driven by unsurpassed labor-saving technologies, and constantly improved by a culture of efficiency, which is why, for Goldberger, the U.S. was a "land of unlimited possibilities."

While the advanced U.S. consumer culture had already become a cipher of American Exceptionalism before World War I, the transformations of the global economic system wrought by the war made this even more pronounced. The U.S. economy had outfitted and fed the armies and societies of Great Britain and France, and U.S. banks had largely financed Europe's warfare before 1917. The U.S. declaration of war on Germany on April 6, 1917, led to a massive economic mobilization that increased the U.S. lead over the rest of the world. With Europe's economies in shambles after four years of industrial warfare, the U.S. economy emerged unscathed and under full steam from the military conflict.

The 1920s witnessed a massive expansion of U.S. businesses into Europe, and New York's Wall Street replaced the City of London as the financial center of the world; along with this came the altogether new presence in Europe of U.S. consumer goods and pop culture like jazz and Hollywood films. From a European perspective, America's economic growth and strength appeared all the more spectacular in light of Europe's postwar decline. In 1925, the German economist Julius Hirsch, who as a Jew was forced to emigrate to the Netherlands and Denmark in the 1930s and came to the U.S. in 1941, published his widely read study *Das amerikanische Wirtschaftswunder*. In it, he analyzed U.S. economic performance in terms of an economic miracle (*Wirtschaftswunder*), and his celebration of the U.S. economy was inextricably tied to a desperate diagnosis of European decline.

During the 1920s, attitudes toward consumption changed significantly and on a broad basis in American society. A growing number of Americans spent their money on things not primarily needed for subsistence (shelter, food, clothing), consumer goods that made life more comfortable and enjoyable and promised social status and standing. This deep cultural change, which began around 1900 but picked up momentum in the 1920s as the new consumer society fully matured in the U.S., was prominently described by two U.S. sociologists, Robert Staughton Lynd and Helen Merrell Lynd, in their study *Middletown: A Study in Contemporary American Culture*, first published in 1929. In the chapter "Why Do They Work So Hard," the Lynds observed a massive multiplication of the "optional occasions for spending money" since the end of World War I, and they detected "rapidly changing habits of thought as to what things are essential to living." Identifying a "rapid growth of subjective wants" among the population, wants that were increasingly divorced from subsistence needs, the Lynds argued that the inhabitants of the fictitious city of Middletown had "countless things they desire"; they attributed the "diffusion of new urgent occasions for spending money" to the "rise of large-scale advertising, popular magazines, movies, radio, and other channels of increased cultural diffusion."

In the 1920s, America's consumer culture, which made a wide range of consumer goods available to the upper and middle classes, became a marker of America's economic exceptionality. The private home became a semipublic showcase of material wealth, while suburban neighborhoods served as semiprivate spaces providing an audience for an individual family's display of wealth. The new middle-class lifestyle emerging in the 1920s was built on the ownership of homes and gardens, automobiles, refrigerators, washing machines, vacuum cleaners, and other household appliances, as well as the availability of leisure activities. The conformity of middle-class life that went with it was seen by some as the democratization of consumption and the final realization of America's promise of equal opportunity, self-determination, and choice. In his bestselling 1925 book *The Man Nobody Knows*, advertising executive Bruce F. Barton even attached a religious meaning to consumption. Presenting Jesus as an advertising man and founder of modern business, Barton encouraged his readers to study the parables of Jesus because their "language and learning" revealed key principles of good advertising like "marvelously condensed" gripping sentences, a "marvelously simple" language, utmost sincerity, and the necessity of repetition. While Henry Ford, Bruce Barton, and others celebrated the widely shared affluence produced by American consumer capitalism as a manifestation of U.S. exceptionality, others, like Sinclair Lewis in his novel *Babbitt*, satirized the emptiness of the new consumer culture and its outer-directed pressures for conformity.

Be that as it may, the U.S. standard of living cemented notions of an American Exceptionalism on both sides of the Atlantic. U.S. political, business, and intellectual elites celebrated America's business culture and consumer capitalism as paving the way for the utopia of a world free of want. In a speech, "The Press under a Free Government," delivered to newspaper editors in January 1925, U.S. president Calvin Coolidge remarked that "the chief business of the American people is business." Americans made no "concealment of the fact" that they wanted wealth. While Coolidge pointed to other things that Americans wanted even more, like peace, honor, and charity, he felt that material wealth was the basis of it all. Coolidge thus praised business leaders and the business community for laying the foundations of an ideal world of equally shared wealth. On October 22, 1928, Coolidge's successor in office, Herbert Hoover, in his speech accepting the nomination as presidential candidate of the Republican Party, declared that the U.S. was nearer "to the ideal of the abolition of poverty and fear from the lives of men and women than ever in any land."

THE GREAT DEPRESSION AND THE CHALLENGES
TO NOTIONS OF EXCEPTIONALISM

The Great Depression, which began with the stock market crash of New York's Wall Street in October 1929, only a year after Hoover had anticipated the end of poverty in the near future, severely challenged all notions of Americans as a people of plenty. The stock market crash was a gigantic destruction of capital, quickly creating a banking crisis that translated into the, up until then, deepest economic depression in U.S. history. Firms collapsed in unprecedented numbers, exceeding one hundred thousand by the end of 1932. Industrial production in 1932 was 54 percent of what it had been in 1929, and the GNP of 1932 was down 43.5 percent compared to 1929. The farming regions of the West and the South were particular economic disaster areas, since the economic slump combined with a severe agrarian crisis that had been building in the course of the 1920s, largely as a result of agricultural overproduction. Farm prices were in free fall, while the costs to operate a farm remained the same or rose. In desperate actions to stabilize the prices for farm products, some farmers ploughed their harvests under or let them rot in the fields since it did not pay for them to bring the harvests in. To make matters worse, a period of severe drought from 1932 to 1941 put additional pressure on U.S. farming regions in what came to be known as the Dust Bowl, where devastating dust storms swept over the country, destroying the little that was left.

Unemployment was high in the 1930s. Between 1930 and 1934, hundreds of thousands of farmers lost their farms due to bankruptcy and foreclosures; in 1933 alone, over 200,000 farms were foreclosed. In the cities, millions of industrial workers lost their jobs. At the height of the Great Depression in 1933, fifteen million Americans were unemployed, about a quarter of America's workforce. As a result, the per capita income declined rapidly, dramatically reducing the purchasing power of potential consumers at a time when it would have been vital for the economy for people to shop. Oscar Ameringer, a newspaper publisher from Oklahoma, analyzed this dilemma in a congressional hearing in February 1932; he said, "The farmers are being pauperized by the poverty of industrial populations, and the industrial populations are being pauperized by the poverty of the farmers. Neither has the money to buy the product of the other, hence we have overproduction and underconsumption at the same time and in the same country."

Hidden beneath these macroeconomic facts, however, lay the misery, hardship, and poverty that the Great Depression brought to millions of individuals, their families, and friends. The economic disaster disrupted or completely destroyed individual lives, their goals, and dreams of happiness. Millions of biographies were changed and transformed. Not only people used to being poor were affected by the economic disaster but also families of the hitherto well-to-do middle classes, who had been the main beneficiaries of the perilous affluence of the 1920s. The sudden experience of poverty and the need to make do in hard times came as life-changing shocks to these circles, and many preferred death over the loss of affluence and status.

The collective experience of hard times undermined, if not invalidated, all notions of exceptionalism based on dreams of material wealth. A very telling documentation in this context was a billboard created by Arthur Rothstein in February 1937. Displayed across the country by the National Association of Manufacturers, the billboard showed the image of a white middle-class family proudly riding in their brand-new car. The scene represented a jolly father in the driver's seat who appeared to be in full command of the car and his family. Joyfully sitting next to him was his beautiful and perfectly styled wife. In the backseat were the couple's two kids, a daughter and a son, and the family dog, who was happily sticking his head out of the car window. Everybody in the car was well dressed. The two female characters were beautiful and very feminine, the two male characters handsome and masculine, and everybody in the car was smiling glowingly, obviously proud to be American. The scene was framed at the top by a three-striped banner in red, white, and blue, with the words "World's Highest Standard of Living" written in bold into the white stripe running across the whole image. To the left of the car was a slogan: "There is no way like the American Way."

While this billboard celebrated U.S. consumer culture and the widely shared affluence produced by it as the manifestation of American Exceptionalism, it did so in the midst of dire poverty. The very disparity between the realities of American life during the Great Depression and the propagandistic celebration of American consumer capitalism deconstructed the whole message of the billboard, letting it appear as an ironic denial of facts. A homeless family on the move in search of jobs passing one of these billboards would have immediately realized this irony, but there were even outspoken visual critiques of the billboard. Margaret Bourke-White's picture taken in the aftermath of the Great Flood of 1937 showed a long line of flood refugees waiting for rations beneath Rothstein's billboard celebrating the highest standard of living as the result of the American way. All of the people waiting in line beneath the all-white middle-class family in the car were African American. This photograph not only deconstructed the propaganda effort of the billboard, but it also revealed the racial and the gender dynamics of America's consumer capitalism and its exceptionalist premises.

The Great Depression shook the foundations of the U.S. political and economic order. The 1930s were a decade of turmoil, violent protests, and militant unrest in the U.S. There were many acts of insubordination, disobedience, and resistance, and countless violent clashes between protesters and police or private security firms. A few examples suffice to illustrate the point: On January 31, 1931, roughly five hundred armed farmers from the vicinity of England, Arkansas, marched through the business district of the town demanding food for themselves and their families. If they did not get it for free, they would help themselves to bread, butter, milk, meat, and vegetables. On April 1, 1932, roughly five hundred ill-fed and ill-clad school children paraded through downtown Chicago, making their way to the local education authority to demand free school meals. Three months later, on June 3, 1932, twenty-five hungry children in Boston took a cold buffet by storm that had been set up for veterans of the Spanish-American War of 1898. They were driven away by two squadrons of police.

In addition to these spontaneous acts of resistance, there were other organized forms of protest, especially union-led strikes. There was an endless series of spontaneous and mostly very militant strikes in the U.S., as strikes by industrial unions that organized all workers of an industry, not only the skilled workers of a trade, were on the rise in the 1930s. In 1934 alone, an estimated 1.5 million workers went on strike, and they were in many cases led by communist labor activists. Communists were very active and present on the local level, and several large unions; the United Electrical Workers and the Mine, Mill, and Smelter Workers were actually controlled by Communist leaders. At the same time,

Margaret Bourke-White, *World's Highest Standard of Living*, black and white photograph, 1937. Art Institute of Chicago. http//:www.artic.edu

writers like John Steinbeck, Sherwood Anderson, and John Dos Passos, as well as many artists and intellectuals, felt very much attracted to communist doctrines in the 1930s.

This constellation of turmoil, protest, and militancy, as well as the visibility and intensity of leftist radicalism, has led many a contemporary—and also many scholars—to think of the 1930s as the "Red Decade." While there are many good points to be made in the case, what is even more remarkable about the 1930s is that a foundation-shaking crisis like the Great Depression did not lead to the destruction of liberal democracy and free-market capitalism. The political response to the economic crisis in the U.S. was not a socialist revolution but the reform of America's order under the auspices of the New Deal, discussed in chapter 7. At a time when liberal democracies all over in Europe were existentially weakened by the Great Depression and fell prey to totalitarian rulers, U.S. democracy was rejuvenated through liberal reform.

The culturally deeply ingrained and widely shared exceptionalist persuasions, as different, diverse, and contested as they may have been, had a lot to with the fact that the crisis of the Great Depression was not perceived as a systemic crisis beyond repair by the majority of Americans but, rather, as another test of America's dedication to its own way of life. In a radio address on the occasion of Abraham Lincoln's birthday on February 12, 1931, President Herbert Hoover rightly stated that there had never been an economic crisis that produced as little social disorder as the current one of unprecedented depth and destructiveness. Hoover argued that the Great Depression had released the "spirit of self-sacrifice and of service," so that the economic misery had actually rejuvenated American values. Hoover said: "We are going through a period when character and courage are on trial, and where the very faith that is within us is under test. Our people are meeting this test. And they are doing more than the immediate task of the day. They are maintaining the ideals of our American system." Hoover, as we saw in chapter 7, authored the essay *American Individualism*, and was no New Dealer, but his analysis made a point, and when his successor in office, Franklin D. Roosevelt, embarked on his reform policy, carried by an understanding of government as actively regulating economic and social processes on behalf of social justice, he understood his reform initiatives as a way to maintain the American way of life.

EXCEPTIONALISM AND AFFLUENCE IN COLD WAR AMERICA

With its economy emerging booming from World War II, the U.S. became the economic superpower of the postwar world, rivaled by none. In contrast to what many contemporaries had expected, the first twenty-five years after World War II were a period of extraordinary economic growth producing one of the longest phases of prosperity in U.S. history. Together with it went a massive expansion of consumer society. Prior to 1945, participation in America's consumer culture had been largely restricted to the upper and upper-middle classes. After 1945, the lower-middle classes, the blue-collar working class, and also the rural areas increasingly became a part of it.

The spectacular success of American consumer capitalism created what John Kenneth Galbraith called an "affluent society" in the 1950s. With this term, he described a society integrated on the basis of a consumerist consensus that saw the constant quest for superior goods and an ever higher standard of living as the principal social goals in life. In Galbraith's analysis of the affluent society, the consumption of goods was largely divorced from the question of need and subsistence. It was no longer primarily driven by the quest for food, clothing, and shelter. Rather, productive energies were used to make things that were of "no great urgency" but that promised to make life nicer and give social status and recognition to their owners. As such, the affluent society essentially was a middle-class society, i.e., a society whose majority was middle class and whose culture was homogenized on the basis of a middle-class way of life and everything that went with it. The period after 1945 saw the rapid expansion of the middle class and its notions of a good life, especially to the blue-collar working classes who, by increasingly participating in mass consumption, began to display a middle-class consciousness. The result was a dramatic improvement of blue-collar living conditions and the gradual *embourgeoisement* of the working class, whose members increasingly ceased to live proletarian lives and began leading affluent and respectable middle-class ones.

In Galbraith's analysis, consumption in the affluent society could take on a life of its own only because economic development and its pecuniary returns were a lot more stable than prior to 1945. Ongoing processes of economic concentration had created huge corporations that monopolized large sections of a market, thereby reducing competition and minimizing the risks of failure. At the same time, government, businesses, and labor organizations all worked together to regulate industrial capitalism on behalf of stability. A policy to systematically promote mass consumption was a shared consensus among political, economic, and labor leaders, who collaborated to keep prices low and wages high in an attempt to generate purchasing power in an economy built on the mass consumption of mass-produced consumer goods.

The pro-growth consensus was complemented by a welfare-state consensus that accepted government as an agent of social and economic change, legislating public measures like unemployment insurance, social security, minimum wage legislation, and public assistance programs like the G.I. Bill of Rights. Add to this the defense spending of the Cold War governments that made them the largest contractors of U.S. businesses, creators of jobs, and financiers of colleges, universities, and research institutes. Overall, therefore, America's culture of mass consumption was based on a mixed economy of public and private spending that stabilized economic development, protected the average wage-earner from the risks of free-market capitalism, and kept mass consumption going.

As the affluent society matured fully in the 1950s and 1960s, poverty became the experience of a minority. Whereas poverty, as Galbraith pointed out, had been the pervasive fact of social life in North America prior to 1945, prosperity became an experience shared by millions in the first twenty-five years after World War II. Individual incomes rose, economic security was high, consumption was ever expanding, and expectations for an even better and more affluent future were widely shared. Although prosperity in general was still unevenly distributed and far from universal, it is important to state that all strata of American society increased their incomes after 1945, two-thirds of U.S. society in one way or another shared in the affluence spreading around them, and even poverty was no longer as grim as it had been before.

We cannot further detail the structures, patterns, aspects, and problems of the post-1945 affluent society of the U.S. here. What is important to note, however, is that the enlargement of consumer society and the sustained period of prosperity carried by mass consumption reinforced notions of American Exceptionalism built on affluence after they had been invalidated during the period of the Great Depression. After 1945, a golden age of widely shared prosperity in the eyes of many a contemporary seemed to demonstrate the superiority of the American way of life. Yet, in the context of the Cold War and its global competition of the two mutually exclusive systems that the U.S. and the Soviet Union stood for, narratives of American Exceptionalism based on affluence took on a new quality insofar as America's consumer capitalism seemed to be on its way to finally realizing the utopian dream of an egalitarian middle-class society of truly free, prosperous, and self-determined citizens that the founders of America's democracy had envisioned at the end of the eighteenth century.

The historian Lizabeth Cohen has coined the term "Consumers' Republic" in a book of that same name to describe what emerged in post-1945 America. With this term, she was referring to "an economy, culture, and politics built around the promises of mass consumption, both in terms of material life and the more idealistic goals of greater freedom, democracy, and equality." This Consumers' Republic did not just materialize as the result of unknown processes and transformations inherent to free-market capitalism. Rather, it was the result of a concerted "strategy" of government, business, and labor "for reconstructing the nation's economy and reaffirming its democratic values through promoting the expansion of mass consumption."

In the Cold War years, the promotion of affluence was seen as the essence of America, and the prosperity produced by America's consumer capitalism was celebrated as a manifestation of progress and human liberation. President Harry Truman, addressing an audience in Oregon in 1950, argued that the "uses of the powers of Government to achieve a higher living standard and a fair deal for all the people" was neither statism nor socialism but "part of the American tradition." In his highly influential 1954 book *People of Plenty: Economic Abundance and the American Character*, David Potter argued that America's national identity had been shaped by the experience of economic abundance throughout history, and he highlighted the mental, cultural, and social predispositions that made Americans more likely to become prosperous than other people in the world. Six years later, economist Walt W. Rostow, in his *Stages of Economic Growth: A Non-Communist Manifesto*, saw the U.S. having reached the stage of "high mass consumption," which for him represented the pinnacle of modernization. A college textbook, *The United States: A History of a Democracy* by Wesley Marsh Gewehr, in the same year, stated:

> The goal of America has been the economic improvement of the masses, and this remains a goal which requires social and economic change. The goal of achieving a decent standard of living for all men, of abolishing poverty and inequality, has come closer to realization in the United States than was dreamed possible. [...] The American standard of living is many times the world average.

In the Cold War context, the promotion of mass consumption was not only an end in itself but also an instrument for fighting the battle against the Soviet Union, and the alternative to liberal democracy and free-market capitalism it represented. Widely shared prosperity was seen as the best bulwark against communism at home and abroad. William Levitt, a pioneer of suburban development after 1945 and creator of Long Island's Levittown, was convinced that "[n]o man who owns his own house and lot can be a Communist. He has too much to do."

However, prosperity, mass consumption, and raising the standard of living were not only economic means to contain the spread of communism. They were also seen and sold as the litmus test for the performance of the American system in the global competition with the Soviet Union. American elites from politics, business, and even labor argued that mass consumption enabled an economic egalitarianism that created a truly classless society peacefully and to the benefit of all. While Soviet communism was promising the same vision of a classless society free of war, want, and misery, and argued that the totalitarian dictatorship of the working class was the means to achieve this goal, U.S. elites argued that the liberal American model was actually superior to the communist way of realizing this utopian vision.

Most telling in this regard is the famous kitchen debate that occurred between U.S. vice president Richard Nixon and Soviet first secretary Nikita Khrushchev at the opening of the American National Exhibition at Sokolniki Park in Moscow on July 24, 1959. To represent the strength and superiority of the American way of life, the U.S. government put the latest-model homes, appliances, cars, fashions, and soft drinks on display—more than 450 consumer goods altogether. When Nixon and Khrushchev reached the fully equipped kitchen filled with labor-saving devices, Nixon said that this was what freedom meant to Americans. Pointing out that three-fourths of America's 44 million families owned their own homes, along with 56 million cars, 50 million television sets, and 143 million radios, Nixon argued that anyone in America could afford such a life of comfort, leisure, and joy. Then he said that the U.S. came "closest to the ideal of prosperity for all in a classless society." A year later, this view was seconded by Wesley Marsh Gewehr, who in his already mentioned history of the U.S., concluded that the country had "largely eliminated those class conflicts which have plagued almost all societies. The 'classless society' which Marxian socialists held up as the goal of proletarian revolution has been largely achieved by American 'capitalism,' mixed with a good deal of government welfare activity." In the global context of the Cold War, the systematic promotion of consumption became a national mission that established a connection between egalitarianism, prosperity, and America's exceptionality.

This enthusiastic celebration of mass consumption should not blind us to the fact that affluence in U.S. consumer society was neither evenly distributed nor universally shared. Rather, the mechanisms of American consumer capitalism created a highly segmented society differentiated along the lines of class, gender, and race. Yet the systematic promotion and growth of mass consumption in the first twenty-five years after World War II enabled a period of prosperity in the U.S. that was longer lasting and more universally enjoyed than ever before in American history. Seen against the backdrop of the poverty and deprivations of the Great Depression and the death, destruction, and hardships of World War II, Americans of the 1950s and 1960s were living far better and more comfortable lives than they could have possibly expected in 1945. This era of exceptional economic growth and widely shared prosperity came to an end in the 1970s—a decade that ushered in a period of crisis and uncertainty with far-reaching effects on the meaning and function of American Exceptionalism in the contemporary U.S.

This chapter has shown that the experience and expectation of affluence were key factors in the conceptual history of American Exceptionalism. They created the idea of an American Dream that took different shapes and forms in the repeatedly changing economic and social contexts of U.S. history. Originally tied to notions of republican virtue and citizenship in an order based on individual freedom, the American Dream, in the course of time, was largely divorced from the complex moral universe in which Benjamin Franklin was moving when he wrote his autobiography in the last quarter of the eighteenth century.

We have seen that affluence and plenty provided a rather frail base to concepts of American Exceptionalism. The validity and acceptance of exceptionalist persuasions was inseparably tied to the ability of the American way of life to actually produce affluence for the many. In this context, it is important to note that the American way of life, and the values it is based on, originated in an agrarian world, and that urbanization, industrialization, and the corporate transformation of American capitalism changed the rules of the game massively, undermining the meritocratic ethos of hard work, frugality, self-reliance, and individual achievement, which the American Dream was originally built on.

Finally, this chapter has shown economic downturns like the Great Depression have the potential to let affluence-centered concepts of American Exceptionalism disintegrate rather quickly. Economic crises have the potential to trigger crises of disorientation and identity in the U.S. that go far beyond material matters. This has to do with the fact that the anticipation of affluence—the hope of getting rich through one's own talents, skills, and hard work—has done more to validate ideas of American Exceptionalism than the actual experience of it.

9

Crisis of Disorientation

Contested Exceptionalisms in Contemporary America

IT DID NOT TAKE THE CORONAVIRUS, the police killing of George Floyd, or the storming of the U.S. Capitol by militant Trump supporters to shatter the belief among Americans that the U.S. was the best country on earth. The "American-Western European Values Gap" survey conducted by the Global Attitudes Project at the Pew Research Center in 2011, already cited in the introduction to this book, showed that just 49 percent of Americans still held their country to be superior, a decline of 11 percent from 2002, when the survey was first conducted. The polling also showed that, while the belief in America's cultural superiority had declined among Americans across all age, gender, and education groups, it was most dramatic in the cohort of those younger than thirty, where 61 percent denied that American culture was superior. The declining belief in America's political and moral superiority defines a deep crisis of uncertainty about American identity that has been building since the 1970s and that grows out of the fundamental and rapidly accelerating transformations the U.S. has gone through in this period.

TRENDS AND TRANSFORMATIONS IN THE U.S. SINCE THE MID-SEVENTIES UNDERMINING EXCEPTIONALIST CERTAINTIES

The history of U.S. politics and government since 1970 is defined by a series of scandals that provide little reason to see America's democracy as a shining example of virtuous politics superior to the rest of the world. In the Watergate scandal, U.S. president Richard Nixon abused his executive powers to cover up the criminal burglary by five men of the Democratic National Committee headquarters at the Watergate office complex in Washington, DC, on June 17, 1972. Only a decade later, the Reagan administration gave the country its Iran-Contra affair: Senior administration officials, circumventing an official arms embargo, secretly facilitated the sale of more than 2,500 U.S.-made missiles to Iran, and used the proceeds to support the Contras in Nicaragua. Thereby, they thereby knowingly violated congressional legislation prohibiting the further funding of Contra warfare against the Sandinista government. The 1990s witnessed the Clinton-Lewinsky affair, a political scandal that had President Clinton lying about his extramarital sexual relationship with the twenty-two-year-old White House intern Monica Lewinsky, which led to his impeachment. The first decade of the new millennium saw the Bush administration lying about the existence of weapons of mass destruction in Iraq to justify an ill-advised and costly war that destabilized the entire Middle East. Finally, there was President Trump, who lived in world of "alternative facts," refused to accept the reality of regular election results, and instigated the sack of the U.S. Capitol in a last desperate attempt to disrupt the constitutional procedures of American democracy. With a disbelieving world watching the events in Washington, DC, unfold, Germany's foreign minister, Heiko Maas, on January 10, 2021, boldly offered the U.S. a "Marshall Plan for Democracy," under which Europeans—led by Germany of all countries—would guide Americans back to the true path of liberal democracy.

In the arena of congressional politics, the period since roughly the mid-1970s was a time of growing, and rapidly accelerating, political polarization that has let the ability and willingness of politicians to compromise erode to a troublesome degree. An increasingly aggressive partisan particularism, the rise of political ideologues in both parties, and the moralization of politics along the lines of *good* and *evil* has marginalized moderates on both sides of the political aisle. As a consequence, the federal government has become largely dysfunctional. The high-flying hopes that many Americans place in government, despite their widespread skepticism about political power as such, have been continuously disappointed.

On a more abstract level, the legitimacy and integrity of the U.S. constitutional order have become increasingly problematic. The two-party system combined with the winner-take-all principle led to the presidential elections of 2000 and 2016 being decided not by the popular majority but by the U.S. Supreme Court and the idiosyncrasies of the U.S. electoral system. Other incidents have called the integrity of the U.S. Constitution into question as well. The filling of U.S. Supreme Court vacancies has become a partisan issue, with the potential to trigger constitutional crises. In 1987, the U.S. Senate rejected Robert Bork's nomination to the U.S. Supreme Court on political grounds; Bork appeared to be too conservative. In 2016, the Republican majority of the Senate refused to process President Obama's nomination of Merrick Garland as successor for Associate U.S. Supreme Court Justice Antonin Scalia, with senators arguing that they wanted to withhold voting on any potential nominee in a presidential-election year. When the newly elected president Trump twice got the chance to nominate U.S. Supreme Court justices, both of his nominations, Neil Gorsuch and Brett Kavanaugh, were highly contested for political and ethical reasons, triggering partisan warfare in the Senate that brought the U.S. to the brink of a constitutional crisis.

While these events all demonstrate a highly troublesome gradual erosion of hitherto accepted institutional procedures and tacit agreements on how things should be decided, President Trump inflicted even greater damage on America's political institutions. Already in 2016, when still a candidate for the presidency, he called the legitimacy of the democratic process as such into question. After keeping the country in suspense for weeks over whether he would accept the election results, he said at an election rally at the Delaware County Fair in Ohio on October 20, 2016: "I will totally accept the results of this great and historic presidential election. If I win." From today's perspective, these lines fatally foreshadowed what would happen in the 2020 elections; Trump's refusal to accept Joe Biden's election victory and his attempts to stop the certification process of the election results by all means did not come out of the blue.

Apart from the integrity of the U.S. Constitution increasingly being called into question under the auspices of extreme political polarization and partisanship, two of the most significant changes in America's democracy over the last fifty years have been declining public participation and the growing influence of money on the outcome of popular elections. Only an average of 54 percent of all eligible voters have turned out for presidential elections since 1976, with the elections of 1988, 1996, and 2000 being decided by only half of the voting-age population. In the three decades before 1976, an average of 59 percent of all voters had cast their ballots in the presidential elections; the 1960s even witnessed a voter turnout of more than 60 percent.

With participation in U.S. democracy declining since the mid-1970s, the influence of money buying political access and influence has increased tremendously. The skyrocketing costs of election campaigns have increased candidates' dependence on their own fortunes and wealthy donors to an unprecedented degree. Lobbying has become a profession pushing special interests at the expense of the common good. All of these developments have largely invalidated all claims to America's democracy being politically and morally superior.

In international politics, the failure of U.S. policy in Vietnam was signed and sealed with the victory of North Vietnam and the unification of the country on Communist terms in 1975. In 1979–1981, the Iranian Revolution and the ensuing hostage crisis at the U.S. embassy in Teheran saw the U.S. acting helplessly. The moment of triumph in 1989–1991, when the Cold War ended with a victory of the U.S.-led Western alliance, was short-lived. A new American world order based on a Pax Americana did not come to pass in the 1990s, and visions of a world made of market democracies peacefully trading with each other and promoting global prosperity and welfare all over the world did not materialize. In contrast to what Francis Fukuyama predicted in his 1992 book *The End of History and the Last Man,* history did not end with the failure of communism as the last great alternative to liberal democracy and free-market capitalism. Even before the turn of the millennium, it had become obvious that liberal democracy and free-market capitalism would not be the only games in town for all of time to come. The terrorist attacks of September 11, 2001, demonstrated the destructive potential of an aggressive Islamic fundamentalism that rejected the American way of life as the purest manifestation of a Western modernity it did not want. While the War on Terror gave U.S. foreign policy a new direction, to be sure, it did so at the price of long, costly, and eventually unwinnable wars in Afghanistan and Iraq, which were a heavy burden on U.S. society.

During the Cold War, U.S. international leadership rested on moral credibility and the widely shared conviction that the U.S., in its conduct as a superpower, had lived up to its own standards, working to protect and spread human rights, and obeying the norms of behavior it promoted all over the world. Since the end of the Cold War, this has changed significantly. Especially after 9/11, the U.S. developed into a hegemon that felt no longer bound by its own values in the pursuit of international policies. Instead of leading by persuasion, the U.S. government spread democracy at gunpoint, denying its terrorist enemies basic rights, preferring military solutions over civilian ones, and adopting a policy of what Godfrey Hodgson, in his *The Myth of American Exceptionalism*, has called "exemptionalism." This term refers to the new conduct of the U.S. in international affairs by which it "exempted itself from standards it wanted to impose on others."

As consequence, the history of both U.S. domestic and foreign policy since the 1970s has produced among Americans a deep frustration with politics that has translated into a rapid decline of trust in government. According to the April 11, 2019, Pew Research Center survey "Little Public Support for Reductions in Federal Spending" (an update of its 2015 "Beyond Distrust: How Americans View Their Government" examination), public trust in the government remained near historic lows. Only 17 percent of Americans said they could trust the government in Washington to do what is right "just about always" (3 percent) or "most of the time" (14 percent). The study explained that trust in government began eroding during the 1960s, amid the escalation of the Vietnam War, and that the decline continued in the 1970s with the Watergate scandal and the economic crisis of that decade. Confidence in government recovered in the mid-1980s without ever reaching its pre-1970 heights, then it fell again in the mid-1990s. Toward the end of the 1990s, trust in government started to rise again briefly, reaching a three-decade high shortly after the 9/11 terrorist attacks. Even this high, however, was a far cry from where figures had been in 1965, and it did not last long, since trust in government quickly declined again in the wake of the Iraq War. Since 2007, the share of the U.S. population saying they can trust the government always or most of the time has never surpassed 30 percent.

However, not only politics undermined exceptionalist persuasions since the 1970s. Economic developments of this period have done their share as well. They may have even greater weight than political developments because much about American Exceptionalism is, as we have seen in chapter 8, connected to the experience of affluence, and even more to the hopeful expectation of it, or even greater affluence for the future.

Concepts of national identity built around American Exceptionalism to a very great extent have been anchored in the conviction that the future would be better than the present, and that children would be even better off economically than their parents. Due to the deep transformations of America's economic order since the 1970s, this widely shared optimism about the future has been clouded, if not shattered altogether.

In the 1970s, the U.S., although remaining the strongest economy in the world, began losing its position in an increasingly globalized economy. The oil crises of the 1970s demonstrated that an economic giant like the U.S. could be easily held hostage by a few oil-producing countries in the less-developed parts of the world. While the U.S. economy had historically been exceptional in its self-sufficiency in raw materials and energy, the oil crises of the 1970s demonstrated the degree to which the U.S. had become dependent on the importation of oil. Furthermore, the 1970s were the decade of "stagflation," a bizarre combination of economic stagnation and high inflation, which had President Jimmy Carter reflect on the limits of growth in his "Crisis of Confidence" speech, delivered to an unbelieving television audience on July 15, 1979. In it, Carter sought to prepare the country for a post-growth era demanding sacrifice from everyone.

While the oil crises were single events, deindustrialization was an ongoing structural transformation that accelerated significantly in the 1970s, turning the U.S. manufacturing belt into the Rust Belt in the 1980s. A large number of factories in the Great Lakes area were closed down, millions of manufacturing jobs were lost to low-wage countries in Asia and Latin America, and cities like Detroit and Youngstown became industrial wastelands. The North American Free Trade Agreement (NAFTA), which went into effect in 1994, only accelerated the deindustrialization of the U.S. industrial heartland.

The new postindustrial order that emerged as manufacturing declined was dominated by the service sector, which offered a few high-paying and lucrative jobs for the already privileged, highly skilled, educated elites, and millions of low-paying, unprotected jobs at or slightly above minimum wage. The technology revolution of the 1980s and 1990s, along with even more efficient and reliable transportation systems on land, on sea, and in the air created a new economic order in a rapidly globalizing world that developed and designed products in the U.S. and had them manufactured in Mexico, Vietnam, or China. Although the 1990s were economically good times for many Americans, the boom did not last long. In 2000, President Bill Clinton, in his State of the Union address, said that the country had never been better off. Unemployment was low, economic activity was high, and the U.S. was experiencing "the longest period of economic growth" in its "entire history." A few weeks later, the dot-com bubble burst in March 2000, triggering a deep recession in 2001, from which the U.S. had barely recovered when the financial crisis of 2007–2008 hit the country and produced the gravest economic crisis since the Great Depression. Finally, the COVID-19 crisis demonstrated for everyone that the global economy is built on the verge of instant chaos.

Overall, the economy of the digital age has not produced new jobs for the many in developed countries. While nineteenth-century technologies like railroads, the electric motor, and the internal combustion engine did create mass employment, there is little evidence that computers and the internet produce a lot of jobs, let alone well-paying jobs. The digital revolution has pushed automation even further. Automation means that machines are supervising and running other machines, that computers and robots are doing the work that human beings used to do. Factories have become smart but largely devoid of human workers; supply chain models, cloud-based forms of work, and artificial intelligence have been reducing the need for human laborers even more. The globalized economy of the digital age produces greater and greater profits and wealth with fewer and fewer workers. Computer and software giants like Apple, Microsoft, Google, and Amazon do not employ very many people, compared to the leading companies of the industrial age like Ford, Kodak, or General Electric. At the same time, the internet economy has destroyed countless jobs in retail, publishing, transportation, travel, entertainment, and other fields. In the mid-1990s, there were around four thousand bookstores in the U.S.; in 2015, there were half that number. The internet economy is squeezing jobs in other retail sectors, too. In 2013, the U.S. Institute of Local Self-Reliance (ILSR) reported that brick-and-mortar retailers employ 47 people for every $10 million in sales. Amazon did the same with only 14 people. Overall, therefore, the combination of deindustrialization, the expansion of the service sector, and the rise of the internet economy has created a structural unemployment crisis in the

U.S. that makes it hard for a growing number of Americans to wholeheartedly embrace exceptionalist narratives built around the ability of the U.S. to provide affluent and comfortable lives to those willing to work hard.

Along with deep economic transformations, dramatic changes in U.S. society have contributed to a widely shared uncertainty about America's exceptional status. Since the 1970s, American society has become more unequal and more diverse, with both developments, each in its own way, unsettling exceptionalist persuasions.

While the decades from 1940 to the mid-1970s witnessed the so-called "Great Compression," the years since the late 1970s have witnessed a dramatic growth in income inequality that has hit middle-income households particularly hard. During the 1950s and 1960s, income inequality in the U.S. was at its twentieth-century low. Real incomes were rising, the American middle class was expanding, the working class was on its way to a middle-class way of life, and in 1970 the top 1 percent of American households earned 9 percent of national income. Large parts of American society were participating in the affluent society, and wealth was more equitably shared than ever before in U.S. history. Then the economic troubles of the 1970s and the hegemony of conservative economic thought in U.S. politics, revolving around deregulation, the reduction of government, and tax breaks (especially for the top echelons of society), ushered in what Nobel laureate, Princeton economist, and *New York Times* columnist Paul Krugman and journalist Timothy Noah have called the "Great Divergence." With this term, they referred to a process of growing income inequality in American society that essentially unfolded as a redistribution of wealth from bottom to top.

According to the Congressional Budget Office's statistical survey "The Distribution of Household Income," published in October 2020, average household income between 1979 and 2017 increased considerably across all five income brackets. The statistics also show, however, that this increase was far from equitably shared. In 2017, average income before transfers and taxes among households in the lowest bracket was about $21,300; among those of the highest bracket it was about $309,400— "more than 14 times the average income of households in the lowest quintile." Looking at long-term developments, average real income among America's top 20 percent in 2017 was 108 percent higher than it was in 1979; for the other four quintiles, it was only 35 percent greater. A closer look at the top bracket also reveals that within this group, the income of the top 1 percent skyrocketed by 261 percent between 1979 and 2017; this figure includes the heavy losses this income group suffered in the financial crisis of 2008. Thus, middle-class households have been confronted with largely stagnating incomes, while the top 20 percent of U.S. households have gotten significantly richer since the mid-seventies.

At the same time, private debt has been rising, with ups and downs. According to the most recent *Quarterly Report on Household Debt and Credit* issued by the Federal Reserve Bank of New York's Center for Microeconomic Data in February 2021, household debt in the U.S. has been continuously on the rise since 2013, standing at a stunning $14.56 trillion at the end of 2020. While disposable income, therefore, has increased across the board since 1979, a significant share of it goes into servicing a dramatically growing private debt. Thus, to agree with Paul Krugman, income distribution in the U.S. since the 1980s has reverted to the Gilded Age pattern, making American incomes currently the most unequal in the world.

The effects of growing income inequality are felt everywhere in contemporary American life. Poverty has become ever more visible in both the countryside and inner-city areas, while those who can afford it are retreating behind the walls of gated communities that seal the affluent off against the rest of U.S. society. The cost of higher education has exploded to a degree that even college professors can hardly afford their children's education; there is a widespread fear of losing one's social status and standing that nurtures an uncertainty if not pessimism about the future. These developments undermine one key idea of American Exceptionalism, namely, that the U.S. is a land where everybody has a fair chance of acquiring wealth.

The second major societal transformation that has let exceptionalist certainties erode since the 1970s is the dramatically growing diversity in U.S. society. Over the last fifty-five years, U.S. society has become more diverse and also more individualistic. While diversification was largely wrought by the new wave of mass immigration triggered by the Immigration and Nationality Act of 1965, also known as the Hart-Celler Act, the processes of individualization were the result of a multiplication of lifestyles in the wake of the civil rights revolution of the 1960s.

Since the 1970s, the U.S. has been fundamentally shaped by a new wave of mass immigration that has not yet ended. This migratory process has changed the demographic, social, and cultural landscape tremendously. The reform legislation of the 1960s ended a forty-year period of highly restrictive immigration policies. The Hart-Celler Act raised the number of immigrants allowed into the country significantly, and it abolished the national quota system introduced by the National Origins Act of 1924, replacing it with a system of hemispheric ceilings instead. In the wake of the Hart-Celler Immigration Reform Act, millions of immigrants flocked to the U.S.: 4.5 million came during the 1970s, 7.3 million during the 1980s, 9.1. million during the 1990s, and an unprecedented 13.9 million from 2000 to 2010. According to estimates of the Census Bureau, another more than 8.4 million immigrants have come to the U.S. since 2010. In addition, there are a significant number of illegal, undocumented immigrants who came to the U.S. by crossing the 3,000-mile border between the U.S. and Mexico. As a recent article, "Frequently Requested Statistics on Immigrants and Immigration in the United States," published by the online journal of the Washington-based Migration Policy Institute on February 11, 2021, shows, more than 44.9 million immigrants resided in the U.S. in 2019, with immigrants' share of the overall U.S. population at 13.7 percent. In 1970, only 4.7 percent of all Americans were foreign born. In all, current immigration surpasses all earlier migration waves by far.

Immigrants' demographic makeup is just as important as their sheer numbers. Roughly three-fourths of all immigrants since 1970 came from Latin America, Asia, and Africa; only about 20 percent arrived from Europe, most of them from successor states to the Soviet Union. This means that the Euro-Atlantic migration system, which dominated and structured voluntary immigration to the U.S. from the sixteenth century to 1914, has dramatically lost importance. Current immigration to the U.S. is fueled by two new migration systems, a Pacific and a hemispheric one. As a result, Latinos and Asian Americans are currently the fastest-growing communities in the U.S., while the number of African Americans is relatively stable, and the percentage of Caucasians with a European background is declining.

The new immigration has led to a considerable de-Europeanization of the U.S. On June 15, 1997, President Clinton was quoted in *The*

Tennessean, stating that the U.S. was in need of a third "great revolution." According to Clinton, the first two revolutions were the American Revolution of the eighteenth century and the civil rights revolution of the 1960s. The third still lay ahead, he said, and it was to prove that Americans "literally can live without having a dominant European culture."

The implications of this statement for the history of American Exceptionalism can hardly be overestimated, given that the measure for America's exceptionality had always been Europe. The different elements, images, symbols, and narratives defining the conceptual history of American Exceptionalism, in one way or another, suggested that America was exceptional because it was *not* Europe, and the main carriers of this idea were European immigrants or Americans of European descent who used the concept to justify the political, economic, and cultural hegemony of white, male, Anglo-Saxon Protestants and their Caucasian friends from northern and western Europe. In a society that has increasingly become a mirror of world society, ideas of American Exceptionalism formulated on the basis of European experiences are losing their grip.

Yet U.S. societal development since the mid-1970s is not only characterized by an ethnic pluralization. In the wake of the civil rights revolution of the 1960s, lifestyle choices have multiplied as well. The 1960s implanted a new rights consciousness in American society that went well beyond the question of equal rights for African Americans. Rather, it took the idea of self-determination to ever-wider contexts, driven by a new individualism that posits every individual's right to be different. This new rights consciousness celebrated the autonomous individual, emancipating him or her from all traditions, conventions, and norms to make lifestyles a matter of choice more than ever before. This trend has multiplied the spectrum of acceptable lifestyles significantly, and it has created a multitude of subcultures, each with their own specific way of life, and largely sealed off against the others. The new digital communication technologies, internet, and new social media platforms like Facebook, Instagram, and Twitter have reinforced both the preoccupation with one's individual self and the fragmentation of lifestyles. The effect of this process of rapidly accelerating individualization is that it becomes increasingly impossible to define what the American way of life actually is and what norms it is built on. This, in turn, also makes it hard to define exactly in which lifestyle American Exceptionalism manifests itself.

In combination with growing inequality, the new degree of ethnic pluralism and the accelerating processes of individualization have fueled a series of violent, and largely moral, debates about the meaning of America and the course of American history. The issues of abortion, extramarital sex, homosexuality, same-sex partnerships, and the seemingly God-forgotten hedonism of American culture have mobilized the Christian Right. Finding their platform in the Republican Party and merging with other conservatives to form the New Right, Christian conservatives have embarked on a crusade against the liberal lifestyles of the 1960s. Their agenda aims at freezing, if not turning back, the ongoing processes of diversification and pluralization on behalf of an alleged "American normalcy" that is essentially white, middle-class, heterosexual, religiously pious, and centered on the normative ideal of the American family as a married heterosexual couple with children.

On the other side of the political spectrum, the rise of the New Right has triggered determined reactions that want to push the rights-consciousness-driven culture of individual self-determination and the diversification of American life even further. The liberal agenda stretches from issues of complete gender equality, minority rights, and the fight against racism to abortion rights, the legalization of same-sex marriages, and the recognition of transgender and non-binary individuals. Overall, therefore, U.S. society has become more and more polarized over questions of morality and lifestyles since the mid-1970, largely as a result of a conservative backlash against the emancipatory gains of the 1960s.

This polarization has triggered a series of culture wars since the end of the Cold War that have contributed massively to the erosion of exceptionalist convictions in the U.S. One major effect of the civil rights revolution of the 1960s was the multiplication of voices and actors in U.S. history. In the wake of the 1960s, not only African Americans but also women, American Indians, and other minorities claimed their right to be recognized as subjects of U.S. history. No longer did they want to be treated as mere objects of an essentially white, male, Anglo-Saxon, and Protestant history but as historical actors in their own right to whom things were not only being done but who had acted themselves in the multiple contexts of the past. A major case in point is the much-debated question of who freed the slaves in the Civil War. Was it President Lincoln acting as the great white male emancipator who finally fulfilled the emancipatory promise of the American Revolution, or did the slaves free themselves by running away from their plantations, following the Union army, or committing countless acts of obstruction and resistance on their plantations during the Civil War?

Wanting to be given their own voice, African Americans, women, American Indians, and other hitherto marginalized groups worked out their own narratives of U.S. history—and most of them unfolded as a determined critique of the exceptionalist master narratives featuring white, Anglo-Saxon, Protestant males as dominant historical actors. In light of this complex and multifaceted criticism, the American Revolution no longer appeared as the forceful beginning of a new era of universal human freedom, but as an event that perpetuated slavery and the patriarchal rule of men over women. Instead of being interpreted as America's "second revolution" ushering in a new birth of freedom, the Civil War and Reconstruction periods were addressed as an "unfinished revolution" (Eric Foner) that petrified racism and racist discrimination against blacks in the U.S. Furthermore, the nation's dynamic westward expansion could no longer be dealt with as the fulfillment of a Manifest Destiny to spread liberty and Euro-American civilization. Rather, it was conceived of as a destructive process exterminating the American Indians, destroying the environment, and cementing inequality along the lines of gender, race, and class. The frontier was no longer the site of equality and the rugged individualism of heroic Anglo-Saxon settlers that rejuvenated American democracy time and again. Quite the contrary, the westernmost settlements were identified as a place of highly primitive living conditions where people were more preoccupied with survival than with the ideals of freedom and participation. Instead of being interpreted as a place where white, Anglo-Saxon Protestant culture was perennially being reborn, the frontier areas were discovered to be sites where several cultures met, interacted, and mingled to produce new and hybrid borderland cultures that were as much Anglo-Saxon as they were pan-European, American Indian, Hispanic, or Asian.

Finally, U.S. expansion abroad and its rise to superpower status was no longer seen as happening against the will of U.S. political leaders and as being driven by the selfless benevolent American quest to enlarge the sphere of freedom, democracy, and prosperity worldwide. Rather, post-1960s historiography, informed by the traumatic experience in Vietnam and carried by a growing anti-exceptionalist critique in U.S. society, tended to feature the imperialist design that U.S. foreign policy had from the start, and highlighted the multiple forms of aggressive domination that the U.S. was capable of abroad. This historiography argued that the U.S. economic penetration of the world was to a very large extent driven by a capitalist quest for profit that exploited less-developed countries abroad, interfered with the integrity of foreign states, infringed upon their right to self-determination, and destroyed environments and people there.

In all, these controversial debates about the course and character of U.S. history have shattered the belief that U.S. history followed unique trajectories. Instead of reflecting U.S. history essentially on its own terms, recent trends in historiography encourage us to think of U.S. history not as an exception to global patterns, trends, and contexts but, rather, as a variation of them. Eminent historians Ian Tyrell, Thomas Bender, David Thelen, and others have reflected U.S. history as the history of a "nation among nations," which, for always having been entangled with developments in other world regions, could not be understood in isolation from the rest of the world.

NEGATIVE EXCEPTIONALISMS

The COVID-19 virus has highlighted once again that there are aspects of life where the U.S. the falls behind the international standards of the developed world. However, the U.S. did not need the coronavirus to reveal the deficiencies of its health care system. It was all out in the open before: The U.S. health care system is by far the most expensive and least accessible in the world, and compared to other developed countries, it is not performing very well. A look at indicators such as life expectancy and infant mortality rates shows that the U.S. has been trailing comparable countries like Japan, Switzerland, Australia, Sweden, France, Germany, and Canada since the 1980s. According to the Peterson-Kaiser Health System Tracker, the U.S. has seen significantly lower life expectancy at birth than the countries mentioned above. With life expectancy at birth in the U.S. standing at 78.6 years in 2017, it was far behind the average of 82.3 years for comparable countries. At the same time, infant mortality in the U.S. was significantly higher. While Japan only lost 2.0 babies per 1,000 births in 2017, the U.S. lost 5.8. U.S. infant mortality rates in 2017 were about 71 percent higher than in the other developed countries of the world. Other indicators show that the U.S., since the 1980s, has routinely been outperformed on many fronts by countries with universal health care.

The U.S. is also negatively exceptional in the criminal justice system: It features the highest incarceration rates in the world. The 2020 Bureau of Justice Statistics (BJS) report "Prisoners in 2019" showed that there were 419 sentenced prisoners per 100,000 U.S. residents in state and federal prisons combined at the end of 2019. While this was the lowest incarceration rate since 1995, the total population of sentenced prisoners in the U.S. still comprised more than 1.4 million people. At its peak in 2009, the Bureau had counted more than 1.6 million inmates in state and federal prisons. These numbers, however, count only prisoners sentenced to serve more than a year. When you add the large number of people locked up on pretrial detention without being convicted of any crime, the U.S. prison population and incarceration rates are significantly higher. The report of the Prison Policy Initiative "Mass Incarceration: The Whole Pie 2020" speaks of almost 2.3 million people held by the American criminal justice system in 1,833 state prisons, 110 federal prisons, 1,772 juvenile correctional facilities, 3,134 local jails, 218 immigration detention facilities, and 80 Indian Country jails as well as in military prisons, civil commitment centers, state psychiatric hospitals, and prisons in the U.S. territories. With this, the U.S. locks up more people per capita than any other nation—its rate currently is 698 prisoners per 100,000 residents. In all, the U.S. represents less than 5 percent of the world's population, and it houses more than 20 percent of its prisoners.

At the same time, incarceration in the U.S. is characterized by a grotesque racial imbalance in that African Americans and Latinos are (measured against their share of the overall adult population) grossly overrepresented in the prison population. At the end of 2019, according to BJS statistics, there were 1,096 sentenced black prisoners per 100,000 black residents, and 525 sentenced Latino prisoners per 100,000 Latino residents, but only 214 sentenced white prisoners per 100,000 white residents in the U.S. In 2018, again according to BJS statistics, African

Americans represented 12 percent of the adult population but 33 percent of the prison population. Latinos, while representing 16 percent of the adult population, accounted for 23 percent of inmates. Whites, by contrast, accounted for 63 percent of all American adults and 30 percent of prisoners. This racial imbalance has led Michelle Alexander to speak of a new Jim Crow regime in the U.S.

Besides incarceration rates, the U.S. is among the leading nations in the world regarding capital punishment. According to the Death Penalty Information Center in Washington, DC, 1,532 criminals have been legally executed since 1977, with 170 executions taking place from 2013 to 2018. With these figures, the U.S. is—and since the 1980s has continuously been—in embarrassingly exceptional company. According to Amnesty International's report for 2019, the U.S., with China, Iran, Saudi Arabia, Iraq, and Egypt, was among the six countries that executed the most criminals in the world.

One could also point to other fields, from public education to environmental protection and gun control, to show how the U.S. has fallen far behind the best international standards. In light of all these developments, wrote Godfrey Hodgson in his *The Myth of American Exceptionalism*, "it can no longer be maintained, without argument, that America is proudly exceptional. In so many fields where Americans long believed, often justifiably, that their society was both exceptionally successful and exceptionally virtuous, it is now just one great, but imperfect, country among others."

AMERICAN EXCEPTIONALISM AS A FACTOR OF DIVISION IN CONTEMPORARY AMERICA

While belief in America's political, social, economic, and cultural superiority has declined in the U.S. since the mid-1970s, ideas, symbols, images, and narratives of American Exceptionalism still continue to matter as a cultural force in today's America. However, instead of creating social cohesion and a sense of unity, the concept of American Exceptionalism not only mirrors the existing divisions but plays a role in deepening socio-moral divides.

In this context, it is telling that only two U.S. presidents since the 1970s, Ronald Reagan and Barack Obama, have enthusiastically embraced concepts of American Exceptionalism without reservations, although they did so in very different ways.

Reagan, whose election as president in 1980 ushered in an era of conservative politics and government in the U.S. that has not yet ended, embraced a narrative of American Exceptionalism that celebrated small government and the free, unregulated market as the essence of the American way of life. Reagan's conservatism unfolded as a rebellion against the New Deal state and the liberal ethos it was built on. The idea of government as an agent of change on behalf of social justice, for Reagan, was destroying liberty, prosperity, and national pride. Charging liberal politics and government with demolishing the very basis of America's exceptionality, Reagan sold his own conservative agenda as a return to the true course of American politics and history that would restore American political and moral superiority.

Reagan's version of American Exceptionalism found its clearest manifestation in his first and last speeches as the fortieth president. In his inaugural address of January 20, 1981, Reagan painted a bleak picture of the deep U.S. economic troubles that had triggered a crisis of disorientation about the meaning of America. The stagflation of the 1970s, he said, had led to idle industries casting "workers into unemployment, causing human misery, and personal indignity. Those who do work are denied a fair return for their labor by a tax system which penalizes successful achievement and keeps us from maintaining full productivity." In this situation, Reagan famously exclaimed, "[G]overnment is not the solution to our problem; government is the problem." He then stated that, although he did not want "to do away with government" altogether, it was his "intention to curb the size and influence of the Federal establishment" to create a government that provided opportunity, not smothered it, and that fostered productivity, not stifled it. This agenda, Reagan anticipated, was the way to make America "a beacon of hope for those who do not now have freedom."

Reagan's dogma of small government translated into a policy of deregulation and a massive reduction of federal income taxes, which curbed the welfare state and significantly limited the options for an active government addressing basic social needs. Supply-side economics and monetarism—both connected to the teachings of Milton Friedman and his Chicago school of economics—replaced the demand-side approach of John Maynard Keynes to become the dominant economic doctrine in the U.S. As the tax-reduction policy was complemented by a policy of military strength translating into a strong military buildup, the "Reagan Revolution" in government created astronomically high budget deficits that actually impoverished the government and limited its range of activity even further.

Be that as it may, Reagan successfully managed to sell his conservative faith in small government, deregulation, tax breaks, and military strength as the true manifestation of American Exceptionalism. In his farewell address to the nation, delivered from the Oval Office on January 11, 1989, he used his last words as president to explain his understanding of the U.S. as a "shining city upon a hill." Pointing out that this phrase came from John Winthrop, who led the Congregationalist Puritans to New England in 1630, Reagan intimated that he himself had spoken of America as "the shining city" all his political life without ever fully explaining what he meant by it. He went on to describe his vision of the U.S. as

> a tall, proud city built on rocks stronger than oceans, wind-swept, God-blessed, and teeming with people of all kinds living in harmony and peace; a city with free ports that hummed with commerce and creativity. And if there had to be city walls, the walls had doors and the doors were open to anyone with the will and the heart to get here. That's how I saw it, and see it still.

Reagan's political mind and persona ushered in a period of conservative hegemony in politics and government, a coherent epoch that eminent liberal historian Sean Wilentz, in a magisterial chronicle of American political history from 1974 to 2008, has defined as the Age of Reagan. This period of U.S. history witnessed the ideologization of conservative politics to an unprecedented degree. Conservatives managed to seize and keep control of the terms of public debate, and they framed politics in terms of binary moral oppositions along the lines of good versus bad, us versus them, conservative versus liberal. In this context, they utilized exceptionalist narratives to justify both their own political agenda and their contempt of liberalism. The right-wing Tea Party movement, which formed as a response to President Obama's health care policy, can serve as a case in point. According to their 2009 mission statement published on their website, Tea Party activists thought of themselves as "patriots" united by "the same set of core principles that brought America together at its founding, that kindled the American Dream in the hearts of those who struggled to build our nation, and made the United States of America the greatest, most successful country in world history." The "Tea Party Patriots" saw "three guiding principles" giving rise to "the freedom necessary to pursue and live the American Dream": personal liberty, economic freedom, and a debt-free future.

In the field of foreign policy, conservative narratives of exceptionalism served to justify a new isolationism that wants the U.S. to retreat from its commitment to the very liberal world order that it created under many sacrifices in the course of the twentieth century. Reflecting on the political outlook of Sarah Palin, a right-wing icon of the Tea Party movement and vice presidential running mate of John McCain in 2008, Roger Cohen argued in his *New York Times* column of September 25, 2008, that American Exceptionalism had

> taken an ugly twist of late. It's become the angry refuge of the America that wants to deny the real state of the world. From an inspirational notion, however flawed in execution, that has buttressed the global spread of liberty, American exceptionalism has morphed into the fortress of those who see themselves threatened by "one-worlders" (read Barack Obama) and who believe it's more important to know how to dress moose than find Mumbai.

Behind the conservative exceptionalism personified by Palin, Cohen argued, lay an anger that had been "growing as America's relative decline has become more manifest in falling incomes, imploding markets, massive debt and rising new centers of wealth and power from Shanghai to Dubai."

While conservative narratives tend to suggest that American Exceptionalism is in need of restoration after the welfare aberrations of the New Deal state and the liberal internationalism of U.S. foreign policy, President Obama and his political followers articulated a different version of American Exceptionalism. Their liberal narrative was largely carried by the theme of the U.S. as a perfectible union and an ongoing experiment whose promise of liberty and self-determination still had to be fulfilled in a more inclusive and just America. The full realization of America's exceptionalist potential thus still lay ahead. Obama inaugurated his presidential campaign in 2007 as a we-the-people movement to create an America that provided a home not only for African Americans, but also for gays and lesbians, the disabled, marginalized ethnic groups, and all those economically left behind in the post-9/11 and post-Katrina worlds. To frame his political campaign and mobilize support for it, Obama utilized the concepts of the American Dream, the perfectible Union, and the land of promise, and he reiterated these themes throughout his two terms in the Oval Office, as we have seen in great detail in chapter 6. Where Ronald Reagan, in his farewell address, described an existing "shining city upon a hill" that he had actually seen through the windows of the White House, Obama, in his own farewell address, delivered on January 10, 2017, to a roaring crowd at the McCormick Place convention center in Chicago, spoke of the U.S. as a country that was still in the process of becoming an ideal place. Describing America as an ever-changing democracy developing toward higher and higher degrees of tolerance, freedom, and justice, he concluded: "So that's what we mean when we say America is exceptional. Not that our nation has been flawless from the start, but that we have shown the capacity to change, and make life better for those who follow."

This liberal version of the U.S. as an exceptional place in the making was embraced by those individuals and groups in contemporary America that wanted to push rights-conscious agendas of emancipation further and further. Thus, on May 1, 2015, GrafZeppelin127 posted an article titled "Marriage and American Exceptionalism" on Daily Kos, an American political blog. In it, the author urged the U.S. to embrace gay marriage as a fundamental right of citizenship; he made his point by asking: "Wouldn't it be perfectly in line with American exceptionalism, and with America being an exceptional nation [. . .] [to] break down one of the last barriers to true liberty and equality, one of the last anachronistic prejudices, that still exists in the world?" Should America allow same-sex marriages, "America will not only be exceptional, it will be *FABULOUS*."

All of the above shows that concepts of American Exceptionalism in contemporary America, instead of uniting the country behind a widely shared, consensual identity narrative, tend to have a divisive effect. They highlight the political-moral cleavages separating liberals and conservatives in a country in which a growing number of citizens refuse to embrace exceptionalist persuasions to begin with. It does not look as if this is going to change any time soon. The case in point is provided by President Donald Trump, who, before being elected to the White House, explicitly denied a belief in American Exceptionalism, and who refused to refer to exceptionalist themes, elements, symbols, and narratives in his dark and gloomy inaugural address, as we saw in the introduction. When, two years into his presidency, he finally did use the whole conceptual toolbox of American Exceptionalism in his "Salute to America" of July 4, 2019, it not only sounded more than hollow but also triggered another round of intense political controversy between conservative and liberal America.

In his Independence Day speech, Trump told the conventional story of America as a heroic quest for freedom and self-determination that was begun by white, male Americans of European descent and then was taken to completion by the freedom struggles of women and African Americans. He acknowledged the 19th Amendment giving women the vote as major step toward enlarging democracy in the U.S., and he celebrated Frederick Douglass, Harriet Tubman, and Dr. Martin Luther King Jr. as great American heroes and champions of liberty. He said that the "story of America" was "one of the greatest stories ever told." It was "the chronicle of brave citizens who never give up on the dream of a better and brighter future. And it is the saga of thirteen separate colonies that united to form the most just and virtuous republic ever conceived." Looking at the crowd chanting "USA, USA," Trump stated that Americans loved their freedom "and no one will ever take it away from us." The story of America was "the epic tale of a great nation whose people have risked everything for what they know is right." While President Trump's speech came across as a nonpartisan celebration of American Exceptionalism, it could not make anyone forget the many racist, misogynist, and xenophobic comments he had made before and during his presidency. The crowd at the Reflecting Pool of Washington's Mall, who braved hours of heavy rains, thunder, and lightning, was almost exclusively white, and the speech was enveloped by a military parade featuring the presentation of tanks and flyovers by military aircraft.

Trump's Independence Day speech, which largely avoided contentious issues and reiterated a conventional, all-American story of

America's exceptionality, did not help to unite the country. On the contrary, it triggered heated political controversies and deepened the existing socio-moral and political divides in the U.S. Some Democrats feared that Trump, politicizing a nonpartisan national holiday, would turn the Independence Day celebration into a campaign rally. Other liberal critics worried about the unprecedented display of military strength, characterizing it as jingoistic, authoritarian, and un-American. Appearing on *Deadline: White House* on July 2, MSNBC's Joy Reid even claimed that Trump, in displaying America's military might, was imitating authoritarian statesmen like North Korean leader Kim Jong-un or Russian President Vladimir Putin. For her, Trump's display of military strength was first and foremost a threat to Americans opposing him and his presidency. On a different note, liberal critics belittled Trump's Fourth of July celebration of America as all too basic, simplistic, and naïve. Appearing on CNN's *The Situation Room* on July 4, 2019, former Admiral John Kirby mocked President Trump's speech as "essentially 8th-grade history that was fairly sepia-toned and saccharine in its depth and context," adding that he could have "gotten this off of watching Schoolhouse Rock." Two days after Trump had sung the song of an American nation dedicated to the cause of freedom against all odds, Joy Reid, referring to the administration's immigration policies, derided Trump supporters as a bunch of sadists who wanted to see people at the border cruelly mistreated.

Faced with such ferocious liberal criticism, Trump's political friends responded that the charges were unfounded, uncalled for, and essentially unpatriotic. Engaging in a vicious debate with Chris Hahn, former aide to Democratic Senator Chuck Schumer, on Fox News on July 3, Kayleigh McEnany, national secretary of the reelection campaign Trump 2020, said that there was absolutely no genuine reason for the Democrats to be upset about the planned Fourth of July celebrations. "Let's be clear what this is about," she said. "Their [the Democrats'] hate for President Trump is clouding their love for this country," and one should leave it to the left to be unpatriotic on Independence Day, when President Trump meant to deliver nothing but a salute to America.

One and a half years after he had saluted America as "the most just and virtuous republic ever conceived," President Trump encouraged his most dedicated followers to storm the U.S. Capitol, attempting to prevent Congress from certifying Joe Biden's Electoral College win. One hundred and fifty years after the first Republican president of the U.S., Abraham Lincoln, had gone to war to save the Union as the basis of America's exceptional experiment in liberty, another Republican president did all he could to disrupt American institutions and democratic procedures. Speaking from the Senate floor during the certification process on January 6, 2021, then Senate Minority Leader, Chuck Schumer wondered, "As we speak, the eyes of the world are on this chamber, questioning whether America is still the shining example of democracy, the shining city on the hill. What message will we send to fledgling democracies, who study our Constitution, mirror our laws and traditions, in the hopes that they, too, can build a country ruled by the consent of the governed?"

Schumer made his remarks before the crowd attacked the U.S. Capitol building, and whatever else the sack of the U.S. Capitol may stand for, it demonstrated that the U.S. was not immune to authoritarian threats and autocratic leaders emerging from within. "As Americans we like to think of ourselves as exceptional," Laura Merrifeld Wilson, assistant professor of political science at the University of Indianapolis, said in an interview with *Deutsche Welle* on January 6, 2021. The armed attack on the U.S. Capitol, she continued, "could be an opportunity for us to learn to do better—see that we are not impervious to challenges like this, that it can happen on American soil, too."

The question remains, however, whether the events of January 6, 2021, mark "the end of the road for American exceptionalism," as Ishaan Tharoor suggested in the *Washington Post* on January 7, 2021. Just fourteen days after the U.S. Capitol raid, the forty-sixth president of the United States, Joe Biden, in his inaugural address, and Amanda Gorman, in her enthusiastically acclaimed poem "The Hill We Climb," reiterated many—if not all—of the ideas, narratives, and images of American Exceptionalism that we have encountered in the pages of this book. This seems to show that American Exceptionalism as an intellectual concept, cognitive map, site of meaning making, and site of identity negotiation continues to matter as a cultural force. While a growing number of Americans have been refusing to embrace American Exceptionalism since roughly the turn of the millennium, the history of the concept has not come to a close yet. However, it is unclear how it will develop in the years to come. Will the conservative narrative continue to dominate, or will the currently marginalized liberal version of American Exceptionalism rise again? Will American Exceptionalism remain a site of contestation and continue to divide U.S. society, or will a new generation develop new narratives that have the power to unite a divided country behind a commonly shared concept of identity? Will future Americans continue to insist on the exceptionality of their country, however exactly they may define it, or will they abandon concepts of political and moral superiority altogether to accept that the U.S. is one great country among many others with its own specific strengths and weaknesses, achievements and failures, and multiple ways of life? As for the future, the concept of American Exceptionalism no doubt will remain complicated, contradictory, elusive, fluid, and nuanced—much like the American experience itself.

Bibliographical Essay

HISTORICAL SOURCES

In writing this book, I have drawn mostly on canonical historical documents and literary texts available online, as paperbacks, or in one of the anthologies of American literature, such as Nina Baym, ed., *The Norton Anthology of American Literature* (8th ed., 4 vols.) (New York: W. W. Norton & Company, 2012), or Paul Lauter and Richard Yarborough, eds., *The Heath Anthology of American Literature* (7th ed., 5 vols.) (Boston: Cengage Learning, 2014).

Timothy Roberts and Lindsay DiCuirci in *American Exceptionalism* (4 vols.) (London: Pickering & Chatto, 2013) collect many valuable historical sources. General collections of documents are *100 Milestone Documents* (http://www.ourdocuments.gov) and the *Avalon Project: Documents in Law, History, and Diplomacy* (https://avalon.law.yale.edu). Readers can find fine selections of historical documents and relevant excerpts from the research literature in the volumes of the Major Problems in American History Series. I have also drawn on less well-known materials, mostly by European authors. These works can be easily found at http://www.worldcat.org.

INTRODUCTION

There are numerous scholarly works reflecting single aspects, dimensions, and problems of American Exceptionalism, but only few systematic overviews of the history of the concept. The following books pave first paths: Seymour Martin Lipset, *American Exceptionalism: A Double-Edged Sword* (New York: Norton, 1996), Deborah L. Madsen, *American Exceptionalism* (Jackson: UP of Mississippi, 1998), and Godfrey Hodgson, *The Myth of American Exceptionalism* (New Haven, CT: Yale UP, 2009). Jack P. Greene's *The Intellectual Construction of America: Exceptionalism and Identity from 1492 to 1800* (Chapel Hill: U of North Carolina P, 1993) is a highly readable account of the intellectual construction of America in the early modern period. David M. Wrobel deals with the years from roughly 1850 to 1940 in *The End of American Exceptionalism: Frontier Anxiety from the Old West to the New Deal* (Lawrence: UP of Kansas, 1993). A book that came out after my manuscript was completed and that approaches the phenomenon rather one-sidedly from a radical tradition is Roberto Sirvent and Danny Haiphong, *American Exceptionalism and American Innocence: A People's History of Fake News: From the Revolutionary War to the War on Terror* (New York: Skyhorse Publishing, 2019).

Since the end of the Cold War, a new interest in American Exceptionalism has produced some very important new theorizations: Michael Kammen, "The Problem of American Exceptionalism: A Reconsideration," *American Quarterly* 45, 1 (March 1993): 1–43, Byron E. Shafer, ed., *Is America Different? A New Look at American Exceptionalism* (Oxford: Clarendon P, 1991), Ian Tyrell, "American Exceptionalism in an Age of International History," *American Historical Review* 96, 4 (October 1991): 1031–55, and, most importantly, Donald E. Pease, *The New American Exceptionalism* (Minneapolis: U of Minnesota P, 2009). The discussion about how to frame American Exceptionalism is also led in collected volumes: Charles W. Dunn, ed., *American Exceptionalism: The Origins, History, and Future of the Nation's Greatest Strength* (Lanham, MD: Rowman & Littlefield, 2013) and Sylvia Söderlind and James Taylor Carson, eds., *American Exceptionalisms: From Winthrop to Winfrey* (Albany: State U of New York P, 2011). Readers interested in comparative approaches can turn to Elisabeth Glaser and Hermann Wellenreuther, eds., *Bridging the Atlantic: The Question of American Exceptionalism in Perspective* (Washington, DC: German Historical Institute; New York: Cambridge UP, 2002).

CHAPTER 1: THE AMERICAN LAND

Readers wishing to learn more about the spaces and landscapes of U.S. history should turn to D. W. Meinig's monumental historical geography *The Shaping of America: A Geographical Perspective on 500 Years of History* (4 vols.) (New Haven, CT: Yale UP, 1986–2004). North America's natural environments in the American experience and imagination were one of the foundational themes of American studies with pathbreaking books by Henry Nash Smith, *Virgin Land: The American West as Symbol and Myth* (Cambridge, MA: Harvard UP, 1950), and Perry Miller, *Nature's Nation* (Cambridge, MA: The Belknap P of Harvard UP, 1967). America's nature also had far-reaching political and economic effects that culminated in the agrarian ideal, as Drew R. McCoy shows in *The Elusive Republic: Political Economy in Jeffersonian America* (Chapel Hill: U of North Carolina P, 1980). Analyzing the visual history of the agrarian ideal with numerous illustrations is Karsten Fitz, *The American Revolution Remembered, 1830s to 1850s: Competing Images and Conflicting Narratives* (Heidelberg: Universitätsverlag Winter, 2010).

Roderick Nash, *Wilderness in the American Mind* (rev. ed.) (New Haven, CT: Yale UP, 1973) is the standard account of the history of the wilderness idea. Max Oelschlaeger's *The Idea of Wilderness: From Prehistory to the Age of Ecology* (New Haven, CT: Yale UP, 1991) provides an intellectual history of the idea of wilderness from a global perspective, with chapters on Henry David Thoreau and John Muir. Critically reflecting the very idea of wilderness as an interest-driven cultural imagination is William Cronon, ed., *Uncommon Ground: Toward Reinventing Nature* (New York: Norton, 1995). Thomas R. Vale investigates movements to protect a vanishing wilderness in *The American Wilderness: Reflections on Nature Protection in the United States* (Charlottesville: U of Virginia P, 2005).

Barbara Novak's *Nature and Culture: American Landscape and Painting 1825–1875* (3rd ed.) (Oxford: Oxford UP, 2007) and Rebecca Bedell's *The Anatomy of Nature: Geology and American Landscape Painting, 1825–1875* (Princeton: Princeton UP, 2001) show how American landscape painting constructed America's natural environments as a source of national identity. In the twentieth century, photography added a new dimension to the iconography of landscape in the U.S., as the third chapter of Miles Orvell's *American Photography* (Oxford: Oxford UP, 2003) demonstrates.

For a comprehensive history of American Transcendentalism and the idea of the sublime, see Philip F. Gura, *American Transcendentalism: A History* (New York: Hill & Wang, 2007). *The Oxford Handbook of Transcendentalism*, edited by Sandra Harbert Petrulionis, Laura Dassow Walls, and Joel Myerson (Oxford: Oxford UP, 2010) is a very useful research tool. More specific titles on nature and the sublime include

John Gatta, *Making Nature Sacred: Literature, Religion, and Environment in America from the Puritans to the Present* (Oxford: Oxford UP, 2004) and Lawrence Buell, *The Environmental Imagination: Thoreau, Nature Writing, and the Formation of American Culture* (Cambridge, MA: The Belknap P of Harvard UP, 1995). On the sublime in the industrial age see David E. Nye's *American Technological Sublime* (Cambridge MA: MIT P, 1994).

Robert F. Berkhofer was among the first to investigate images of American Indians in U.S. culture in *The White Man's Indian: Images of the American Indian, from Columbus to the Present* (New York: Knopf, 1978). The topic was explored further by S. Elizabeth Bird, ed., *Dressing in Feathers: The Construction of the Indian in American Popular Culture* (Boulder, CO: Westview P, 1996) and Shari M. Huhndorf, *Going Native: Indians in the American Cultural Imagination* (Ithaca, NY: Cornell UP 2001). Richard Slotkin, *Regeneration through Violence: The Mythology of the American Frontier, 1600–1860* (Middletown, CT: Wesleyan UP, 1973) explores how American myths about theAmerican Indians and the frontier served to justify the violent removal of the indigenous peoples.

CHAPTER 2: THE WEST AND THE SOUTH

Readers interested in learning more about the West as a region in U.S. history are recommended to turn to Robert V. Hine and John Mack Faragher's *Frontiers: A Short History of the American West* (New Haven: Yale UP, 2008). Karen R. Jones and John Wills give a good overview of how historians and popular culture have reflected the West in *The American West: Competing Visions* (Edinburgh: Edinburgh UP, 2009).

Richard Slotkin, *Gunfighter Nation: The Myth of the Frontier in Twentieth-Century America* (New York: Atheneum, 1992), David H. Murdoch, *The American West: The Invention of a Myth* (Reno: U of Nevada P, 2001), and Gary J. Hausladen, *Western Places, American Myths: How We Think about the West* (Reno: U of Nevada P, 2006) analyze the West as myth in U.S. history and popular culture.

Frederick Jackson Turner's collected his essay "The Significance of the Frontier in American History" and other writings as *The Frontier in American History* (New York: H. Holt & Co, 1920). The best biography of

Turner is Ray A. Billington, *Frederick Jackson Turner: Historian, Scholar, Teacher* (New York: Oxford UP, 1973). Contextualizing Turner's work in the academic contexts of its time is Richard Hofstadter, *The Progressive Historians: Turner, Beard, Parrington* (New York: Knopf, 1969). Richard W. Etulain has edited a great selection of readings critically discussing the frontier thesis in *Does the Frontier Experience Make America Exceptional?* (Boston: St. Martin's, 1999). The single most important book initiating New Western History is Patricia Nelson Limerick, *The Legacy of Conquest: The Unbroken Past of the American West* (New York: Norton, 1987).

The contributions to *James Fenimore Cooper: The Critical Heritage*, edited by George Dekker and John P. Williams (London: Routledge, 1997) analyze the author's pathbreaking work from multiple perspectives. Standard studies of Cooper's Leatherstocking Tales are Warren Motley, *The American Abraham: James Fenimore Cooper and the Frontier Patriarch* (Cambridge: Cambridge UP, 1987), Kay Seymour House, *Cooper's Americans* (Columbus: Ohio State UP, 1965), and William P. Kelly, *Plotting America's Past: Fenimore Cooper and the Leatherstocking Tales* (Carbondale: Southern Illinois UP, 1983).

For detailed analyses of the Western genre see James Folsom, *The Western: A Collection of Critical Essays* (Englewood Cliffs, NJ: Prentice Hall, 1979), Kim Newman, *Wild West Movies: How the West Was Found, Won, Lost, Lied About, Filmed and Forgotten* (London: Bloomsbury, 1990), and Jane P. Tompkins, *West of Everything: The Inner Life of Westerns* (New York: Oxford UP, 1992). Collecting many interesting perspectives on the cinematic representations of the American West is John E. O'Connor and Peter C. Rollins, eds., *Hollywood's West: The American Frontier in Film, Television, and History* (Lexington: UP of Kentucky, 2005).

Still unsurpassed on Tocqueville's travel in the U.S. is George Wilson Pierson's 1938 book *Tocqueville in America*, which was reissued as a paperback by Johns Hopkins UP (Baltimore, 1996).

Literature on the history and culture of the South is just as vast as that of the West, if not more so. Good places to start explorations into the topic are the twenty-four volumes of *The New Encyclopedia of Southern Culture*, published by the Center for the Study of Southern Culture at the University of Mississippi under the general editorship of Charles Reagan Wilson. Another helpful tool to study Southern history and culture is *A Companion to the American South*, edited by John B. Boles (Malden: Blackwell Publishers, 2002).

In the field of Southern history, the question of Southern exceptionalism is a major topic. Many discussions depart from Wilbur J. Cash, *The Mind of the South* (New York: Vintage Books, 1941). Opening up multiple perspectives on the South as a distinctive region, a worldview, and an idea is John David Smith and Thomas H. Appleton Jr., eds., *A Mythic Land Apart: Reassessing Southerners and Their History* (Westport, CT: Greenwood P, 1997). Laura F. Edwards problematizes Southern exceptionalism in the contexts of U.S. history in her well-researched and heavily documented article "Southern History as U.S. History," *Journal of Southern History* 75, 3 (August 2009): 533–64, while *The Myth of Southern Exceptionalism*, edited by Matthew D. Lassiter and Joseph Crespino (Oxford: Oxford UP, 2010), revisits the debate especially for the post-1945 era.

The question of when, if at all, the South ceased to be distinct, unique, and exceptional and how to interpret it in the context of U.S. history has garnered a lot of scholarly attention. Reflecting this question from a political science point of view is Byron E. Shafer and Richard Johnston, *The End of Southern Exceptionalism: Class, Race, and Partisan Change in the Postwar South* (Cambridge, MA: Harvard UP, 2006). Historians, however, are rather skeptical about the end of Southern distinctness, given the many continuities of racism, distribution of property, religious fundamentalism, and political conservatism in that region. The work of Charles P. Roland is especially important in this respect. See his *The Improbable Era: The South Since World War II* (Lexington: UP of Kentucky, 1975), or his shorter, more thesis-driven article "The Ever-Vanishing South," *Journal of Southern History* 48, 1 (Feb. 1982): 3–20.

Key to white Southerners' defense of slavery was the plantation myth that represented slavery as a benign and innocent institution based on the paternalistic care of masters for their slaves. This plantation myth emerged in the antebellum period, as William R. Taylor masterfully demonstrates in *Cavalier and Yankee: The Old South and American National Character* (New York: G. Braziller, 1961), and after the Civil War, it merged with the narrative of an allegedly "lost cause," as is shown by Gaines M. Foster, *Ghosts of the Confederacy: Defeat, the Lost Cause, and the Emergence of the New South, 1865 to 1913* (New York: Oxford UP,

1985), and Charles Reagan Wilson, *Baptized in Blood: The Religion of the Lost Cause, 1865–1920* (Athens: U of Georgia P, 1980).

The plantation myth has been thoroughly deconstructed by historians of American slavery. Peter Kolchin, *American Slavery, 1619–1877* (New York: Hill & Wang, 1993) is still the most concise and comprehensive one-volume history of slavery in the U.S. His book is nicely complemented by James Oliver Horton and Lois E. Horton, *Slavery and the Making of America* (Oxford: Oxford UP, 2005). A pathbreaking early book destroying the argument that antebellum slavery was a benign institution is Kenneth M. Stampp, *The Peculiar Institution: Slavery in the Ante-Bellum South* (New York: Vintage Books, 1956). James Oakes, *The Ruling Race: A History of American Slaveholders* (New York: Vintage Books, 1983) is an important study on the social history of Southern slaveholders that systematically deconstructs the plantation myth.

In recent years, the work of Sven Beckert on the centrality of cotton to the evolution of global capitalism has shed new light on slavery and the Southern planters as global economic actors: Sven Beckert, *Empire of Cotton: A Global History* (New York: Knopf, 2014). See also *Slavery's Capitalism: A New History of American Economic Development*, which Beckert edited together with Seth Rockman (Philadelphia: U of Pennsylvania P, 2018). A pioneering study approaching the history of American slavery from the perspective of slaves as actors and not just as objects and victims of the institution is Eugene D. Genovese, *Roll, Jordan, Roll: The World the Slaves Made* (New York: Pantheon Books, 1972).

Henry Mayer, *All on Fire: William Lloyd Garrison and the Abolition of Slavery* (New York: St. Martin's P, 1998), Richard S. Newman, *The Transformation of American Abolitionism: Fighting Slavery in the Early Republic* (Chapel Hill: U of North Carolina P, 2002), as well as Timothy Patrick McCarthy and John Stauffer, *Prophets of Protest: Reconsidering the History of American Abolitionism* (New York: New Press, 2006), all ably capture the history of abolitionism and its development into a national opposition. Julie Roy Jeffrey, *The Great Silent Army of Abolitionism: Ordinary Women in the Antislavery Movement* (Chapel Hill: U of North Carolina P, 1998) unearths the significant female presence in the abolitionist movement.

Southern nationalism formed as a response to the growing and increasingly militant national critique of slavery. John McCardell demonstrates how, beginning in the 1820s, Southerners increasingly imagined themselves as a distinct community in *The Idea of a Southern Nation: Southern Nationalists and Southern Nationalism, 1830–1860* (New York: Norton, 1979). Recently, Paul Quigley has published the most systematic and conceptually innovative inquiry into Southern nationalism with *Shifting Grounds: Nationalism and the American South, 1848–1865* (New York: Oxford UP, 2012). A masterful analysis of the secessionist sentiment in the antebellum period, including a sharp analysis of the role slavery played in the Nullification Crisis is William W. Freehling, *The Road to Disunion*, vol. I: *Secessionists at Bay, 1776–1854* (New York: Oxford UP, 1990). A brilliant interpretation of the Great Seal of the Confederacy is Emory M. Thomas's *The Confederacy as a Revolutionary Experience* (Englewood Cliffs, NJ: Prentice Hall, 1971).

The historiographical debate on the postbellum South is largely structured by the concept of a "New South," which C. Vann Woodward developed in his *Origins of the New South* (Baton Rouge: Louisiana State UP, 1951). Pursuing Woodward's arguments further are Edward L. Ayers, *The Promise of the New South: Life after Reconstruction* (Oxford: Oxford UP, 1992), and George B. Tindall, *The Emergence of the New South, 1913–1945* (Baton Rouge: Louisiana State UP, 1967). Paul K. Conkin discusses the Southern Agrarians of the 1930s in *The Southern Agrarians* (Knoxville: U of Tennessee P, 1988).

The classic study on the history of racial segregation is C. Vann Woodward, *The Strange Career of Jim Crow* (New York: Oxford UP, 1955). More recent studies on the system of de jure segregation in the South, which always went hand in hand with de facto segregation, are Jerrold M. Packard, *American Nightmare: The History of Jim Crow* (New York: St. Martin's P, 2002), and Paul Finkelman, ed., *The Age of Jim Crow: Segregation from the End of Reconstruction to the Great Depression* (New York: Garland, 1992). A very informative and concrete history of the U.S. Supreme Court ruling declaring de jure segregation constitutional is Brook Thomas, ed., *Plessy v. Ferguson: A Brief History with Documents* (Boston: Bedford Books, 1997).

V. O. Key Jr., in *Southern Politics in State and Nation* (New York: Knopf, 1949), reflects the one-party rule of the Democrats over the Solid South prior to 1945 as a key feature of Southern exceptionalism. Ira Katznelson demonstrates how Southern Democrats acted as a powerful

BIBLIOGRAPHICAL ESSAY 245

check on Roosevelt's New Deal policy in *Fear Itself: The New Deal and the Origins of Our Time* (New York: Liveright, 2013), while Kari A. Frederickson discusses Southern estrangement from the Democratic Party in *The Dixiecrat Revolt and the End of the Solid South, 1932–1968* (Chapel Hill: U of North Carolina P, 2001).

CHAPTER 3: CITIES UPON HILLS

J. H. Elliott reconstructs the history of colonial British North America from an imperial perspective in *Empires of the Atlantic World: Britain and Spain in America, 1492–1830* (New Haven, CT: Yale UP, 2006), as do David Armitage and Michael J. Braddick in their edited volume *The British Atlantic World, 1500–1800* (2nd ed.) (Basingstoke: Palgrave Macmillan, 2009). Taking a continental approach is Alan Taylor, *American Colonies: The Settling of North America* (New York: Penguin, 2002). Focused on Massachusetts and Virginia as the two paradigmatic models of English colonization: Jack P. Greene, *Pursuits of Happiness: The Social Development of Early Modern British Colonies and the Formation of American Culture* (Chapel Hill: U of North Carolina P, 1988). Joseph E. Illick, *Colonial Pennsylvania: A History* (New York: Scribner's, 1976) is a still valid account of that colony's past. Readers will learn much about colonial Georgia and its founder James Oglethorpe from Trevor Richard Reese, *Colonial Georgia: A Study in British Imperial Policy in the Eighteenth Century* (Athens: U of Georgia P, 1963), and the worthwhile collection of essays edited by Harvey H. Jackson and Phinizy Spalding, *Forty Years of Diversity: Essays on Colonial Georgia* (Athens: U of Georgia P, 1984).

The importance of Puritan New England for the history of American Exceptionalism is beyond doubt, and Perry Miller masterfully reconstructs Puritan worldviews in *The New England Mind: The Seventeenth Century* (Cambridge, MA: Harvard UP, 1954) and *Errand into the Wilderness* (Cambridge, MA: Harvard UP, 1956). Sacvan Bercovitch reflects on the significance of Puritan mindsets for U.S. cultural history in *The Puritan Origins of the American Self* (New Haven, CT: Yale UP, 1975).

An indispensable book on John Winthrop's sermon "Model of Christian Charity" is Daniel T. Rodgers's *As a City on a Hill: The Story of America's Most Famous Lay Sermon* (Princeton: Princeton UP, 2018). Tracing the city-on-a-hill motif in narratives of American Exceptionalism into the twentieth century is Abram C. Van Engen, *City on a Hill: A History of American Exceptionalism* (New Haven, CT: Yale UP, 2020).

The Congregationalist project in New England was informed by millennial utopianism, which James Holstun analyzes in *A Rational Millenium: Puritan Utopias of Seventeenth-Century England and America* (New York: Oxford UP, 1987). The most extensive study of millennialism in the second half of the eighteenth century is Ruth H. Bloch, *Visionary Republic: Millennial Themes in American Thought, 1756–1800* (Cambridge: Cambridge UP, 1985). One major concept of millennial thinking framed New England as the New Canaan. Mason I. Lowance Jr. traces this concept in *The Language of Canaan: Metaphor and Symbol in New England from the Puritan to the Transcendentalists* (Cambridge, MA: Harvard UP, 1980), while Sacvan Bercovitch studies the fear of declension connected to millennial thinking in *The American Jeremiad* (Madison: U of Wisconsin P, 1978).

CHAPTER 4: SACRED FIRE OF LIBERTY

The best overview of the political history of the American Revolution is Francis D. Cogliano, *Revolutionary America, 1763–1815: A Political History* (3rd ed.) (New York: Routledge, 2017). A monumental study covering the many aspects of the revolutionary process is Robert Middlekauff, *The Glorious Cause: The American Revolution, 1763–1789* (rev. and expanded ed.) (New York: Oxford UP, 2007). *The Oxford Handbook of the American Revolution*, edited by Edward G. Gray and Jane Kamensky (Oxford: Oxford UP, 2015), has several authors dealing with most of the major problems of that period. A thought-provoking interpretation of radical egalitarianism as the American Revolution's core idea is Gordon S. Wood, *The Radicalism of the American Revolution* (New York: Knopf, 1993).

The classic study on the ideology of the American Revolutions is Bernard Bailyn's *The Ideological Origins of the American Revolution* (Cambridge, MA: The Belknap P of Harvard UP, 1967). Tracing the ideological foundations of the U.S. Constitution and the political interests behind it is Gordon S. Wood, *The Creation of the American Republic,*

1776–1787 (Chapel Hill: U of North Carolina P, 1969). Parts of America's revolutionary ideology were anchored in Enlightenment philosophy, as is shown by Jonathan I. Israel's *A Revolution of the Mind: Radical Enlightenment and the Intellectual Origins of Modern Democracy* (Princeton: Princeton UP, 2010). Focused on the Enlightenment in revolutionary America is Henry F. May, *The Enlightenment in America* (New York: Oxford UP, 1976), and Henry Steele Commager, *The Empire of Reason: How Europe Imagined and America Realized the Enlightenment* (Garden City, NY: Doubleday, 1977).

Sophia A. Rosenfeld treats the effects of Thomas Paine's *Common Sense* on revolutionary America in the fourth chapter of her *Common Sense: A Political History* (Cambridge, MA: Harvard UP, 2011). Gregory Claeys comprehensively analyzes Paine's political thinking in *Thomas Paine: Social and Political Thought* (London: Unwin Hyman, 1989), as does Jack Fruchtman in *The Political Philosophy of Thomas Paine* (Baltimore: Johns Hopkins UP, 2009). The major texts of the so-called Revolution Debate between Paine and Edmund Burke are collected and commented upon in Marylin Butler, ed., *Burke, Paine, Godwin, and the Revolution Controversy* (London: Cambridge UP, 1984).

The Declaration of Independence, its ideological contexts, its making, and its effects have been thoroughly analyzed by Carl L. Becker, *The Declaration of Independence* (New York: P. Smith, 1933), Pauline Maier, *American Scripture: Making the Declaration of Independence* (New York: Knopf, 1997), and Jayne Allen, *Jefferson's Declaration of Independence: Origins, Philosophy, and Theology* (Lexington: UP of Kentucky, 1998). Interpreting the document from a global perspective is David Armitage, *The Declaration of Independence: A Global History* (Cambridge, MA: Harvard UP, 2008).

Most relevant for this chapter's remarks about Benjamin Franklin's social and political ideas were Douglas Anderson, *The Unfinished Life of Benjamin Franklin* (Baltimore: Johns Hopkins UP, 2012), and Kevin Slack, *Benjamin Franklin, Natural Right, and the Art of Virtue* (Rochester: U of Rochester P, 2017). James N. Green and Peter Stallybrass do a wonderful job in connecting Franklin's biography and professional life to his writings in *Benjamin Franklin: Writer and Printer* (New Castle: Oak Knoll P; London: British Library, 2006). A concise synthesis of the genesis, content, and afterlife of Benjamin Franklin's autobiography is my own

"Benjamin Franklin: The Autobiography of Benjamin Franklin (1791 sq.)," in *Handbook of Autobiography/Autofiction*, vol. III: *Exemplary Texts*, ed. Martina Wagner-Egelhaaf (Boston: De Gruyter, 2019), 1539–53.

The first study of the Articles of Confederation to turn to is Merrill Jensen's *The Articles of Confederation: An Interpretation of the Social-Constitutional History of the American Revolution, 1774–1781* (Madison: U of Wisconsin P, 1959). The volume edited by Richard R. Beeman, Stephen Botein, and Edward C. Carter, *Beyond Confederation: Origins of the Constitutions and American National Identity* (Chapel Hill: U of North Carolina P, 1987), offers many insights into the constitutional contexts, debates, and problems under the Articles. The state constitutions of revolutionary America have been masterfully analyzed by Willi Paul Adams in *The First American Constitutions: Republican Ideology and the Making of the State Constitutions in the Revolutionary Era* (expanded ed.) (Lanham, MD: Rowman & Littlefield, 2001). Gordon S. Wood's *The Creation of the Republic*, cited above, is the standard study on the genesis of the Constitution, while Jürgen Heidenking's *The Constitution before the Judgment Seat: The Prehistory and Ratification of the American Constitution, 1787–1791* (Charlottesville: U of Virginia P, 2012) is the most detailed account of the ratification debate. Glenn A. Phelps, *George Washington and American Constitutionalism* (Lawrence: UP of Kansas, 1993) shows how Washington was the first Federalist president. Alison L. LaCroix, *The Ideological Origins of American Federalism* (Cambridge, MA: Harvard UP, 2010) demonstrates how modern federalism was invented by the American founding fathers.

On the *Federalist Papers*, which offer an authoritative interpretation of the U.S. Constitution, see Garry Wills, *Explaining America: The Federalist* (New York: Penguin, 2001). Although the Anti-Federalists, who opposed the ratification of the Constitution, were for a long time treated as the losers of history, Saul Cornell has rescued them in *The Other Founders: Anti-Federalism and the Dissenting Tradition in America, 1788–1828* (Chapel Hill: U of North Carolina P, 1999).

The concept of Atlantic Revolutions goes back to R. R. Palmer, *The Age of the Democratic Revolution* (2 vols.) (Princeton: Princeton UP, 1959–1964). Palmer's suggestion that the American and European revolutions of the age were integral parts of one, unilinear historical movement to spread liberal democracy has recently been challenged by Wim Klooster, *Revolutions in the Atlantic World: A Comparative History* (new ed.) (New York: New York UP, 2018).

CHAPTER 5: THE AMERICAN WAY OF EMPIRE

The New Cambridge History of American Foreign Relations (Cambridge: Cambridge UP, 2013) provides a concise overview of the history of U.S. foreign policy. Its four volumes are William Earl Weeks, *Dimensions of the Early American Empire, 1754–1865*; Walter LaFeber, *The American Search for Opportunity, 1865–1913*; Akira Iriye, *The Globalizing of America, 1913–1945*, and Warren I. Cohen, *Challenges to American Primacy, 1945 to the Present*. Two seminal works have informed my chapter without being literally present in it. These are Smith's *The Virgin Land*, cited above, and R. W. B. Lewis, *The American Adam: Innocence, Tragedy and Tradition and the Nineteenth Century* (Chicago: U of Chicago P, 1955). The latter, although focusing on literary texts, investigates the myth of American innocence in contrast to European corruption, which also informed U.S. foreign policy from early on.

Richard Van Alstyne, *Empire and Independence: The International History of the American Revolution* (New York: John Wiley and Sons, 1965), Samuel Flagg Bemis, *The Diplomacy of the American Revolution* (Bloomington: Indiana UP, 1957), and Jonathan R. Dull, *Diplomatic History of the American Revolution* (New Haven, CT: Yale UP, 1985) investigate the revolutionary foundations of U.S. foreign policy. David C. Hendrickson, *Peace Pact: The Lost World of the American Founding* (Lawrence: UP of Kansas, 2003) shows that the Articles of Confederation constituted a confederacy between states to guarantee peace between them and, therefore, must be interpreted within the context of U.S. foreign policy in the revolutionary period. David M. Fitzsimons reconstructs Paine's vision of the independent America's role in international relations in "Tom Paine's New World Order: Idealistic Internationalism in the Ideology of Early American Foreign Relations," *Diplomatic History* 19, 4 (Fall 1995): 569–82.

Felix Gilbert, *To the Farewell Address: Ideas of Early American Foreign Policy* (Princeton: Princeton UP, 1961), Burton Kaufman, ed.,

Washington's Farewell Address: The View from the 20th Century (Chicago: Quadrangle Books, 1969), and Lawrence S. Kaplan, *Entangling Alliances with None: American Foreign Policy in the Age of Jefferson* (Kent: Kent State UP, 1987) are important studies on the subject. Robert W. Tucker and David C. Hendrickson scrutinize Jefferson's foreign policy agenda in *Empire of Liberty: The Statecraft of Thomas Jefferson* (New York: Oxford UP, 1990).

The extent to which early U.S. foreign policy was a matter of identity politics is the subject of Jasper Trautsch's *The Genesis of America: U.S. Foreign Policy and the Formation of National Identity, 1793–1815* (Cambridge: Cambridge UP, 2018), and Robert W. Smith's *Keeping the Republic: Ideology and Early American Diplomacy* (DeKalb: Northern Illinois UP, 2004).

An influential study on the Monroe Doctrine is Ernest R. May, *The Making of the Monroe Doctrine* (Cambridge, MA: Harvard UP, 1975). Gretchen Murphy, *Hemispheric Imaginings: The Monroe Doctrine and Narratives of U.S. Empire* (Durham, NC: Duke UP, 2005) unearths the cultural and racial implications of the Monroe Doctrine, while Jay Sexton reflects its imperial aspirations in *The Monroe Doctrine: Empire and Nation in Nineteenth Century America* (New York: Hill & Wang, 2011).

The westward expansion of the U.S. is a major topic of Daniel Walker Howe's magisterial *"What Hath God Wrought?" The Transformation of America, 1815–1848* (New York: Oxford UP, 2009). Regarding the origins and function of the Manifest Destiny idea, Albert K. Weinberg's *Manifest Destiny: A Study of Nationalist Expansionism in American History* (Baltimore: Johns Hopkins P, 1935) remains important, so too does John Carl Parish, *The Emergence of the Idea of Manifest Destiny* (Los Angeles: U of California P, 1932). Reginald Horsman exposes racial dynamics that go way beyond slavery in *Race and Manifest Destiny: The Origins of American Racial Anglo-Saxonism* (Cambridge, MA: Harvard UP, 1981). Showing how the problem of slavery let the expansionist consensus erode well before the Civil War are Michael A. Morrison, *Slavery and the American West: The Eclipse of Manifest Destiny and the Coming of the Civil War* (Chapel Hill: U of North Carolina P, 1997), and Matthew Mason, *Slavery and Politics in the Early American Republic* (Chapel Hill: U of North Carolina P, 2006).

The controversial annexation of Texas is the subject of Joel H. Silbey, *Storm over Texas: The Annexation Controversy and the Road to Civil War* (Oxford: Oxford UP, 2005), while Robert W. Johannsen, *To the Halls of the Montezumas: The Mexican War in the American Imagination* (New York: Oxford UP, 1985) deals with the cultural impact of the war.

A classic study on U.S. imperialism is Walter LaFeber, *The New Empire: An Interpretation of American Expansion 1860–1898* (Ithaca, NY: Cornell UP, 1963). LaFeber's concept of the U.S. as a market empire was taken to the twentieth century by Emily S. Rosenberg, *Financial Missionaries to the World: The Politics and Culture of Dollar Diplomacy, 1900–1930* (Durham, NC: Duke UP, 2003), and Victoria de Grazia, *Irresistible Empire: America's Advance through Twentieth-Century Europe* (Cambridge, MA: Harvard UP, 2005). More generally reflecting on the nature of U.S. imperialism is Ernest R. May, *American Imperialism: A Speculative Essay* (Chicago: Imprint Publications, 1991). Frank A. Ninkovich, *The United States and Imperialism* (Malden: Blackwell Publishers, 2001) responds to May's interpretation. Putting U.S. imperialism into a comparative perspective is Geir Lundestad, *The American "Empire" and Other Studies of U.S. Foreign Policy in a Comparative Perspective* (Oxford: Oxford UP, 1990).

While imperialists used exceptionalist rhetoric to justify their cause, anti-imperialists also employed it to justify theirs. Robert L. Beisner, *Twelve against Empire: The Anti-Imperialist Movement in the United States, 1898–1900* (New York: McGraw Hill, 1968) remains the best monograph on the subject. It is nicely complemented by the sources collected in Philip S. Foner and Richard C. Winchester, eds., *Anti-Imperialist Reader: A Documentary History of Anti-Imperialism in the United States*, vol. I: *From the Mexican War to the Election of 1900* (New York: Holmes & Meier, 1984).

Matthew Frye Jacobson delivers a broad sweep that links the controversies over immigration and the deep social transformations resulting from industrialization to U.S. overseas expansion in *Barbarian Virtues: The United States Encounters Foreign Peoples at Home and Abroad, 1876–1917* (New York: Hill & Wang, 2000). Eric T. L. Love, *Race over Empire: Racism and U.S. Imperialism, 1865–1900* (Chapel Hill: U of North Carolina P, 2004) investigates how the issue of race was employed by both imperialists and anti-imperialists, and Paul A. Kramer, *The Blood of*

Government: Race, Empire, the United States, and the Philippines (Chapel Hill: U of North Carolina P, 2006) shows how racism informed U.S. policies in the Philippines.

Fighting for American Manhood: How Gender Politics Provoked the Spanish-American and Philippine-American Wars (New Haven, CT: Yale UP, 1998), by Kristin L. Hoganson, unearths issues of gender, and especially masculinity, in U.S. imperialism. Not specifically focused on imperialism, but nonetheless helpful to understand its gender dynamics, is Gail Bederman, *Manliness and Civilization: A Cultural History of Gender and Race in the United States, 1880-1917* (Chicago: U of Chicago P, 1995). On the role of Protestant missionaries in American imperialism, see Ian Tyrell, *Reforming the World: The Creation of America's Moral Empire* (Princeton: Princeton UP, 2010). More specifically on the Philippines, see Kenton J. Clymer, *Protestant Missionaries in the Philippines, 1898-1916: An Inquiry into the American Colonial Mentality* (Urbana: U of Illinois P, 1986).

America's mission to make the world safe for democracy was first formulated by Woodrow Wilson, whose political agenda is analyzed by Lloyd E. Ambrosius, *Wilsonianism: Woodrow Wilson and His Legacy in American Foreign Relations* (Houndsmills: Macmillan, 2002), and John Milton Cooper Jr., *Breaking the Heart of the World: Woodrow Wilson and the Fight for the League of Nations* (Cambridge: Cambridge UP, 2001). Tony Smith traces the history of liberal internationalism in twentieth-century U.S. foreign policy in *America's Mission: The United States and the Worldwide Struggle for Democracy in the Twentieth Century* (Princeton: Princeton UP, 1994), as do the contributions to *American Democracy Promotion: Impulses, Strategies, and Impacts*, edited by Michael G. Cox, G. John Ikenberry, and Takashi Inoguchi (Oxford: Oxford UP, 2000).

Mary Nolan thematizes the new economic, cultural, and military presence of a globalizing America in Europe in *The Transatlantic Century: Europe and the United States, 1890-2010* (Cambridge: Cambridge UP, 2012), and in *The Deluge: The Great War and the Remaking of Global Order 1916-1931* (New York: Viking, 2014), Adam Tooze shows how the U.S. was unwilling to confront its new responsibilities as a world power.

An altogether brilliant account of U.S. history in the era of Franklin D. Roosevelt is David M. Kennedy, *Freedom from Fear: The American People in Depression and War, 1929-1945* (New York: Oxford UP, 1999).

The isolationist mood during the 1930s is the topic of Manfred Jonas, *Isolationism in America* (Ithaca, NY: Cornell UP, 1966). Robert Dallek, *Franklin D. Roosevelt and American Foreign Policy, 1932–1945* (New York: Oxford UP, 1979) is the authoritative study on Roosevelt's thinking about foreign policy; the best biography on Henry Luce is Alan Brinkley, *The Publisher: Henry Luce and His American Century* (New York: Knopf, 2010).

Paving paths into the thickets of Cold War history are Richard H. Immerman and Petra Goedde, eds., *The Oxford Handbook of the Cold War* (Oxford: Oxford UP, 2013), and Melvyn P. Leffler and Odd A. Westad, eds., *The Cambridge History of the Cold War* (3 vols.) (Cambridge: Cambridge UP, 2010). Analyzing the Cold War from a global perspective are Simon J. Ball, *The Cold War: An International History, 1947–1991* (London: Arnold, 1996), and Odd A. Westad, *Cold War: A World History* (New York: Basic Books, 2019). Approaching the history of the Cold War from a U.S. perspective are John L. Gaddis, *The United States and the Origins of the Cold War* (New York: Columbia UP, 1972), Gaddis, *We Now Know: Rethinking Cold War History* (Oxford: Oxford UP, 1997), and Melvyn P. Leffler, *A Preponderance of Power: National Security, the Truman Administration, and the Cold War* (Stanford: Stanford UP, 1992). For a thick contextualization of George Kennan's Long Telegram, see Kenneth M. Jensen, *Origins of the Cold War: The Novikov, Kennan, and Roberts "Long Telegrams" of 1946* (rev. ed.) (Washington DC: United States Institute of Peace P, 1993). The Cold War culture of paranoia about communists at home is the subject of Ellen Schrecker's *Many Are the Crimes: McCarthyism in America* (Princeton: Princeton UP, 1998), and Landon R. Y. Storrs, *The Second Red Scare and the Unmaking of the New Deal Left* (Princeton: Princeton UP, 2012).

William Hyland analyzes the erratic internationalism of the U.S. foreign policy of the 1990s in *Clinton's World: Remaking American Foreign Policy* (Westport: Praeger, 1999). James M. Goldgeier, *America Between the Wars: From 11/9 to 9/11* (New York: PublicAffairs, 2008) is the best account of U.S. foreign policy from the end of the Cold War to the War on Terror, while the contributions collected by Michael Ignatieff in *American Exceptionalism and Human Rights* (Princeton: Princeton UP, 2005) show how the War on Terror demonstrated that America's approach to human rights differs from that of most other Western nations.

CHAPTER 6: PROMISSORY NOTES

The chapter's argument is indebted to the concept of the Dialectic of Enlightenment as it was first formulated by Max Horkheimer and Theodor W. Adorno in 1944, and translated into English by Edmund Jephcott in 2002. I have reflected on how this concept can be applied to the American case in my article "The Double Dialectic of the American Enlightenment," in *Das Prinzip Aufklärung zwischen Universalismus und Partikularem Anspruch*, ed. Kristina-Monika Hinneburg and Grazyna Jurewicz (Paderborn: W. Fink, 2014), 137–65.

An early overview of the history of African Americans that remains in print is John Hope Franklin and Alfred A. Moss, *From Slavery to Freedom: A History of African Americans* (New York: Knopf, 1947). More recent comprehensive and problem-oriented overviews and introductions are Raymond Gavins, *The Cambridge Guide to African American History* (New York: Cambridge UP, 2016), Kevin Kelly Gaines, *African-American History* (Washington, DC: American Historical Association, 2012), Clayborne Carson, Emma J. Lapsansky-Werner, and Gary B. Nash, *The Struggle for Freedom: A History of African Americans* (Boston: Prentice Hall, 2011), and Henry Louis Gates Jr., *Life upon These Shores: Looking at African American History, 1513–2008* (New York: Knopf, 2011). A highly thought-provoking book investigating African American history from a global perspective and in international contexts is Molefi Kete Asante, *The African American People: A Global History* (New York: Routledge, 2012).

For the problem of slavery in the American Revolution, see Paul Finkelman, *Slavery and the Founders: Race and Liberty in the Age of Jefferson* (Armonk: M.E. Sharpe, 1996), and David Brion Davis, *The Problem of Slavery in the Age of Emancipation* (New York: Knopf, 2014). Many of the African American voices cited in my chapter are from Frank Kelleter, *Amerikanische Aufklärung: Sprachen der Rationalität im Zeitalter der Revolution* (Paderborn: Schönigh, 2002), chapter 11.

Readers wishing to learn more about Frederick Douglass can learn much from the contributions collected by Eric J. Sundquist in *Frederick Douglass: New Literary and Historical Essays* (New York: Cambridge UP, 1990). Lincoln's Gettysburg Address is thickly contextualized by Garry Wills, *Lincoln at Gettysburg: The Words that Remade America* (New York: Simon & Schuster, 1992). However, not only the abolitionists drew on exceptionalist persuasions to justify their cause; the advocates of slavery did so, too, as is shown in *The Ideology of Slavery: Proslavery Thought in the Antebellum South, 1830–1860*, edited by Drew Gilpin Faust (Baton Rouge: Louisiana State UP, 1981).

David Lucander investigates the effect of World War II on the struggle for civil rights at home in *Winning the War for Democracy: The March on Washington Movement, 1941–1946* (Urbana: U of Illinois P, 2014), as does the volume *Fog of War: The Second World War and the Civil Rights Movement*, edited by Kevin M. Kruse and Stephen Tuck (New York: Oxford UP, 2012). Mary L. Dudziak, *Cold War Civil Rights: Race and the Image of American Democracy* (Princeton: Princeton UP, 2002) discusses the international dimension of the civil rights struggle during the Cold War.

The best overview of the long history of the civil rights movement in the U.S. is Harvard Sitkoff, *The Struggle for Black Equality 1954–1992* (rev. ed.) (New York: Hill & Wang, 1993). An influential history of the NAACP is Manfred Berg, *The Ticket to Freedom: The NAACP and the Struggle for Black Political Integration* (Gainesville: UP of Florida, 2005). The role of the U.S. Supreme Court in the process is scrutinized by Michael J. Klarman in *From Jim Crow to Civil Rights: The Supreme Court and the Struggle for Racial Equality* (Oxford: Oxford UP, 2006). Among the many books on the post-1945 civil rights movement, Taylor Branch's monumental account stands largely unrivaled: *Parting the Waters: America in the King Years, 1954–63* (New York: Simon and Schuster, 1988) and *Pillar of Fire: America in the King Years, 1963–1965* (New York: Simon & Schuster, 1998).

For biographies on Martin Luther King Jr. see Thomas F. Jackson, *From Civil Rights to Human Rights: Martin Luther King, Jr., and the Struggle for Economic Justice* (Philadelphia: U of Pennsylvania P, 2007), and Troy Jackson, *Becoming King: Martin Luther King Jr. and the Making of a National Leader* (Lexington: UP of Kentucky, 2008). Michael E. Dyson, *The Black Presidency: Barack Obama and the Politics of Race in America* (Boston: Houghton Mifflin Harcourt, 2016) critically assesses Obama's presidency and his integrationist understanding of American Exceptionalism.

My discussion of black nationalism is very much informed by Critical Race Theory, with a good introduction into the field having been edited by Kimberlé Crenshaw et al., *Critical Race Theory: The Key Writings That Formed the Movement* (New York: New Press, 1995). On the life, thought, and activism of Malcolm X, see Michael E. Dyson, *Making Malcolm: The Myth and Meaning of Malcolm X* (Oxford: Oxford UP, 1995), and Rachel A. Koestler-Grack, *Malcolm X: A Biography* (Westport: Greenwood P, 2007). A very interesting and thought-provoking comparison of King and Malcolm X in terms of differences but also commonalities is Britta Waldschmidt-Nelson, *Dreams and Nightmares: Martin Luther King Jr., Malcolm X, and the Struggle for Black Equality in America* (Gainesville: UP of Florida, 2012). Regarding the history of the Black Power movement, I learned much from William L. Van Deburg, *New Day in Babylon: The Black Power Movement and American Culture, 1965–1975* (Chicago: U of Chicago P, 1992).

CHAPTER 7: PERFECTIBLE UNION

Readers will find an indispensable source of information on nineteenth-century reform movements in William D. P. Bliss, ed., *The Encyclopedia of Social Reform: Including Political Economy, Political Science, Sociology and Statistics, Covering Anarchism, Charities, Civil Service, Currency, Land and Legislation Reform, Penology, Socialism, Social Purity, Trades Unions, Woman Suffrage, etc.* (New York: Funk & Wagnalls, 1897).

Timothy L. Smith, *Revivalism and Social Reform: American Protestantism on the Eve of the Civil War* scrutinizes the religious dynamics of social reform movements (Baltimore: Johns Hopkins UP, 1957). A more recent book is Michael P. Young, *Bearing Witness against Sin: The Evangelical Birth of the American Social Movement* (Chicago: U of Chicago P, 2006).

The pathbreaking study on Jacksonian America as an age of reform under the auspices of the *common man* is Arthur M. Schlesinger Jr., *The Age of Jackson* (Boston: Little, Brown and Co, 1945). The liberal narrative of Jacksonian America as a reform period is essentially reaffirmed—although with major qualifications regarding the supposed egalitarianism of the age and with much greater emphasis on social conflict instead of consensus—in Sean Wilentz, *The Rise of American Democracy: Jefferson to Lincoln* (New York: Norton, 2005).

Besides the 1830–1840s, the years from roughly 1880 to 1920 were another major reform period, frequently termed the Progressive Era. For overviews see Robert H. Wiebe, *The Search for Order 1877–1920* (New York: Hill & Wang, 1967), John Whiteclay Chambers II, *The Tyranny of Change: America in the Progressive Era, 1890–1920* (2nd ed.) (New Brunswick, NJ: Rutgers UP, 2000), and Michael McGerr, *A Fierce Discontent: The Rise and Fall of the Progressive Movement in America, 1870–1920* (Oxford: Oxford UP, 2005).

Progressivism led to new thinking about the role and function of government, which Robert Harrison analyzes in *Congress, Progressive Reform, and the New American State* (Cambridge: Cambridge UP, 2004), as does Will Morrisey in *The Dilemma of Progressivism: How Roosevelt, Taft, and Wilson Reshaped the American Regime of Self-Government* (Lanham, MD: Rowman & Littlefield, 2009). Reflecting this transformation from an Atlantic perspective are Daniel T. Rodgers, *Atlantic Crossings: Social Politics in a Progressive Age* (Cambridge, MA: The Belknap P of Harvard UP, 1998), and James T. Kloppenberg, *Uncertain Victory: Social Democracy and Progressivism in European and American Thought, 1870–1920* (New York: Oxford UP, 1986).

Women's movements in U.S. history were frequently driven by a liberal feminism that is reflected in Nancy F. Cott, *The Grounding of Modern Feminism* (New Haven, CT: Yale UP, 1987). Linda Kerber highlights the effects of the American Revolution on women and gender concepts in *Women of the Republic: Intellect and Ideology in Revolutionary America* (Chapel Hill: U of North Carolina P, 1980). Mary Beth Norton's *Liberty's Daughters: The Revolutionary Experience of American Women, 1750–1800* (Boston: Little, Brown and Co., 1980) nicely complements Kerber's book. The life and thought of Abigail Adams are the topic of Edith B. Gelles, *Abigail Adams: A Writing Life* (London: Routledge, 2002), and Woody Holton, *Abigail Adams: A Life* (New York: Free Press, 2009).

In the second half of the nineteenth century, the women's movement zeroed in on the suffrage question. The respective material cited in my chapter is to a very large extent drawn from Borislava Borisova Probst's dissertation: "Dialectic of the Enlightenment in America: The Woman Suffrage Debate 1865–1919" (PhD diss., U of Regensburg, 2015), http://

www.urn:nbn:de:bvb:355-epub-316611. A detailed and lively account of the Seneca Falls Convention and its aftermath appears in Elizabeth Cady Stanton et al., *History of Woman Suffrage: Volume I, 1848–1861* (New York: Fowler & Wells, 1881). Its appendix to chapter IV collects a great number of newspaper commentaries and other materials that are cited in my chapter.

The account of the Seneca Falls Convention to turn to is Miriam Gurko, *The Ladies of Seneca Falls: The Birth of the Woman's Rights Movement* (New York: Macmillan, 1974). Additional sources and material on the women's suffrage movement are collected in Charles L. Zelden, *Voting Rights on Trial: A Sourcebook with Cases, Laws, and Documents* (Indianapolis: Hackett, 2004). Two key studies on the suffrage movement still in print are Aileen S. Kraditor, *The Ideas of the Woman Suffrage Movement, 1890–1920* (New York: Columbia UP, 1965), and Eleanor Flexner, *Century of Struggle: The Woman's Rights Movement in the United States* (rev. ed.) (Cambridge, MA: The Belknap P of Harvard UP, 1995). Revisiting the movement is Jean H. Baker, ed., *Votes for Women: The Struggle for Suffrage Revisited* (Oxford: Oxford UP, 2002).

The industrial transformation of the U.S. and the corporate reconstruction of American capitalism is detailed in the works of Robert Sobel, *The Age of Giant Corporations: A Microeconomic History of American Business, 1914–1992* (3rd ed.) (Westport: Greenwood P, 1993), and Wesley B. Truitt, *The Corporation* (Westport: Greenwood P, 2006). Reflecting the legal, institutional, and political frameworks of this process is Martin J. Sklar, *The Corporate Reconstruction of American Capitalism, 1890–1916: The Market, the Law, and Politics* (Cambridge: Cambridge UP, 1987). Tracing the emergence of a new class of professional managers are Alfred D. Chandler, *The Visible Hand: The Managerial Revolution in American Business* (Cambridge, MA: The Belknap P of Harvard UP, 1977), and Olivier Zunz, *Making America Corporate, 1870–1920* (Chicago: U of Chicago P, 1990).

Daniel Nelson, *Managers and Workers: Origins of the Twentieth-Century Factory System in the United States, 1880–1920* (2nd ed.) (Madison: U of Wisconsin P, 1995) analyzes the emergence of the factory as a new mode of production. Reflecting the corporate reconstruction in a broader context that transcends the narrow view on corporations is Philip Scranton,

Endless Novelty: Specialty Production and American Industrialization, 1865–1925 (Princeton: Princeton UP, 1997).

On Henry Ford and his business philosophy, see Douglas Brinkley, *Wheels for the World: Henry Ford, His Company, and a Century of Progress, 1903–2003* (New York: Penguin, 2004), Steven Watts, *The People's Tycoon: Henry Ford and the American Century* (New York: Knopf, 2005), and Robert Lacey, *Ford, the Men and the Machine* (Boston: Little, Brown and Co., 1986). Frederick Winslow Taylor and his idea of scientific management are ably discussed by Robert Kanigel, *The One Best Way: Frederick Winslow Taylor and the Enigma of Efficiency* (Cambridge, MA: MIT P, 2005), and Daniel Nelson, *Frederick W. Taylor and the Rise of Scientific Management* (Madison: U of Wisconsin P, 1980).

Readers interested in learning more about Andrew Carnegie are recommended to turn to Harold C. Livesay, *Andrew Carnegie and the Rise of Big Business* (3rd ed.) (New York: Longman, 2006), and David Nasaw, *Andrew Carnegie* (New York: Penguin, 2006). The Social Darwinism embraced by Carnegie and other business leaders appears in Robert C. Bannister, *Social Darwinism: Science and Myth in Anglo-American Social Thought* (Philadelphia: Temple UP, 1988), and Carl N. Degler, *In Search of Human Nature: The Decline and Revival of Darwinism in American Social Thought* (New York: Oxford UP, 1993).

How the industrial transformation of the U.S. created a "post-frontier anxiety" about the future of American Exceptionalism that fed into the reform efforts of the New Deal is reflected in Wrobel's, *The End of American Exceptionalism*, cited above. David M. Kennedy, in *Freedom from Fear*, also cited above, gives a detailed and comprehensive overview of the U.S. in the 1930s. A gripping oral history of the Great Depression's hardships and plights is Studs Terkel's *Hard Times*, which was published as an illustrated version by the New Press in New York in 2013.

A classic study of the New Deal is William E. Leuchtenburg, *Franklin D. Roosevelt and the New Deal, 1932–1940* (New York: Harper & Row, 1963). Colin Gordon analyzes labor relations in *New Deals: Business, Labor, and Politics in America, 1920–1935* (Cambridge: Cambridge UP, 1994). Ira Katznelson's *Fear Itself* (see above), and Alan Brinkley, *The End of Reform: New Deal Liberalism in Recession and War* (New York: Knopf, 1995) highlight the many limits to reform in the New Deal era and beyond. Meanwhile, Klaus Kiran Patel, *The New Deal: A Global History* (Princeton: Princeton UP, 2016), positions the New Deal in a global perspective. The history of the welfare state beyond the 1930s appears in William E. Leuchtenburg, *In the Shadow of FDR: From Harry Truman to Barack Obama* (4th ed.) (Ithaca, NY: Cornell UP, 2009), and Jill S. Quadagno reflects the narrow limits racism set to the unfolding of the welfare state in *The Color of Welfare: How Racism Undermined the War on Poverty* (New York: Oxford UP, 1996).

Kim Voss reflects the problem of American Exceptionalism in U.S. labor history in *The Making of American Exceptionalism: The Knights of Labor and Class Formation in the Nineteenth Century* (Ithaca, NY: Cornell UP, 1993). On the history of unions, see Philip Dray's sweeping *There Is Power in a Union: The Epic Story of Labor in America* (New York: Doubleday, 2010), and Nelson Lichtenstein, *State of the Union: A Century of American Labor* (Princeton: Princeton UP, 2003). Alice Kessler-Harris, *Out to Work: A History of Wage-Earning Women in the United States* (New York: Oxford UP, 1982) is the standard study on women in the American labor force. The history of the mill girls of Lowell, Massachusetts, is detailed by JoAnne Weisman Deitch, *The Lowell Mill Girls: Life in the Factory* (2nd ed.) (Carlisle: Discovery Enterprises, 1998), and Jeff Levinson, ed., *Mill Girls of Lowell* (Boston: History Compass, 2014).

Rich insights into the mentality and everyday experiences of Americans and their still-limited radicalism even in the midst of a severe economic crisis like the Great Depression are provided by Studs Terkel's oral history of that period, cited above, and by chapter 15 of Howard Zinn, *A People's History of the United States* (New York: Harper & Row, 1980).

CHAPTER 8: PEOPLE OF PLENTY

David M. Potter's *People of Plenty: Economic Abundance and the American Character* (Chicago: U of Chicago P, 1954) is a very influential book tracing the mental, cultural, and social predispositions for material success in America. Jim Cullen's *The American Dream: A Short History of an Idea That Shaped a Nation* (Oxford: Oxford UP, 2004) is a concise history of the concept. More detailed and focused on the period of industrial and postindustrial America is Esmond Wright, *The American Dream: From Reconstruction to Reagan* (Cambridge, MA: Blackwell, 1996). John G. Cawelti, *Apostles of the Self-Made Man* (Chicago: U of Chicago P, 1965) investigates the concept of the self-made man as an integral part of the American Dream, while Roland Marchand focuses on how the American Dream was visualized in commercials in *Advertising the American Dream: Making Way for Modernity, 1920–1940* (Berkeley: U of California P, 1985). Calvin C. Jillson elaborates on the dilemma of participation and exclusion in *Pursuing the American Dream: Opportunity and Exclusion over Four Centuries* (Lawrence: UP of Kansas, 2004).

Literature on Benjamin Franklin and his autobiography is discussed in the bibliographical essay for chapter 4. On Horatio Alger, see James V. Catano, *Ragged Dicks: Masculinity, Steel, and the Rhetoric of the Self-Made Man* (Carbondale: Southern Illinois UP, 2001), Charles Orson Cook, *Horatio Alger: Gender and Success in the Gilded Age* (St. James, NY: Brandywine P, 2001), and Carol Nackenoff, *The Fictional Republic: Horatio Alger and American Political Discourse* (Oxford: Oxford UP, 1994). Susan Goodman and Carl Dawson provide a useful overview of William Dean Howells's life in *William Dean Howells: A Writer's Life* (Berkeley: U of California P, 2005), while Theodore Dreiser's literary works are examined in Donald Pizer, *The Novels of Theodore Dreiser: A Critical Study* (Minneapolis: U of Minnesota P, 1976). A good introduction to the life and writings of F. Scott Fitzgerald is provided by Kirk Curnutt, *The Cambridge Introduction to F. Scott Fitzgerald* (Cambridge: Cambridge UP, 2007).

A good place to start investigations of American consumer capitalism is *Consumer Society in American History: A Reader*, edited by Lawrence B. Glickman (Ithaca, NY: Cornell UP, 1999). Susan J. Matt, *Keeping Up with the Joneses: Envy in American Consumer Society, 1890–1930* (Philadelphia: U of Pennsylvania P, 2003), Charles F. McGovern, *Sold American: Consumption and Citizenship, 1890–1945* (Chapel Hill: U of North Carolina P, 2006), and Lizabeth Cohen, *A Consumers' Republic: The Politics of Mass Consumption in Postwar America* (New York: Vintage Books, 2003) all trace the history of American consumerism. The texts collected by Jennifer Scanlon in *The Gender and Consumer Culture Reader* (New York: New York UP, 2000) reflect the complex gender dynamics of a consumer culture that positions women at the center of consumerism. Offering multiple perspectives on the history of U.S. consumer culture is Richard Wightman Fox and T. J. Jackson Lears, eds., *The Culture of Consumption: Critical Essays in American History, 1880–1980* (New York: Pantheon Books, 1983).

Richard H. Pells discusses the paradoxical constellation of leftist radicalism and the reaffirmation of American core values in the 1930s in his *Radical Visions and American Dreams: Culture and Social Thought in the Depression Years* (New York: Harper & Row, 1973). Most of the historical episodes about the American people during the Great Depression mentioned in chapter 8 derive from chapter 15 of Zinn's *People's History of the United States*, cited above.

Readers interested in the history of consumption in the Cold War context and the formation of the affluent society in the U.S. after 1945 are recommended to turn first to Cohen, *A Consumer Republic* and then to John Kenneth Galbraith's influential *The Affluent Society* (Boston: Houghton Mifflin, 1958). Generally, the new mass consumer culture emerging after 1945 is a major topic of that period and is concisely narrated by James T. Patterson in *Grand Expectations: Postwar America, 1945–1974* (New York: Oxford UP, 1995), and H. W. Brands, *American Dreams: The United States since 1945* (New York: Penguin, 2010).

CHAPTER 9: CRISIS OF DISORIENTATION

For general accounts of U.S. history since 1975, see James T. Patterson, *Restless Giant: The United States from Watergate to Bush v. Gore* (New York: Oxford UP, 2005), Sean Wilentz, *The Age of Reagan: A History, 1974–2008* (New York: HarperCollins, 2008), and Godfrey Hodgson, *More Equal Than Others: America from Nixon to the New Century* (Princeton: Princeton UP, 2004).

The economic history of the U.S. since 1975 is treated in the third volume of Stanley L. Engerman and Robert E. Gallman's *The Cambridge Economic History of the United States* (Cambridge: Cambridge UP, 2000). Stephen High analyzes the process of deindustrialization from a continental perspective in *Industrial Sunset: The Making of North America's Rust Belt, 1969–1984* (Toronto: U of Toronto P, 2003). Judith Stein identifies the 1970s as a crucial period in explaining both the deindustrialization of the U.S. and the enormous growth of the financial capital sector, in *Pivotal Decade: How the United States Traded Factories for Finance in the Seventies* (New Haven, CT: Yale UP, 2010), while Andrew Keen elaborates on the effects of the internet economy in *The Internet Is Not the Answer: Why the Internet Has Been an Economic, Political and Cultural Disaster—and How It Can Be Transformed* (London: Atlantic Books, 2014).

The growing inequality in the U.S. since the 1980s is analyzed by Paul R. Krugman, *The Conscience of a Liberal* (New York: W.W. Norton & Co., 2007), and Timothy Noah, *The Great Divergence: America's Growing Inequality Crisis and What We Can Do about It* (New York: Bloomsbury, 2012). Colin Gordon has an informative website on inequality in the U.S.: https://inequality.org/research/growing-apart-political-history-american-inequality/, accessed June 2021.

On the history of immigration to the U.S. since 1975, see Leonard Dinnerstein and David M. Reimers, *The World Comes to America: Immigration to the United States since 1945* (New York: Oxford UP, 2014), and Mary C. Waters and Reed Ueda, eds., *The New Americans: A Guide to Immigration since 1965* (Cambridge, MA: Harvard UP, 2007)

The rise of the New Right and the history of American conservatism since the mid-1960s is ably discussed by the general overviews of Patterson, Hodgson, and especially Wilentz cited above. In addition, readers wanting to learn more about the political persuasions of Ronald Reagan are recommended to read Gil Troy, *Morning in America: How Ronald Reagan Invented the 1980s* (Princeton: Princeton UP, 2005), and Steven F. Hayward's monumental two-volume *The Age of Reagan: The Fall of the Old Liberal Order, 1964–1980* (Roseville, CA: Forum, 2001) and *The Age of Reagan: The Conservative Counterrevolution, 1980–1989* (New York: Crown Forum, 2009).

The culture wars beginning in the 1990s were first identified by James Davison Hunter, *Culture Wars: The Struggle to Define America* (New York: BasicBooks, 1991).

The question of who freed the slaves has long preoccupied historians, with no end to that discussion in sight. The current state of the debate over how African American slaves were simultaneously being emancipated and emancipating themselves during the Civil War is presented in Glenn David Brasher, *The Peninsula Campaign and the Necessity of*

Emancipation: African Americans and the Fight for Freedom (Chapel Hill: U of North Carolina P, 2012), James Oakes, *Freedom National: The Destruction of Slavery in the United States, 1861–1865* (New York: Norton, 2013), and Leonard L. Richards, *Who Freed the Slaves?: The Fight over the Thirteenth Amendment* (Chicago: U of Chicago P, 2015).

The debate about transnationalizing U.S. history has produced substantial reinterpretations of U.S. history, such as Thomas Bender, *A Nation among Nations: America's Place in World History* (New York: Hill & Wang, 2006) and Ian Tyrrell, *Transnational Nation: United States History in Global Perspective Since 1789* (Basingstoke: Palgrave Macmillan, 2007).

Regarding the negative exceptionalism of the U.S. in the field of criminal justice, Marie Gottschalk, *The Prison and the Gallows: The Politics of Mass Incarceration in America* (New York: Cambridge UP, 2006), and Michelle Alexander, *The New Jim Crow: Mass Incarceration in the Age of Colorblindness* (rev. ed.) (New York: New P, 2012) are the most eminent studies. See also Tony G. Poveda, "American Exceptionalism and the Death Penalty," Social Justice 27, 2 (Summer 2000): 252–67. America's negative exceptionalism in the field of health care is highlighted by Gunnar Almgren, *Health Care as a Right of Citizenship: The Continuing Evolution of Reform* (New York: Columbia UP, 2017).

Index

Page references for figures are italicized.

9/11 attacks, 129, 131, 133, 216, 217, 232
abolitionists, abolitionist movement, 34, 36, 37–40, 100, 137, 139–43, 157, 159, 161
abundance:
  in agricultural America, 2–10, 186–87;
  in industrial America, 10–11, 170–71;
  as theme of American Exceptionalism, xviii, xxi, 1, 23, 185, 208.
  See also American Dream; poverty; prosperity; resources, natural
Adams, Abigail, 158–59
Adams, Ansel, 22
Adams, John, 72, 136–37, 158–59
Adams, John Quincy, 20, 100–101
AF of L. *See* American Federation of Labor
affluence. *See* prosperity
Afghanistan, 130, 133, 216
Africa, 104, 139–40, 222
African Americans, xx–xxi, 135–55, 162, 173, 203, 204, 222, 223, 224–25, 232, 233;
  and democracy, 136, 139–40, 142–43, 154;
  in the Early Republic, 139–41;
  and education, 149;
  and equality of opportunity, 35–36, 147–49, 151, 173–74, 223;
  on the frontier, 31–32;
  labor unions and, 176, 183;
  and police violence, xiii, 151, 213;
  and poverty, 35, 143, 146, 147, 152, 174;
  representations of, 38–39;
  in revolutionary America, 138–39;
  in U.S. prisons, 152, 227–28;
  in the U.S. South, 34, 35–36, 44, 45, 47;
  and the U.S. welfare state, 173–74;
  in World War I, 143–44;
  in World War II, 144–45.
  See also American Revolution; civil rights movement; discrimination, racial; Myrdal, Gunnar; slavery
agrarianism, 164, 210;
  Thomas Jefferson on, 6–7, 98;
  in landscape painting, 7–8, 9;
  Southern Agrarians, 43–44.
  See also agriculture; Crèvecœur, John Hector St. John de; industrial society; industrial workers; industrialization
agriculture:
  during Great Depression, 173, 201;
  and industry, 10, 166–67;
  and progress, notions of, 8, 13–14, 27;
  and prosperity, 9–10, 186.
  See also agrarianism; Crèvecœur, John Hector St. John de; industrialization; Jefferson, Thomas; resources, natural; settlement colony
Aguinaldo, Emilio, 109
Al Qaeda, 129–30. *See also* terrorism
Alabama, 14, 44, 150

Alger, Horatio, 191–93
American Civil War, 10, 33, 34, 36, 104, 143, 150, 161, 165, 166, 181, 191, 192;
  historical interpretations of, 141–42, 224–25;
  and Southern exceptionalism, xix, 43, 46;
  states' rights and, 38, 82.
  See also American Revolution; Confederate States of America; secession; slavery
American Dream, xxi, 181, 185–94;
  Horatio Alger and, 191–93;
  John Hector St. John de Crèvecœur and, 186–87;
  definitions of, 185, 187, 210;
  Benjamin Franklin and, 186, 188–89;
  Lyndon B. Johnson and, 171;
  Martin Luther King and, 148;
  Malcolm X and, 154;
  Barack Obama and 149, 150, 232;
  Tea Party Movement and, 231.
  See also abundance; equality; individualism; inequality; poverty; prosperity
American Federation of Labor, 175, 176, 177. See also labor unions
American Indians, 26, 32, 66, 68, 69, 162, 224–25;
  representations of, 13–14, *15*, 83, *84*;
  Puritan perception of, 59–60
American Revolution, 5–6, 7, 71–91, 98, 115, 185, 223, 225;
  and African American emancipation, xxi, 136, 137–43;
  and American Exceptionalism, transformation of, xviii, xix–xx, 71, 90–91;
  and discrimination, patterns of, 135–36;
  the Federalist interpretation of, 82–83, *84*, 85;
  and the French Revolution, 71, 85–89;
  radicalism of, 77;
  revolutionary turn of, 73–74;
  and slavery, 34, 36, 136–37;
  and U.S. foreign policy, 93–94, 114;
  the Southern interpretation of, 41–43;
  and women's rights, 158–59, 162–63.
  See also Articles of Confederation; Declaration of Independence; egalitarianism; U.S. Constitution
Ameringer, Oscar, 201
Anderson, Sherwood, 204
Anthony, Susan B., 161
Anti-Federalists. See Federalists
Antin, Mary, 181
Arendt, Hannah, 185
Articles of Confederation, 79–80;
  and American Exceptionalism, notions of, 81.
  See also states' rights; U.S. Constitution
Ashe, Thomas, 45
Asia, 46, 121, 133;
  immigration from, 34, 222;
  U.S. economic relations with, 104, 218;
  U.S. expansion to, 104, 106, 110.
Asian Americans, 31, 222, 225
Australia, 26, 162, 226
autocracy:
  as significant other of American Exceptionalism, 103, 113, 122, 163, 235

Baltimore, Lord George Calvert, 1st Baron of, 62
Banneker, Benjamin, 138
Bannon, Stephen, 157

Baraka, Amiri, 153
Barralet, John J.:
  Apotheosis of George Washington, 83, *84*
Barton, Bruce F.:
  The Man Nobody Knows, 200
Benton, Thomas Hart, 99
Biden, Joe, 134, 215, 234, 235
Bierstadt, Albert, 20
  The Domes of Yosemite, 20, *21*
black nationalism, 139, 153–55
blacks. *See* African Americans.
Borah, William, 116
Bork, Robert, 215
Boston, 58, 74, 137, 138, 161, 181, 193, 203
Bourke-White, Margaret:
  World's Highest Standard of Living, 203, *204*
Bradford, William, 12;
  Of Plymouth Plantation, 13, 56
Bremer, Frederica, 45
Burke, Edmund, 72, 85–87
Bush, George H. W., 128
Bush, George W., 103, 129–31, 133, 214

Calhoun, John C., 102;
  South Carolina Exposition and Protest, 38, 41
California, 20, 25, 31
Canada, 26, 32, 226
Carmichael, Stokely, 153
Carnegie, Andrew, 110, 164, 191;
  Triumphant Democracy, 10;
  "The Gospel of Wealth," 165–66, 192–93
Carter, Jimmy, 218
Cass, Lewis, 102
Catt, Carrie Chapman, 161;
  "Will of the People," 162
Charles I, King of England, 52
Charles II, King of England, 61

Chauvin, Derek, xiii
Chicago, 33, 107, 191, 193, 203, 230, 232
China, 126, 129, 162, 219, 228
church, churches:
  Anglican church, 51–53;
  and civil rights movement, 146;
  established churches, 60, 64, 68, 86;
  Puritan thinking about, 53–54, 55, 57, 77;
  and slavery, 40–41, 46;
  and U.S. imperialism, 106–7;
  in the U.S. South, 36
Church, Frederic Edwin, 7
city upon a hill, xiv, 23, 51, 54–55, 57, 60, 75, 90, 115, 162, 183, 230, 232, 235
civil rights, xx–xxi, 170, 172, 174;
  Anti-Federalists and, 81.
  See also civil rights movement; human rights; natural rights
civil rights movement, xx–xxi, 47, 143–52, 221, 224;
  and black nationalism, 153–54;
  Bill Clinton on, 223;
  and Cold War, 145–46;
  March on Washington, 147–48;
  Barack Obama on, 150–51;
  and World War I, 143–44;
  and World War II, 144–45.
  See also African Americans
Clay, Henry, 96, 99, 100, 101
Clinton, Bill, 128–29, 214, 219, 222–23
Cohen, Roger, 231
Cold War, 121–29, 205–9, 216–17, 224;
  and consumer culture in the U.S., 208–9;
  definition of, 121;
  effect on racial segregation in U.S., 145–46;
  and welfare reform in the U.S., 169, 171, 172

Cole, Thomas, 7;
  View from Mount Holyoke, Northampton, Massachusetts, after a Thunderstorm, 7–8, 9
Colonial British North America, xvi, 51–70, 97;
  England's colonial policies, 2, 65–66, 72–73, 136–37;
  descriptions of, 2–5, 26–27;
  religious tolerance in, 60–64.
  See also American Revolution; settlement colony
Columbus, Christopher, 2–3, 29
communism, communists:
  effects on U.S. domestic policies, 145, 171–72;
  as ideological enemy, 122–23, 145, 166, 209, 216;
  and totalitarianism, 118, 121, 209;
  U.S. working class and, 181–82, 203–4.
  See also containment; labor unions; socialism, socialists; Soviet Union
Confederate States of America, 33, 42;
  in Gettysburg Address, 141–42;
  Great Seal of, 42.
  See also American Civil War; secession
Congregationalists. *See* Puritans
conservatism, conservatives, xxi, 166–67, 220, 229–31;
  of the Christian Right, 224;
  conservative populism, 157;
  in Europe, x, 85–86, 88;
  and labor unions, 175, 178;
  and southern exceptionalism, 33;
  and the Tea Party Movement, 230–31;
  and U.S. foreign policy, 128, 131–33;
  and the welfare state, 168, 170, 173–74, 229.
  See also liberalism, liberals; Republican Party, Republicans
Constitutional Convention, 36, 80, 81, 82, 137–38
consumers, consumption, 193–200, 205–11;
  during the Cold War, 208–9;
  consumer goods, 117, 195–96, 199–200, 202;
  critique of, 108, 193–94, 200;
  and overproduction, 104, 125, 201–2;
  and welfare state, 171, 206–7.
  See also American Dream; poverty; prosperity; Veblen, Thorstein
containment, 123–27, 128, 208–9. *See also* Kennan, George F.; Lake, Anthony
Coolidge, Calvin, 200
Cooper, Brittney, 152
Cooper, Gary, 31
Cooper, James Fenimore, 16, 29;
  Leatherstocking Tales, 28, 31
corporations, 195, 197–98;
  corporate transformation of U.S. economy, 107, 165–67, 176, 192–93, 210;
  overseas expansion of, 117;
  regulation of, 168, 172, 206
Cotton, John, 56
Covid-19, xiii–xiv, 213, 219, 226
Crèvecœur, John Hector St. John de, 28, 30;
  Letters from an American Farmer, xv–xvi, 13, 26–27, 44–45, 64, 186–87
Cuba, 105, 107

Danforth, Samuel, 59–60
Daniel, John W., 110
Debs, Eugene V., 177
Declaration of Independence, 73, 142, 147, 151;

and American constitutions, 78–79, 82–85, 90, 148;
and U.S. foreign policy, 94;
and slavery, 137–40;
political values of, 76–77, 87;
and women's movement, 158–61.
See also egalitarianism; French Revolution; liberalism, liberals; natural rights
Delany, Martin, 139, 153
democracy, xv, xx, 46, 49, 164, 232;
and Atlantic Revolutions, 71, 85, 114;
fragility of, 6–7, 79, 134, 142, 164, 213–16, 235;
and frontier, 30–31, 225;
ideologization of, 128, 131, 143, 163;
as inherently peaceful order, 113;
participation in, 135–36, 139, 143, 154, 158–59, 162–63, 215–16;
popular sovereignty, 76–77;
representative democracy, 80–81.
See also African Americans; autocracy; Carnegie, Andrew, *Triumphant Democracy*; internationalism, liberal internationalism; monarchy; Myrdal, Gunnar; racism, racial discrimination; Tocqueville, Alexis de; totalitarianism; Whitman, Walt; women's movement
Democratic Party, Democrats, 37, 100, 102, 110, 172, 173–74, 214, 234, 235
Detroit, MI, 218
Dickens, Charles, 45
Dos Passos, John, 204
Douglass, Frederick, 161, 233;
"What to the Slave Is the Fourth of July," 140–41, 142
Dreiser, Theodore:

Sister Carrie, 193–94
Du Bois, W. E. B., 153;
"Returning Soldiers," 144;
The Souls of Black Folk, 143;
Duden, Gottfried, 9–10
Durand, Asher B., 7
Dyson, Michael Eric, 152

Eastman, Max, 163
education, xv, 65, 68–69, 78, 99, 131, 213, 218, 221, 228;
U.S. colonial rule and, 105, 109;
the federal government and, 170, 171.
See also African Americans; Alger, Horatio; women's movement
Egypt, 288
Eisenhower, Dwight D., 167, 168
El Salvador, 122
Emerson, Ralph Waldo, 16–18;
"Nature," 18
empire of liberty, 98, 101, 115
England. See Great Britain
Enlightenment philosophy, 17, 27, 68, 74, 75, 77, 113
egalitarianism, x, 46, 48, 135–36;
radical, of American Revolution, xx–xxi, 36, 76, 158–59.
See also Declaration of Independence; equality; inequality; Myrdal, Gunnar; racism, racial discrimination; segregation, racial; Tocqueville, Alexis de
equality, 98, 141, 145, 160–61, 165, 208, 224, 225, 232;
Edmund Burke's rejection of, 86;
of opportunity, 49, 87, 164, 166–67, 168, 186, 193, 200;
and welfare state, 169, 172–74.
See also African Americans; egalitarianism; Hoover, Herbert; inequality; segregation, racial;

racism, racial discrimination;
Tocqueville, Alexis de
Europe as significant other, defining the exceptionality of America, 8, 24, 107, 223;
corruption, 6–7, 53, 62, 75, 111;
European revolutions, 85, 88, 91;
feudalism, xvi, 60;
history, 1, 27–28, 78, 80–81, 98;
imperialism, 103–4, 108–10, 117–18;
industrialization, 6–7, 22, 175;
natural environments, 17, 19–21;
prosperity, 4–6, 164–65, 185–87, 189, 198;
religious freedom, 62–64;
war, 93, 95–96, 97, 111, 131;
welfare state, 172–73.
See also agrarianism; city upon a hill; Crèvecœur, John Hector St. John; frontier; labor unions; monarchy; Sombart, Werner; socialism, socialists; Tocqueville, Alexis de
European-American relations:
Atlantic revolutions, 85–91;
economic relations, 38, 41, 93–94, 111, 117, 125–26, 198–99;
European expansion to North America, xix–xx, 2–5, 27–28, 51–70, 233;
European images of America, 2–5, 9–11, 56–57, 63, 69, 71–72, 199;
European travelers to America, 45;
political relations, 95–97, 101–2, 121, 125–26, 130–31, 214;
U.S. expansion to, 117, 198–99.
See also France; Germany; Great Britain; immigrants, immigration; Russia; Soviet Union; Spain; World War I; World War II
extended republic, 14, 79–81, 99, 103

Falwell, Jeremy, 157
fascism, 118, 122, 130
federal government, 38, 41, 44, 99, 170–71, 173, 214, 217, 229
federalism, 79–80, 82, 96;
and slavery, 99–101.
See also Articles of Confederation; extended republic; Federalists; states' rights; U.S. Constitution
Federalists:
Federalist Papers, 5, 81;
Federalists v. Anti-Federalists, 81–85;
Federalist Party, 95, 99.
See also Articles of Confederation; federalism; U.S. Constitution
Ferguson, MO, 151
Fitzgerald, F. Scott:
The Great Gatsby, 194
Fitzhugh, George:
Canibals All! or, Slaves Without Masters, 39;
Sociology of the South, or the Failure of Free Society, 39, 40
Floyd, George, xiii, 213
Ford, Henry, 164, 200;
Ford Motor Company, 23, 117, 164, 219;
Fordism, 196–98.
See also corporations; Taylor, Frederick Winslow
Ford, John, 31
France, xvi, 66, 68, 72, 73, 104, 130, 143–44, 198, 226. See also French Revolution; Tocqueville, Alexis de
Franklin, Benjamin, 7, 82, 186, 191;
Autobiography, 77–78, 188–89, 194, 210;
"Observations Concerning the Increase of Mankind," 4–5.
See also American Dream
freedom. See liberty

French Revolution, 29, 71, 85–91;
  and U.S. foreign policy, 94–95
Friedman, Milton, 230
frontier, xix, 25–32, 48–49, 183, 225;
  and U.S. imperialism, 31, 105–8.
  See also U.S. West
Fukuyama, Francis, 127–28, 216

Gable, Clark, 43
Galbraith, John Kenneth, 205–6, 207
Garland, Merrick, 215
Garrison, William Llyod, 139
Garvey, Marcus, 153
Gast, John:
  American Progress, 14, *15*, 16
George II, King of England, 65
Georgia, 14, 42, 51, 64–70
Germany, Germans, 29, 87, 119, 126, 130, 214, 226;
  economic relations with U.S., 104, 191, 198–99;
  images of America, ix–x, 5, 9–11, 198–99;
  immigrants to America, 9, 62, 66;
  racism in, 144–45;
  World War I, 111–16, 144, 163–64, 198.
  See also Sombart, Werner
Gewehr, Wesley Marsh, 208, 209
Gifford, Charles, 173
Gilded Age, 107, 164, 193, 221
Goldberger, Max, 10–11, 198
Goldwater, Barry, 173
Gompers, Samuel, 176
Gorman, Amanda, 235
Gorsuch, Neil, 215
Grand Canyon, 1, 22, 23
Great Britain, 5, 51–53, 56, 57, 59, 75, 87, 104;
  as colonial power, 2–4, 61, 65–66, 68–69, 72–74, 136–39, 158;
  dissenting Protestantism in, 51, 61;
  philanthropism in, 65–66;
  Reformation in, 51, 55;
  Roman Catholics in, 62–63;
  U.S. economic relations with, 41, 191, 198;
  U.S. political relations with, 95, 119–20, 124–25, 198.
  See also Burke, Edmund; U.S. foreign policy
Great Depression, 118, 150, 167–70, 172, 177, 181–82, 201–5, 207, 210, 211, 219
Greece, 124–25
Grosscup, Peter, 176

Hahn, Chris, 234
Haiti, 129
Hamilton, Alexander, 81, 95, 99
Hammond, Henry, 41
Harriot, Thomas, 3
Harris, Frederick, 152
Hay, John, 109
Hecht, Ben, 43
Hirsch, Julius, 199
Hollywood, 117, 122, 199
homosexuality, homosexuals, 224, 232
Hooker, Isabella Beecher, 161–62
Hoover, Herbert, 166, 168, 200–201, 205;
  American Individualism, 166–67, 173, 205
Howells, William Dean, 194;
  The Rise of Silas Lapham, 193
Hudson River School, 7–8
human rights, 112, 113, 120, 128, 160, 216. See also civil rights; natural rights; rights consciousness
Hussein, Saddam, 130

immigration, immigrants, xix–xx, 149–50, 162, 234;
  to colonial America, 4–5, 51–54, 57, 62–63, 66, 187;

and diversification, 34, 70, 222–23;
and labor unions, 176;
nineteenth-century, 8–9, 181;
since, 1970s, 221–23.
See also Asia; Germany, Germans; settlement colony
imperialism. See U.S. imperialism
individualism, 48, 58, 98, 154, 223
and black nationalism, 153;
and Declaration of Independence, 76;
and frontier, 30, 225;
in industrial America, 164, 176, 179–81;
and social cohesion, 89;
and totalitarianism, 118, 121.
See also American Dream; Hoover, Herbert, *American Individualism*
industry, industrial economy, 16, 23, 24, 27, 30, 35, 122, 198, 218–19, 229;
lack of, xvi, 6–7;
and global economy, 41, 94, 198–99;
New Deal and, 167–71, 173;
and sectional conflict in the U.S., 38–41, 43–46;
and U.S. imperialism, 103–108;
and war, 111, 119, 132, 144.
See also agrarianism; corporations; Ford, Henry; Great Depression; labor unions; socialism, socialists; Taylor, Frederick Winslow
industrial society, 7, 157, 191–92
industrial workers, 173, 175–83, 191;
in affluent society, 205–6, 220;
Henry Ford on, 196–97;
Thomas Jefferson on, 7;
and poverty, 7, 164, 191;
skilled and unskilled, 175, 178, 191, 203.
See also communism, communists; labor; labor history; labor unions

industrialization, 8, 10–11, 22, 35, 164–67, 175–76, 181, 185–86, 191, 210;
in France, 29;
in Soviet Union, 123.
inequality, xiv, 152, 153, 154, 165–66, 191–93, 208, 224, 225;
in Europe, 24;
of income, 220–21;
in U.S. South, 35–36.
See also African Americans; egalitarianism; equality; racism, racial discrimination; segregation, racial
internationalism, 116, 128–29;
liberal internationalism, 93, 112–15, 118–34, 143, 163, 231;
multilateral v. unilateral internationalism, 116–18, 130, 134
See also U.S. foreign policy
internet economy, 219–20
Iran, 122, 130, 214, 216, 228
Iraq, 130–31, 133, 214, 216, 217, 228
isolationism, isolationists, 116, 117, 118, 121, 134, 231

Jackson, Andrew:
"Message to Congress on Indian Removal," 14
Jacksonian America, 157, 159, 161, 189–90
James I, King of England, 52
Jamestown, VA, 3, 119
Japan, 119, 226–27
Jay, John, 5, 81
Jefferson, Thomas, 72, 95, 98, 100, 101, 138;
"Notes on the State of Virginia," 6–7, 17, 64;
on progress, 27–28
Jeremiad, 58–60
Jim Crow. See segregation, racial

Johnson, Hiram, 116
Johnson, Lyndon B., 167;
    War on Poverty, 171–74

Kagan, Robert, 131
Kant, Immanuel, 113
Kavanaugh, Brett, 215
Kennan, George F., 126, 127;
    "Long Telegram," 123–24
Kennedy, John F., 167
Keynes, John Maynard, 230
Khrushchev, Nikita, 209
Kim Jong-un, 234
King, Martin Luther, 150, 154, 233;
    "I Have a Dream," 147–48
Kirby, John, 234
Korea, 122, 130, 234
Krugman, Paul, 220–21

La Follette, Robert, 116
labor, 41, 44, 131, 165–66, 170, 176,
    192, 197, 219, 229;
    in colonial America, 4, 65, 69, 187;
    free labor, 39–40, 45, 46, 195.
    See also industrial workers; labor
        history; labor unions; slavery
labor history, xviii, 175, 176, 178–79,
    183, 203
labor movement. *See* labor unions
labor unions, xxi, 124, 158, 174–83,
    197, 203, 206, 208, 209;
    the New Deal and, 168;
    trade unions v. industrial unions,
        175–77.
    See also industrial workers; labor
        history
LaHaye, Beverly, 157
landscape. *See* natural environments
Lake, Anthony:
    "From Containment to
        Enlargement," 128–29
Larcom, Lucy, 180–81

Latin America, Latin Americans, 32,
    104, 218, 222
Latin American Revolutions, 96–97
Latinos, 222, 225, 227–28

Laud, William, 52
League of Nations, 114, 116–17
Leigh, Vivien, 43
Levitt, William, 208–9
Lewinsky, Monica, 214
Lewis, John L., 177
Lewis, Sinclair, 200
Lexington, MA, 72, 74
liberal internationalism. *See*
    internationalism
liberalism, liberals, 36, 131, 152, 224,
    230;
    concepts of history, 87–88, 98;
    European, x, 85, 88;
    liberal narratives of American
        Exceptionalism, xiv, 33, 44, 49,
        231–32, 234–36;
    New Deal liberalism, 167–74, 204,
        229;
    and the idea of progress, 71, 98;
    values, 10, 94, 101, 103, 114, 118,
        154, 164.
    See also conservatism,
        conservatives; democracy;
        Declaration of Independence;
        internationalism, liberal
        internationalism; natural rights;
        Paine, Thomas; southern
        exceptionalism; totalitarianism
liberty (freedom), 73, 78, 81, 83, 90,
    157, 163, 166, 168, 171–72, 176, 181,
    185, 195, 210, 229, 231;
    and agrarianism, 6–8;
    and American Exceptionalism, xv,
        xvi, xx, 48–49, 79, 139, 150–52,
        173, 174, 186–87, 190, 231–35;
    American Revolution and, 36,

41–42, 71, 76–77, 87–88, 95, 114, 147–48, 158;
and consumption, 207–9;
European debates on, x, 86;
and U.S. expansion, 14, 96–97, 98–99, 101, 108, 115, 225;
and federal union, 82, 96;
the frontier and, 27, 30–31, 108, 225;
and racial discrimination, 145, 152;
and slavery, xiii–xiv, 36, 38, 40–41, 45, 136–43, 150;
and wilderness, 19.
See also African Americans; Declaration of Independence; internationalism, liberal internationalism; religious freedom; Roosevelt, Franklin D., Four Freedoms speech; totalitarianism; women's movement
Lincoln, Abraham, 42, 149–50, 205, 235;
Emancipation Proclamation, 141, 147, 224;
Gettysburg Address, 141–42, 147;
House Divided speech, 46;
on westward expansion, 99, 101, 102
Lippmann, Walter, 145
London, 42, 66, 68, 73, 117, 198
Louis-Philippe, King of France, 89
Louisiana Purchase, 38, 99
Lowell, MA, 180–81
Luce, Henry, 120–21
Lynd, Helen Merrell, 199
Lynd, Robert Staughton, 199

Madison, James, 81, 95
Malcolm X, 153–54
Manifest Destiny, xv, 93, 97–103, 105, 115, 225
manufacturing. *See* industry, industrial economy; industrialization

Marshall, George C.:
Marshall Plan, 125–26, 214
Martineau, Harriet, 45
Marx, Karl, 175, 209
Maryland, 62–63, 70, 137, 138
Massachusetts, 3, 7, 9, 12, 51, 55, 59, 60–61, 62, 68, 69, 70, 74, 99, 138, 158, 173, 180, 191
McCain, John, 231
McClellan, George B., 23
McEnany, Kayleigh, 234
McKinley, William, 109
Mencken, Henry Louis, 36
Mennonites, 51, 62, 69
Mexican War, 101–3, 112. *See also* Texas, annexation of
Mexico, 25, 26, 100, 112, 219, 222
Mississippi, 14, 47, 148
Mississippi River, 14, 20, 33, 38
Missouri, 9–10, 37–38, 151
Mitchell, Margaret, 43
Mitchum, Robert, 31
Mittelberger, Gottlieb, 5
monarchy, xvi, 52, 74, 80–81, 83, 86, 87, 88–89, 113, 158
Monroe James, 100;
Monroe Doctrine, 96–97
Montgomery, AL, 150
Monument Valley, 1
Moravians, 51, 62
Morgan, John Pierpont, 191
Morris, Gouverneur, 138
Moscow, 123–24, 209
Mott, Lucretia, 159–61
Muir, John, 21, 22
Murray, Judith Sargent, 159
Myrdal, Gunnar, 46–47, 135, 137

National Security Council Memorandum No 68 (NSC–68), 126–27
National Socialism, National Socialists, 130, 135, 144

Native Americans. *See* American Indians
natural environments, xix, 1, 17–18, 23–24, 31, 57;
destruction of, 48, 129, 225, 226;
protection of, 21–22, 168, 228.
See also wilderness.
natural rights, xx, 34, 36, 71, 74, 76–77, 86–87, 89, 90, 98, 135–40, 148, 153, 158, 160, 161, 176. *See also* civil rights; human rights; rights consciousness
Netherlands, 80, 199
neutrality, neutral rights, 94–95, 110–12, 118
New Canaan, 56–57, 63
New Deal, xxi, 158, 164–74, 177–78, 204, 205, 229, 231. See also liberalism, liberals; welfare state
New England, xviii, xix, 3–4, 12–13, 25, 44, 51, 53–60, 63, 100, 137, 158, 180–81, 230
New York City, 23, 33, 117, 139, 161, 162, 194, 198, 201, 221
New York, state of, xvi, 46, 64, 140, 160
Nguyen, Viet Thanh, xiv
Niagara Falls, 1, 20, 22, 23
Nicaragua, 122, 214
Niebuhr, Reinhold, 117–18
Nitze, Paul, 126
Nixon, Richard, 209, 213
Noah, Timothy, 220
North Carolina, 14, 66

O'Sullivan, John L.:
"The Great Nation of Futurity," 98–99;
"Annexation," 101.
See also Manifest Destiny; U.S. imperialism; westward expansion
Obama, Barack, 215, 231;
and American Exceptionalism, 149–52, 154, 229, 232;
U.S. foreign policy under, 133, 231
Ochs, Phil, 47
Oglethorpe, James Edward, 65–69
Olmsted, Frederick Law, 45
Oregon, 100, 208
Osama bin Laden, 130

Paine, Thomas, 162;
Burke-Paine controversy, 85–88;
Common Sense, 5, 74–76, 77, 93–94;
Rights of Man, 87–88;
and U.S. foreign policy, 94
Palin, Sarah, 231
Paris, 72, 73, 88, 115
Parker, Alan, 47
Parker, Theodore, 46
Paulding, James Kirke, 45
Penn, William, 61–63
Pennsylvania, 5, 61–64, 69, 70, 137–38, 141, 189
perfectible union, xxi, 157, 231–32
Philadelphia, 62, 74–75, 80, 137, 188–89
philanthropy, 65–69
Philippines. See U.S. imperialism
Pilgrim Fathers. *See* Puritans
Plymouth Plantation, 12, 53, 56, 119
police, xiii, 150, 151, 203, 213
Polk, James K., 100–103
Potter, David, 208
poverty, xv, 19, 168, 170, 187, 188, 192, 221;
in affluent society, 146, 147, 207;
end of, 67–68, 121, 149, 185, 200–201, 208;
in Europe, 24, 65, 125, 186–87;
in Great Depression, 150, 202, 210;
and individualism, 179, 181;
in U.S. South, 35, 45, 47.
See also African Americans;

industrial workers; Johnson, Lyndon B.; New Deal
prisons, 28, 65, 89, 152, 159, 227–28
progress, idea of, xvi, xx, 98, 108, 152, 162, 208;
  critique of, 8;
  and frontier, 30;
  representations of, 13–14, *15*, 16, 27–28, 165–66;
  and American Revolution, 71, 75, 90, 98
Progressive Era, 157, 193
Promised Land, 12, 56–57, 174, 181, 232
property, xvi, 174;
  distribution of, 35, 154;
  right to, 90, 131, 160–61, 182;
  slaves as, 137–38;
  visions of society anchoring in, 66, 86, 185, 187.
  See also American Dream; poverty; prosperity
prosperity, affluence, 13, 14, 28, 65, 66, 68, 70, 72–73, 82, 96, 112, 116;
  and American Exceptionalism, xvi, xxi, 90, 118, 180–81, 185–211, 217–18, 220–21, 225;
  and Cold War, 124–26;
  as middle-class ideal, 149;
  in Puritan New England, 54, 58;
  religious tolerance and, 64;
  the U.S. South and, 40–41;
  and welfare state, 170–72, 174, 177, 206, 209, 229.
  See also American Dream; Franklin, Benjamin; poverty
Prosser, Gabriel, 138
Puritans, xviii, xix, 23, 51–60, 68, 69, 77, 90, 162;
  Pilgrims, 12, 13, 53, 56–57;
  Congregationalists, xx, 12–13, 51, 53–60, 61, 63, 230;
  as Calvinists, 52, 53

Putin, Vladimir, 234

Quakers, 51, 61–62, 63, 69

racism, racial discrimination, xiii–xiv, 29, 136, 152, 153–54, 203, 224, 225, 233;
  in the Cold War context, 145;
  and U.S. criminal justice system, xiii, 151, 227–28;
  in Germany, 144–45;
  and U.S. imperialism, 104, 110, 134;
  and labor unions, 176, 183;
  in the North, 48;
  and slavery, 38, 39–40;
  and the welfare state, 170, 172, 173, 174.
  See also Myrdal, Gunnar; segregation, racial; slavery; white supremacy
Randolph, A. Philip, 147
Reagan, Ronald, 103, 122, 172, 214;
  and American Exceptionalism, 149, 173, 229–30, 232
Reconstruction period, 33, 36, 43, 225
reform, xx–xxi, 157–83;
  and Benjamin Franklin's autobiography, 78;
  immigration reform legislation, 222;
  projects in colonial America, 53–55, 57, 60, 63, 64–70, 204–5.
  See also New Deal
Reid, Joy, 234
religion, 14, 23, 32, 36, 200, 224;
  and civil rights movement, 146;
  religious foundations of American Exceptionalism, xviii, 51–64, 69–70, 83, *84*, 90;
  religious perceptions of American nature, 12–13, 17–20;
  and slavery, 39–40;
  and U.S. imperialism, 106–7.

religious freedom, 60–62, 120, 130, 131. *See also* liberty (freedom)
Republican Party, Republicans, 37, 46, 172, 173, 215, 224, 235. *See also* Hoover, Herbert
republican motherhood, 159
republicanism, 6, 71, 75, 78, 95, 113, 210. *See also* extended republic
resources, natural, 21, 93–94;
   agrarian America, 2–6, 186–87;
   industrial America, 10–11, 41, 218.
Rhode Island, 60–61, 63, 70
rights consciousness, 143, 223–24, 232. *See also* civil rights; civil rights movement; natural rights
Riis, Jacob, 191
Rio Grande, 102–3
Robinson, Harriet H., 180–81
Rockefeller, John D., 164, 191
Rocky Mountains, 20, 27
Roosevelt, Franklin D., 35, 118, 167–69, 205;
   Four Freedoms speech, 119–20
Roosevelt, Theodore, 22, 105;
   The Strenuous Life speech, 107–8
Rostow, Walt W., 208
Rothstein, Arthur, 202
Rumsfeld, Donald, 131
Russia, 26, 32, 129, 166, 181, 234. *See also* Soviet Union
Rutledge, John, 99

Salzburg, Austria, 66
Santa Anna, Antonio López de, 100
Santángel, Luis de, 3
Sargent, Aaron A., 164
Saudi Arabia, 228
Scalia, Antonin, 215
Schlafly, Phyllis, 157, 173
Schumer, Chuck, 234, 235
Schurman, Jacob Gould, 109
secession, 33, 150;
   perspectives on of civil rights movement, 47;
   and American Revolution, 42–43;
   and states' rights, 38, 82.
   See also American Civil War; Confederate States of America
segregation, racial, xix, 33, 34, 44, 48, 150, 173, 228;
   in the armed forces, 143–44;
   and the civil rights movement, 146–47;
   in the Cold War context, 145;
   legal vs de facto, 142–43, 152;
   and U.S. Constitution, 35–36, 143, 148.
   See also racism, racial discrimination
Selma, AL, 150–51
Seneca Falls, NY, 160–61
settlement colony, 2, 68
Seward, William H., 46
Sheeler, Charles:
   American Landscape, 23, 24
Silver, James W., 47
Sinclair, Upton, 191
slavery, slaves, xiv, xix, 33, 34, 35, 136–43, 148, 150, 152, 161, 187;
   depictions of, 38–40, 43, 44–46;
   in colonial Georgia, 67–68, 69;
   in memory wars, 224–25;
   and Southern nationalism, 36–42;
   and westward expansion, 99–101.
Smith, Captain John:
   A Briefe and True Report of the New Found Land of Virginia, 3;
   A Description of New England, 3–4
socialism, socialists, xxi, 121, 123, 204, 208, 209;
   lack of in the U.S., 174–75, 179, 182–83.
   See also communism, communists
Socialist Party of America, 176–77
Sombart, Werner, 174–75, 178–80

South Carolina, 41, 44, 61, 65, 66, 68, 99, 102. *See also* Calhoun, John C.
southern exceptionalism, xix, 32–49. *See also* U.S. South
southern nationalism, 33, 37–42, 82. *See also* U.S. South
Soviet Union, 121–27, 145, 166, 207–9, 222. *See also* Russia
Spain, 2–3, 32, 66, 68
Spanish-American War, 105, 107, 203
Stalin, Josef, 123
Stanton, Elizabeth Cady, 159–61
states' rights, 37–38, 82, 85
Steinbeck, John, 204
Stockton, Robert, 102
Stone, Lucy, 161
Stowe, Harriet Beecher:
    Uncle Tom's Cabin, 38
Stringfellow, Thornton, 40
Strong, Josiah, 105–7
The Sublime, 12, 16–21, 23
Sweden, 46, 135, 226
Switzerland, 66, 80, 226

Taylor, Frederick Winslow:
    Taylorism, 196–98
Tea Party Movement. *See* conservatism, conservatives
Teheran, 216
terrorism, xx, 129–33, 216–17
Texas, 31, 102, 103;
    Annexation of, 100–101
Tharoor, Ishaan, 235
Thoreau, Henry David, 16, 17–19
Thornwell, James Henry, 42
Tocqueville, Alexis de, 88–89;
    Democracy in America, 45, 85, 89–90, 189–90;
    Quinze Jours dans le Désert, 28–29
totalitarianism, 46, 47, 118–19, 121, 125, 130, 143, 145, 204, 209
transcendentalism, 16–18, 46. *See also* Thoreau, Henry David

Truman, Harry S., 126, 167;
    Truman Doctrine, 124–25;
    Fair Deal, 169–71, 208
Trump, Donald, xiv, xv, 133–34, 157, 213, 214, 215, 233–35
Tubman, Harriet, 233
Turkey, 124–25, 162
Turner, Frederick Jackson, 29, 48;
    "The Significance of the Frontier in American History," 25, 29–32, 105–6;
    The Frontier in American History, 30, 106.
    See also U.S. West
Turner, Joseph A., 41

U.S. Capitol, xiv, 213, 214, 234–35
U.S. Congress, xiv, 14, 38, 41, 96–97, 100, 112–13, 118, 125, 129–30, 151, 154, 162, 164, 171–72, 173, 201, 214, 220, 234
U.S. Constitution, 78–85, 214–15;
    and American Exceptionalism, 90, 169, 235;
    Latin America and, 96;
    and New Deal, 169, 173;
    and slavery, 140–41;
    Donald Trump and, xiv, xv, 214;
    and women's suffrage, 161–64.
    See also Constitutional Convention; segregation, racial; states' rights
U.S. foreign policy, xviii, xx, 93–134, 216–17, 226, 231. *See also* 9/11 attacks; American Revolution; Cold War; containment; Declaration of Independence; empire of liberty; French Revolution; internationalism; isolationism, isolationists; Latin American Revolutions; League of Nations; Manifest Destiny; Marshall, George C.; Mexican War; Monroe, James; National

INDEX

Security Council Memorandum No 68; Paine, Thomas; Roosevelt, Franklin D.; terrorism; Texas; Truman, Harry S.; U.S. imperialism; U.S. National Security Strategy (2002); War on Terror; Washington, George, Farewell Address; Wilson, Woodrow; World War I; World War II
U.S. House of Representatives, 99, 114, 173
U.S. imperialism, 103–10, 226;
  anti-imperialism, anti-imperialists, 103, 105, 110, 114;
  definition of, 103–4;
  and Mexican War, 101–3;
  Monroe Doctrine and, 96–97;
  and the Philippines, 105, 108–10.
  See also empire of liberty; Manifest Destiny; westward expansion
U.S. National Security Strategy (2002), 131–33
U.S. Senate, 41, 99, 102, 110, 111, 114, 115–16, 164, 172, 173, 215, 234, 235
U.S. South, xix, 25, 32–49, 100, 102, 137–38, 142, 144, 150, 172, 173, 174, 201. *See also* secession; southern exceptionalism; southern nationalism
U.S. Supreme Court, 36, 173, 215
U.S. West, xix, 14, 20, 25–32, 34, 48–49, 107, 150;
  agriculture in, 8, 9, 14, 15, 16, 20, 21;
  visual representations of, 8–9, 14–16, 20, 22.
  See also frontier; Turner, Frederick Jackson; westward expansion
United Nations, 123, 130, 145

Van Buren, Martin, 99, 100, 101
Veblen, Thorstein:
  The Theory of the Leisure Class, 195
Versailles, 89;
  Versailles Peace Treaty, 111, 115–16
Vietnam, 219;
  Vietnam War, 122, 216, 217, 226
Virginia, 3, 6, 17, 64, 82, 110
virtue, 83, 108, 165;
  and agriculture, 6–7, 187–88;
  as element of American Exceptionalism, 8, 24, 213, 228, 233–34;
  republican virtue, 6–7, 210.
  See also Franklin, Benjamin

Walker, Quock, 138
Wallace, George, 44
War on Terror, xx, 129–34, 216
Washington, DC, 42, 128, 144, 214, 217, 222, 228, 233;
  March on Washington, 147–48
Washington, George, 42, 71, 72, 82, 116, 138;
  Farewell Address, 82, 83, 95–96.
  See also, Barralet, John J.
Watergate Affair, 213–14, 217
Wayne, John, 31
welfare state, xxi, 167–69, 229;
  and American Exceptionalism, 168, 172–73, 174, 183, 231;
  and labor unions, 177;
  See also African Americans; conservatism, conservatives; equality; liberalism, liberals; New Deal; prosperity; racism
Wells, Richard, 137
Westerns, 31
westward expansion, 8, 25, 97–103;
  conceptualizations of, 14, 28–29, 30–31;
  as element of American Exceptionalism, 98–100, 164, 225;

and destruction of American Indians, 14;
and U.S. imperialism, 31, 48, 98, 101–3;
and slavery, 36–38, 99–100;
visualizations of, 8, 9, 14, *15*, 16.
See also frontier; Turner, Frederick Jackson; U.S. West
white supremacy, 33–34, 44, 49, 99, 102, 106
Whitman, Walt, 16, 164–65
wilderness, 1, 11–16, 23, 26, 28–29, 32, 63, 88, 108;
American Indians as part of, 13–15, 56;
definitions of, 11–12;
the Puritans and, 12–13, 56, 58–59, 77;
as a source of American Exceptionalism, 21–22;
visual representations of, 7–8, 9, 14, *15*, 16.
See also frontier; the Sublime; transcendentalism; Turner, Frederick Jackson
Wilhelm II, emperor of Germany, 163
Williams, Roger, 60–61
Wilson, James, 137
Wilson, Laura Merrifield, 235
Wilson, Woodrow, 111–16, 119, 120, 130, 133, 163;
Fourteen Points, 114;
War Message, 112–14.
See also internationalism, liberal internationalism

Winthrop, John, xix–xx, 12, 51, 56, 57, 59, 62, 75, 115, 172, 230;
"A Model of Christian Charity," xix, 53–55.
See also city upon a hill
Wister, Owen, 31
women, 31, 36, 43, 83, 139, 180–81, 224, 225
women's movement, 124, 157, 160, 233;
and education, 158–59, 161;
women's suffrage movement, xxi, 160–64, 183.
World War I, 35, 120, 122, 177;
African Americans in, 143, 144;
U.S. Economy and, 111, 117, 198–99;
the U.S. and, 110–14;
and women's suffrage, 163.
See also internationalism; Wilson, Woodrow, War Message; Versailles
World War II, 36, 118, 122, 125, 207, 210, 220;
African Americans in, 143–45;
U.S. Economy and, 182, 205
Wyoming, 163

Yellowstone National Park, 20
Yosemite National Park, 20–22

Zedong, Mao, 126
Zimmermann, Arthur, 112

About the Author

Volker Depkat is a professor in the Department of British and American Studies at the University of Regensburg, Germany.

www.ingramcontent.com/pod-product-compliance
Lightning Source LLC
Chambersburg PA
CBHW052055230426
43671CB00011B/1903